MW01156568

SHORT CYCLE SELLING

BEATING YOUR COMPETITORS IN THE SALES RACE

JIM KASPER

MCGRAW-HILL

NEW YORK   CHICAGO   SAN FRANCISCO.   LISBON
LONDON   MADRID   MEXICO CITY   MILAN   NEW DELHI
SAN JUAN   SEOUL   SINGAPORE   SYDNEY   TORONTO

The McGraw·Hill Companies

Copyright © 2002 by James P. Kasper. All rights reserved. Printed in the United States of America. Except as permitted under the United States Copyright Act of 1976, no part of this publication may be reproduced or distributed in any form or by any means, or stored in a data base or retrieval system, without the prior written permission of the publisher.

2   3   4   5   6   7   8   9   0   AGM/AGM   0   9   8   7   6   5   4

ISBN 0-07-138873-7

This book was set in New Times Roman by MM Design 2000, Inc.

Printed and bound by Quebecor World/Martinsburg.

Short Cycle Selling, Compression Selling, Participative Distance Learning, A.R.E.B.A., and S.A.F.E. Closing are trademarks of James P. Kasper. An application for registration of these trademarks has been filed with the U.S. Patent and Trademark Office.

Realtor is a registered trademark of the National Association of Realtors.

McGraw-Hill books are available at special quantity discounts to use as premiums and sales promotions, or for use in corporate training programs. For more information, please write to the Director of Special Sales, McGraw-Hill, 2 Penn Plaza, New York, NY 10121-2298. Or contact your local bookstore.

This book is printed on recycled, acid-free paper containing a minimum of 50% recycled, de-inked fiber

Library of Congress Cataloging-in-Publication Data

Kasper, Jim.
   Short cycle selling : beating your competitors in the sales race / Jim Kasper.
     p. cm.
   Includes bibliographical references and index.
   ISBN 0-07-138873-7 (alk. paper)
   1. Selling diets. 2. Competition. I. Title.
   HF5438.25.K375 2002
   658.8'1—dc21

                                                 2002021938

I am dedicating this book to:

My best friend, soul mate, and wife, Ginny.
Thank you for your help, guidance, advice,
inspiration, encouragement, and most of all,
the countless sacrifices you've made
in order for this book to become a reality.

My personal hero and son, Todd Kasper,
whose perseverance toward reaching his goals, words of
encouragement, and keen sense of humor
have always been huge motivators for me.
Your mother and I are truly blessed to have a son like you.

CONTENTS

Acknowledgments • **ix**

Why Short Cycle Sellers Win the Sales Race • **xi**

1. Identify Your Sales Cycle: Champion Racers
   Know Their Racecourses • **1**
   Compression Concept: Sales Cycles Have Stages • **2**
   Compression Concept: Not All Sales Cycles Are Alike • **8**

2. Size Up Your Competition: Identifying When and
   Where to Make Your Move • **15**
   Internal Competition • **16**
   External Competition • **18**
   Compression Concept: Competitive Analysis Based on Your
      Customers' Perceptions • **19**

3. Target Selling: Plan Your Sales Race • **27**
   Compression Concept: The Market Segmentation and Target Process • **30**
   Compression Concept: Do Your Homework Before You Call • **33**
   Compression Concept: Develop a Unique Selling Proposition • **34**

4. Get New Business More Quickly: Race on the
   Fastest Course • **40**
   Compression Concept: Customer Internal Opportunity Analysis • **43**
   Compression Concept: Account Management Plan • **45**
   Compression Concept: Your Customers Want to Help You • **47**

Compression Concept: The Five Steps to Take to Train Your Customers to Shorten Your Sales Cycle • **50**

5. A.R.E.B.A.! The Quickest Track to the First Appointment • **55**
The A.R.E.B.A. Model • **56**
E-Technology Will Save You Thousands in Literature Costs and Sales Cycle Time • **62**

6. Compression Objectives: A Big Key to Winning the Sales Race • **65**
Focusing on the Wrong Sales Objective • **66**
Conceding Control of the Sales Cycle to the Customer • **67**
Compression Concept: The Compression Objective • **67**
Compression Concept: The Customer Must Take Some Form of Action • **70**
E-Selling and Compression Objectives • **75**

7. Let the Customer Tell You How to Win: It's Her Job! • **78**
Compression Concept: The Race Winning Discovery Strategy • **80**
Preparation Phase: Using Internet Technology • **81**
Scenario Planning • **83**
The Sales Interview • **87**
Compression Concept: The Five Questions That Cut to the Essence of the Sales Process • **88**
Compression Concept: Discover the Motivation Behind Your Customers' Questions • **92**
Compression Concept: Asking for Your Compression Objective • **94**

8. Familiarity Breeds Sales Race Winners • **99**
Compression Concept: Understanding Your Customer's Perception Is a Key to Affecting It • **102**
Compression Concept: The Two Basic Buyer Personality Types— Bottom Liner and Top Liner • **103**
Compression Concept: Sell to the Behavioral Style That You Identify • **113**

9. Shorten Your Sales Cycle: Using Strong Sales
Presentations, Demonstrations, and Proposals • **120**

Compression Concept: Customer Involvement Cuts Time from
Your Sales Cycle • **121**

Phase I: Pre-presentation Involvement • **125**

Phase II: Presentation Engagement • **127**

Phase III: Post-presentation Connection • **131**

The Virtual Sales Presentation • **133**

10. Condense Your Sales Negotiations: Jockeying
for a Better Position Near the Finish Line • **137**

Compression Concept: Guiding Your Customer to the Negotiating Stage • **138**

Compression Concept: Keeping Your Prospect Engaged in Negotiations • **140**

Compression Concept: The Two Facets of the Negotiating Process
That Encourage Short Cycle Selling—Time and Information • **145**

Compression Concept: Get Something Every Time That You Give Something • **147**

Compression Concept: Take Control of Your Sales Cycle by Negotiating
Your Issues One by One, but Bring Multiple Issues to the Table • **149**

Compression Concept: Speak to the Behavioral Style of Your
Customer during Sales Negotiations • **150**

11. Eliminate Road Course Obstacles: Control the
Staller or Objector • **156**

Compression Concept: An Objector Has Questions—Just Questions • **157**

Compression Concept: A Staller Will Try to End Your Sales Cycle • **160**

Compression Concept: Six Steps to Isolate the Objection and Move On • **162**

Compression Concept: Four Steps to Help You Get Commitment
from a Staller • **166**

12. S.A.F.E. Closing: It Means You Win • **174**

Compression Concept: Closing Is . . . • **177**

Compression Concept: Sales Race Winners Know When to Ask • **180**

Compression Concept: It's S.A.F.E. to Ask • **182**

Compression Concept: The "No" Game Plan Restores Your Sales Cycle • **185**

Compression Concept: Postclosing Analysis Compresses the Next Sale • **187**

13. Fastest Time Wins: Control Your Time and Shorten Your Sales Cycle • **192**

Compression Concept: Overcoming the Four Skill Deficiencies That Prolong Your Sales Cycle • **195**

Your Sales Cycle Is Your Sales Plan • **196**

Getting Organized Means a Shorter Sales Cycle • **199**

Short Cycle Sellers Find Ways to Delegate • **203**

Call Reluctance Definitely Lengthens Your Sales Cycle • **207**

14. Sales Technology and Automation = Shortened Sales Cycles • **214**

Compression Concept: What a Good CRM System Can Do to Shorten Your Sales Cycle • **219**

Compression Concept: Other Sales Technologies That Will Help You Shorten Your Sales Cycle • **225**

15. Marketing Will Help You Finish First • **231**

Compression Concept: Affect Your Customers' Perceptions by Positioning, Not by Product Features • **232**

Compression Concept: Other Marketing Activities Should Be Aimed at Helping You Shorten Your Sales Cycle • **236**

Compression Concept: Using Marketing to Attack the Market from All Angles • **241**

16. Hone Your Mental Game: Put Your Racing Face On • **245**

Compression Concept: Know Your Selling Self • **247**

Compression Concept: Focus on Short Cycle Selling Success • **249**

The 25 Sales Race Rules That Ensure Your Short Cycle Selling Success • **259**

The Resource Center • **261**

Index • **265**

ACKNOWLEDGMENTS

This book was written in memory of

> Bernard James Fair, Loves Park, Illinois—Killed in action, World War II
>
> George Nicholas Fanis, Loves Park, Illinois—Killed in action, Vietnam
>
> Terry Lee Larson, Loves Park, Illinois—Killed in action, Vietnam
>
> U.S. Navy Commander Dan Shanower, Phi Theta Pi—Killed in the attack on the Pentagon, September 11, 2001

You fellows never had a chance to write your own books. This one is for you!

I want to thank and honor the three top sellers in my life:

> Jack Kasper, my father and best "shade tree" salesperson in the world. Your tenacity was my model.
>
> My late father-in-law, Charles T. Nelson, who always said I belonged in a sales career. Your people skills are still unsurpassed.
>
> My friend and sales champion, Charlie Johnson. I learned so much from watching you.

A special thanks to my colleague Tom Rothrock for his patience and command of the English language, and to the new generation of top-performing Short Cycle sales "pros":

Stacey Brown	Valeria Kartisek
Andrew Kartisek	Jeffrey Lewis
Timothy Kartisek, Jr.	

I've known all along that you all would have great sales careers.

ACKNOWLEDGMENTS

A very special thank you to my mother, Lorraine Kasper, and my mother-in-law, Nell P. Nagle. You've both battled and won! Thank you so much for your encouragement.

Laurie Harper, thank you. You're a real pro, great agent, and good friend!

Jim Kasper

WHY SHORT CYCLE SELLERS WIN THE SALES RACE

I contend that my firm's resource center library truly rivals any university's library in the country when it comes to reference books on sales and selling. The shelves are crammed with a multitude of fine books including *SPIN Selling, Solution Selling, Selling to Very Important Top Officer, Selling to the Top, Collaborative Selling, The New Strategic Selling, Conceptual Selling, 434 Fast Tips for Sales Success, Relationship Selling, The Best Seller, Key Account Selling, Partner Sell, Secrets for Closing Sales, Integrity Selling, Guerilla Selling,* and just plain *Selling.* I've read each of them, some twice. They all profess to hone your already proficient sales skills in their respective areas of sales expertise. Many of them do just that and more. Many of them fall short.

What they don't do is address the hottest and most rapidly growing concern in selling today, shortening your *sales cycle.* Why have the two top professional sales trade publications, *Selling Power* and *Sales and Marketing Management,* begun writing about sales cycle topics in almost every monthly issue? Because they know from their research that in the corporate boardrooms of today and global sales meetings of tomorrow, the sales cycle is where competitive advantage will be established. They know that the world economy demands more performance in shorter time. Officers of top Fortune 500 companies know that in today's competitive global markets, the sales cycle cannot afford to be prolonged. They have the foresight to know that tomorrow's sales cycles must be even shorter. The sales race winners of tomorrow will be the Short Cycle sellers.

The benefits to you of shortening your particular sales cycle are many:

1. You will beat your competition to the punch.

2. You will sell more in a shorter time.

3. You will open many more new accounts.

4. Your earnings will increase dramatically.

5. Your proposals will be accepted more readily.

6. Your customers will remain more loyal and appreciative of your efforts.

7. You will be able to serve your current accounts in a more expeditious and capable manner.

THE ROLE OF TIME-BASED COMPETITION IN SHORTENING YOUR SALES CYCLE

In the early 1990s, George Stalk, Jr., then a vice president, of Boston Consulting promoted a competitive differentiation concept known as *time-based competition.* The idea behind time-based competition is that all of a company's operations departments must understand, control, and reduce the time it takes to perform each departmental process activity. *Process activities* are defined as business functions such as, but not limited to, order entry, shipping, production, invoicing, collections, and inspection. The time it takes to complete these process activities is expressed as *cycle time.* This can best be illustrated by example. The actual amount of time it takes to price, input, print, and send one order to the shipping department is called the *order-entry cycle time.* It is the time required to complete one order-entry cycle. By mastering this notion and identifying opportunities to condense each business function's cycle time, companies have given themselves a tremendous competitive advantage over industry rivals. Therefore, they have provided superior reaction intervals to their customers allowing them to win the race for their customers' businesses.

Time-based competition was conceived originally for the operations side of organizations. After years of direct sales and sales management experience, and 9 years of studying and teaching sales skills, I have discovered that by applying time-based competition concepts to the sales function you will shorten your sales cycle. Your *sales cycle*, like any departmental process function, consists of the steps that take you from initial customer contact to order placement. Each step affords you a wonderful opportunity to beat your competitors by condensing the sales cycle (sales process time).

After identifying the stages in your respective sales cycle, we will walk you through the process that will shorten the time it takes to successfully complete your sales cycle. In this book, you will learn how to

- Identify and analyze your sales cycle.
- Shorten the time needed to complete your sales cycle.
- Gain a competitive time advantage by utilizing market segmentation.
- Recognize your competitor's weaknesses and develop your competitive advantage.
- Form a prospecting system that will yield more prospects in a shorter time.
- Quickly get the prospect's attention.
- Make more appointments with your prospects than your competitors ever hoped to.
- Establish customer objectives and learn how they affect sales cycle compression.
- Let customers tell you what to tell them.
- Compress the time and hassles of sales negotiations.
- Expeditiously turn objections into sales in seven steps.
- Promptly disarm a staller.
- Zero in your sales proposals based on your buyer's behavior.
- Get the order more quickly by using S.A.F.E. Closing techniques.
- Find more time to spend in front of customers while your competitors fiddle away.
- Utilize sales automation to sell to your customers while your competitors sleep at night.
- Develop a fantastic mental sales game plan that will keep your edge up.

Shortening the sales cycle is a hot topic with both sales executives and field sales representatives. Why? It means more income for both. It means more is accomplished with less expended. Psychologically, from the buyer's standpoint, there is only a limited number of buying days in any given year. Compressing the sales cycle allows the sales professional to reach more buyers on their buying days. It means that scaled-down sales forces can compete effectively and even grow their volume. It means the best salespeople will become better.

Every day I hear sales managers and sales forces explain why their sales cycles are so long and why their sales process is so much different than that of anyone else in the world. The medical supply sales representative tells me that doctors are difficult people. The fiber-optic cabling salesperson tells me about the endless engineering requirements. The senior loan officers at banks tell me that they have so much paperwork to do that they can only make five or six calls a month. Every one of them will tell me at least once, "You don't understand. Our sales process is so much different than any other." My general response is

- A sales cycle is only as long as the *seller* allows it to be. It is ultimately the seller who should control the sales process. It is the seller's job!

- As far as the uniqueness of a respective sales method is concerned, I offer that the fundamental process in buying is very similar for all consumer and business-to-business purchasing. All buyers go through the following steps, albeit some business purchase decisions do require a committee and some purchase decisions are impulsive and routine:

  1. Problem recognition and identification
  2. Search for solutions
  3. Evaluation of alternatives
  4. Purchase
  5. Assessment of purchase satisfaction
  6. Alleviation of postpurchase dissonance (eliminate buyer's remorse)

- My experience shows me that differing culture is the only real significant factor that affects the uniqueness or difference of a selling process. The job of selling an environmental consulting contract consists of the same skills as selling a house or selling a plumbing job. If you sell office supplies, you can sell fiber-optic catheters for heart surgery. The selling and buying principles are the same, and you can apply the concepts of Short Cycle Selling to both.

Many of our clients, to whom I have introduced the principles of Short Cycle Selling, are in mature industries. They sell paper products, fossil fuels, chemicals, signage, and financial products. Total market potential is expanding slowly, and if their sales are increasing, it's at the expense of a competitor. They have found that by practicing these doctrines, they are able to sell more new accounts in a shorter time period than their competitors. For some, it has been a matter of survival.

Several of my high-technology clients are still in emerging automation and data industries. Contrary to mature markets, they are operating in growth industries and there are plenty of new applications and customers every day. Some of them are suffering from the latest washouts in technology markets, and competitive pressures are life threatening to their organizations. Companies in both situations have found that instituting a Short Cycle Selling culture helps them capture new customers and market share more quickly than their competitors. This new culture keeps their prospects and customers up to date with the rapidly changing new technologies and market conditions.

When reading this book, I highly recommend that in order to provide a basic understanding of Short Cycle Selling, you start with Chapter 1, Identify Your Sales Cycle, and then you can go to any chapter that peaks your interest. All chapters illustrate distinctly separate approaches for shortening your sales cycle, with representative case studies. Each chapter contains *Compression Concepts*, which are ideas that explain proven sales practices that will compress your sales cycle. You will notice that throughout the book, *Sales Race Rules* are presented as your guidelines to Short Cycle Selling. There are 25 such rules strategically placed throughout the book. Heed them and you'll win the sales race. Ignore them, and your competitors will beat you. The view and the paycheck are always better for the winner.

Today, you have taken the first step toward being in the top 5 percent. For you winners who are already in the top 5 percent, you have taken the next step to being in the top 1 percent. I think that you'll find this book will be a tremendous resource that you can come back to, time and again, as you progress throughout your sales career. Many of our clients have used these concepts to break out of sales slumps and jump-start their careers.

Try Short Cycle Selling. Practice it religiously for at least 30 days or until the principles become habit. It works, and you *will* win many more sales races!

CHAPTER ONE

IDENTIFY YOUR SALES CYCLE

Champion Racers Know
Their Racecourses

The race is on! It's on every day of the week, and it's a race between competing salespersons to be the first to get to the account and sell it. The results for the winner, and there is only one winner, are tremendous psychological and monetary rewards.

The concept of the sales cycle has enjoyed immense popularity in contemporary business and academic circles. From board meetings to sales meetings, sales and marketing executives have been wrestling with the impact that their customers make on their sales cycles. I am offering a new concept to these sultans of sales: a race to shorten your sales cycle by the salesperson, who has the greatest impact on the sales cycle.

The new compression sales culture insists that salespeople make the greatest impression on the sales cycle, not the customer. The complete cycle time of a sale rests squarely on the shoulders of the salesperson. It is up to the salesperson to actively prospect or promptly respond to an inquiry; determine the customer's needs and wants as accurately and expeditiously as possible; expertly dispense with objections and stalls; gain some form of commitment, preferably an order; and ask for referrals so that this process may occur again with someone else. The activities that transpire in this entire sales process are referred to as the *sales cycle*. The sales cycle is just that, a cycle. It consists of several logical steps that take you from the beginning to the end. Each step within the sales cycle is called a *stage*. For instance, the beginning stage in a typical sales cycle is prospecting. The standard sales cycle usually ends with the transaction closure or referral stage. Inside each sales cycle stage are two basic components:

1. The predominant (or principal) activity
2. The compression objective

The *predominant activity* is the basic task you will need to perform within each stage of the sales cycle. It may consist of data collection, information gathering, determining needs or wants, or making a telephone call. As I explain each sales cycle stage, I will discuss the predominant activity or, as my time-based manufacturing friends refer to it, the process.

The compression objective is the primary focus of each stage of your sales cycle. It is the basis for all sales success. Each stage of the sales cycle has a compression objective. You, as the professional salesperson, determine in each stage of the sales cycle what action you want your customer to take to move your sale to the next stage. Unless your customer makes some form of commitment to you, your chances of reaching transaction closure are slim. The compression objective can range from setting up another appointment to gaining your customer's commitment to presenting and supporting your product or service to her boss. Since this is a predominant concept in *Short Cycle Selling*, I have dedicated the entirety of Chapter 5 to its explanation.

COMPRESSION CONCEPT: SALES CYCLES HAVE STAGES

In order to understand better the notion of a sales cycle, we have developed a generic example in Exhibit 1-1.

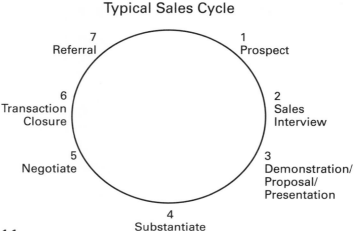

Exhibit 1-1

Stage 1: Prospect

In the first stage of the standard sales cycle, you identify and try to un-cover and penetrate a prospect by attempting to make an appointment with the decision maker or within the decision making sphere of in-fluence. This is not as easy as it was a few years ago because many companies have adopted the *participative management* style of deci-sion making. Participative management means that many people within your customer's organization have input into major decisions, such as specifying and purchasing your product or service. Most com-panies have taken the concept of participative management to limits far beyond its original intent by involving many employees, also known as committee, in the simplest of purchase decisions. It is my experience that the larger the organizations I'm selling to, the more committees are involved at every level in the decision process. This means that you as a sales professional must not only determine the de-cision makers, but must impress the purchase influencers on these committees. This has made the job of separating prospects and sus-pects very difficult. Short Cycle sellers know that prospects have three elements:

1. The authority to make a buying decision

2. Control over the budget

3. A need or want for your service or product

Suspects are missing one of these three elements.

The predominant activity in the prospect stage of the sales cycle is to determine who are suspects and who are prospects.

Stage 2: Sales Interview

The second stage in the sales cycle takes place once you have sold the prospect on seeing you. In the past, this has been commonly referred to as the *sales call*. The concept of the traditional sales call has changed with the advent of *consultative selling*. As Tom Hopkins says so succinctly, "selling isn't telling" anymore. The customer's needs and wants have become predominant over *telling* about features and benefits. Therefore, the sales call has become a questioning or discovery event rather than a selling event. In order to further this concept, we have renamed the sales call the *sales interview*.

The interview stage is characterized by the predominant activity of fact- and emotion-finding about your prospects.

Stage 3: Demonstration/Proposal/Presentation

The third stage in the generic sales cycle involves the demonstration, proposal, or presentation of your product or service. An old sales cliché that I learned over 20 years ago states, "The sale is made at the point of demonstration." This was very true 20 years ago. You may not have necessarily received the commitment at that point, but your customer did make up her mind right then and there. With the emergence of the sophisticated buyer, this expression has changed to, "The purchase decision is influenced at the point of demonstration." In other words, in today's business-to-business (B2B) marketplace, our product or service is subject to much more scrutiny. The customer is more sophisticated due to technology and may have to solicit many opinions before the actual order is placed, regardless of the size of purchase. Obviously, this is affected by the nature of your product or service. If you sell a product or service that is a routinely or repeat purchased item, the sale will be made at the point of price proposal or bid. On the other hand, if you sell an item or service that is either high-priced or quite technical, you can no longer count on the purchase decision being made at the point of demonstration, proposal, or presentation. More than likely it will be made at the point of collaboration or committee. Regardless, there is a stage called demonstration/proposal/presentation.

The predominant activity in the demonstration/proposal/presentation stage is to present and reinforce the benefits of certain features of your product or service that will satisfy your customer's needs and wants.

Stage 4: Substantiate

The fourth stage in the sales cycle is the substantiate stage. The activity that transpires here is often referred to as establishing credibility and believability, or substantiating your competencies. Two factors will affect the exact location of the substantiation stage in your sales cycle:

1. *Your industry.* For instance, in the consulting business, the substantiation stage takes place either in the prospecting or the interview stage. Consultants must be able to validate their competencies before they can move the sales cycle to the demonstration/proposal/presentation stage. In insurance sales the substantiation process occurs in every stage of the sales cycle. Why? Because insurance is a mature industry and there are many perfect substitutes or alternatives for prospects to buy from.

2. *Your previous experience with a prospect or customer.* If you've had positive significant experience selling to a particular customer, you will not have to validate your competencies unless you are selling a product that your customer has never purchased from you before. If you have had negative prior experience with a specific customer, the substantiation stage may be the first stage in your sales cycle.

This stage of the sales cycle is most affected by brand identification or market presence. If you are a leader in your industry and well known

5

to your prospects or customers, you may even be able to skip the substantiate stage because credibility is already established. If you are a relatively unknown entity to your customer or prospect, you may need to substantiate continuously throughout your sales cycle. Another factor that affects the importance of substantiation is the industry life cycle. Once your industry becomes mature, you will have many competitors fighting for a slowly growing or even diminishing marketplace. Substantiating your credibility may be what gives you the edge. This means that you must substantiate at the beginning of your sales cycle.

The predominant activity in the substantiate stage is the establishment of credibility, which gives your customer confidence and comfort in purchasing from you.

Stage 5: Negotiate

In the traditional world of selling, the word *negotiate* sends chills up the spine of even the most seasoned sales pro. Believe it or not, the thought of price dickering is what keeps many salespeople from making a full list price quotation to their customers or prospects.

When we first begin a training program with a client, the very first event that takes place is an interview with every salesperson. Among the many questions that we ask each person is, "Tell me what you like least about selling." Looking back over all the answers that our thousands of training participants have given to this question, dealing with price objection is the most prominent by far. To the contrary, Short Cycle sellers welcome the negotiation stage. They know that by engaging their customers in negotiations they have a better than 85 percent shot of closing the business. They are also aware that negotiations can take place over more than just price and at any stage in the sales cycle. For sales race winners, getting to negotiations is what it's all about. Price should be the last issue to be discussed.

The predominant activity in the negotiation stage is to engage the prospect or customer in a negotiation and keep the negotiations going until you close.

Stage 6: Transaction Closure

In the transaction closure stage of the sales cycle, you experience what many sales managers refer to as *THE CLOSE*. This term seems a bit incongruent with the basic philosophies of relationship and consultative selling. THE CLOSE sounds so conclusive and final. Many salespeople view each individual sale with a certain element of finality. My feeling is that this logic is one of the reasons so many salespeople just can't grasp the concept of nurturing a relationship with their customers. The sales cycle is indeed a continuous closed loop. Look at the sales cycle example in Exhibit 1-1. There is no break in the circle. There is no terminality to the process. After the last stage, the sales cycle continues again or it reproduces itself with another prospect being created, much like living cells split. Short Cycle sellers view each sale as a *transaction being brought to a close*. Therefore, THE CLOSE cannot exist, but the transaction closure can.

The predominant activity at the transaction closure stage is to bring each transaction to an end by taking an order.

Stage 7: Referral

The transaction closure is just one of the many benefits of your efforts. It is your payday. However, if approached properly, your customer should reward you with a bonus in addition to an order. It's called a *referral* and is responsible for the continuation of your sales cycle with another true prospect. This is a crucial point in the continued success of your sales efforts. We all know salespeople who are too busy to breathe (hopefully, one of them is you). If you ask them what is their key to continued success, they will always mention referrals as their number one prospecting tool.

The predominant activity at the referral stage is to accurately describe your prospect profile and gather data on at least three prospects.

COMPRESSION CONCEPT: NOT ALL SALES CYCLES ARE ALIKE

After carefully studying the typical sales cycle, I'm sure you are saying to yourself, "Hey, wait a minute. He forgot the objection stage or the product design stage." Remember that Exhibit 1-1 is just an example of a sales cycle containing steps that appear in different industries. It is very possible, in fact, very probable, that you follow the exact same steps as we have shown, but may use different nomenclature or may, in fact, add, delete, or combine steps. Also, you may have realized by now that your sales cycle with a prospect or new customer will probably be much different than a sales cycle for a repeat sale to a current customer. To illustrate the point about differing sales cycles, let's take a look at some sales cycles from different industries in which I've conducted sales training. The sales cycles for a business banker and a medical equipment salesperson in Exhibit 1-2 are representative of calling on prospects, not reselling to a current customer.

Exhibit 1-2

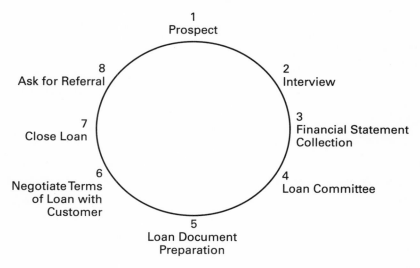

Business Banking: Loans

1
Prospect

8
Ask for Referral

2
Interview

7
Close Loan

3
Financial Statement
Collection

6
Negotiate Terms
of Loan with
Customer

4
Loan Committee

5
Loan Document
Preparation

Medical Capital Equipment

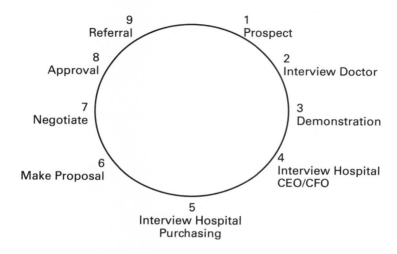

Upon examination, you will immediately note the differences in the respective stages of the two sales cycles. Stage 3 for the medical equipment manufacturer involves a predominant activity consisting of a product demonstration. Stage 3 for the business banker revolves around collecting financial statements of the prospective new client. In stage 6, the medical equipment salesperson is making a proposal and the business banker is already negotiating.

After more careful scrutiny, you will notice that there are also many common stages. Both the business banker and the medical equipment salesperson have to find a prospect. It is very difficult to have a sales cycle without a prospect. Their qualifications for a prospect may differ, but they both need to have a prospect. This selling twosome must conduct interviews, negotiate, ask for business, and ask for referrals. Even though one is selling the invisible and the other is selling a tangible fixed asset, key components of the sale are alike. Despite the similarities and differences between sales cycles, each salesperson, regardless of what he sells, has to go through his own sales cycle dealing with respective customer-, company-, and industry-specific conditions that will affect each stage of the sales cycle.

What conditions affect the stages of *your* sales cycle?

- *Selling a product or service to a prospect who is buying from you for the first time.* Selling to a first-time buyer generally will require you to follow all the stages in your sales cycle. In fact, you may need to repeat some of them. The net effect is that your sales cycle will be longer on a first-time sale if you don't practice the principles of Short Cycle Selling.

- *Selling the same product or service to a current customer who has previously purchased from you.* Selling the same product or service to a current customer who frequently purchases from you should allow you to delete some stages of your sales cycle. For example, you won't need to prospect or go through the interview and negotiation stages. Obviously, if your customer is a repeat buyer, there is no need for product demonstration or substantiation of your competencies. The net effect is a shortened sales cycle.

- *Selling a totally new product or service to a current customer.* On the other hand, if you are selling a current customer a totally new product or service that your company has developed, you will want to demonstrate and substantiate your competencies in that product line. Also, you will find yourself negotiating terms and pricing on totally new products and asking for names of others that could use this new product or service. The net effect is that you may experience a shorter sales cycle than if selling to a completely new prospect that doesn't know you, but a longer one than if selling the repeat product to the same customer.

- *Selling an existing product or service to a current customer who has never purchased that product or service from you before, but has bought it from a competitor.* If you are selling a product or service to a current customer who has never purchased that product or service from you before, but has purchased it from a competitor, you definitely will want to conduct a sales interview and demonstrate and substantiate your competencies. You may not have to penetrate your customer's organization, but you will have to penetrate the organization's buying sphere for that product or service. Someone in your customer's company was purchasing this product from someone they liked. In this case, I guarantee you that there will be substantiation and negotiations involved. The net effect will be a shorter sales cycle than if selling to a new prospect, but a longer one than if repeat selling to the same people.

- *Frequency of purchase.* If what you sell has a low repeat buying pattern or frequency of purchase from your customers, your sales cycle will be longer on a repeat sale. I say this because many times when we go back to resell to a customer after a lengthy period of time, things have changed. Your customer may have changed personnel, the decision-making process or the use of your product or service, or have a lower profitability. In any case, the frequency of purchase will have a tremendous impact on actions that you will need to take to practice Short Cycle Selling.

- *Your reputation or credibility (or lack thereof) in the marketplace.* This is one factor that has tremendous influence on the length of your sales cycle. If you or your company has a strong reputation in your marketplace, you still may have to go through all the stages of your sales cycle, but the time spent in each stage may be significantly shortened. Your prospects' and customers' perceptions of your competency, service levels, and quality are based on your reputation. If your reputation is favorable, then people are predisposed to doing business with you. If your reputation is tarnished, your sales cycle will definitely be longer and you will find yourself spending significant time working on validation and substantiation issues. It doesn't take long to damage a reputation, but it takes years to repair that damage. Changing your marketplace's perception of your reputation is one area that your marketing department can help you with. We will examine that in detail in Chapter 15.

- *Control of the sales cycle.* I will be preaching this throughout the entire book: *It is your job to take control of the sales cycle and guide your customer through it.* If you let the customer control it, you *will* end up with a significantly longer sales cycle. This book will provide you with numerous ways to gain and retain control of your sales cycle.

SALES RACE WRAP-UP

There are a series of sequential steps that comprise your sales process. Collectively these steps are referred to as your *sales cycle*. Individually, the steps are called *stages* in the sales cycle. Each stage has two major components, the *predominant activity* and the *compression objective*.

The predominant activity is the primary task of a specific stage in your sales cycle. A predominant activity can best be illustrated by example. Determining your customer's needs and wants in an interview; relating specific product features and benefits during a demonstration; and gaining customer participation during a presentation are classic examples of predominant activities. They are what customer contact is all about.

The Compression Objective is the primary focus of each stage of your sales cycle. To reach the Compression Objective takes a concentrated effort to elicit some form of commitment or action from the customer that will move the sale to the next stage of your sales cycle. It is your responsibility to establish the Compression Objective and guide your customer to it. There is a Compression Objective for each customer contact. That objective is to move your customer to the next stage in your sales cycle. Before you can accomplish this objective, you must have a thorough understanding of all the stages in your sales cycle.

There are numerous conditions that affect each stage of your sales cycle. Some of them are first-time sale to a prospect, repeat sale to current customer, first-time sale of a new product to a current customer, and first-time sale of a product to a current customer who has been buying that product or service from a competitor. Each has its own effect on shortening or lengthening your sales cycle. The most important thing to remember is that the first salesperson through all of the stages wins the sales race. There is only one winner.

MASTERING YOUR OWN SALES CYCLE

Because it is so important for you to understand your sales cycle, space is provided for you to create your own sales cycle. Below your sales cycle, describe the predominant activity for each stage of your sales cycle. Space is provided for 10 stages in your sales cycle; however, you may not need to use it all.

Your Sales Cycle

STAGE 1: _____

The predominant activity is _____

STAGE 2: _____

The predominant activity is _____

STAGE 3: _____

The predominant activity is _____

STAGE 4: _____

The predominant activity is _____

STAGE 5: _____

The predominant activity is _____

STAGE 6: _____

The predominant activity is _____

STAGE 7: _____

The predominant activity is _____

STAGE 8: _____

The predominant activity is _____

STAGE 9: _____

The predominant activity is _____

STAGE 10:_____

The predominant activity is _____

CHAPTER TWO

SIZE UP YOUR COMPETITION

Identifying When and Where to Make Your Move

Think about this one . . . Competition is the real reason you are in sales.

Competition is the driving force behind all innovative and technological advancements in the world. It is what motivated you to read this book. It provides motivation for the top 20 percent of the world's salespeople to attain their sales goals month after month. Competition is the dynamic that provides the basis of our free-enterprise economy. Quite simply, America would not have developed so rapidly without it.

As salespeople we have a tendency to internalize competition. Good salespeople modify their behavior to either meet or beat competition. While good salespeople do not take rejection personally, they take competition to heart and perpetually think about it. Proof of this is the fact that rarely a week goes by without one of my clients' salespeople telling me about something that their competitors have done to them.

Competition is what drives us to accomplishment. There are two forms of competition that exist in the profession of sales: internal and external.

INTERNAL COMPETITION

Internal competition is the fire that burns within Short Cycle salespeople. It is the motivating stimulus to sell more each year. It is that intangible that compels top producers to beat last month's sales numbers or take control of their sales cycles. Internal competitiveness is embedded within certain personality types. It can be fostered through recognition and positive reinforcement. This personality type is encouraged through early childhood teaching, development, or experience. Intense internal competitiveness is best reflected by five personality traits:

1. Self-starter

2. Aggressiveness

3. Tenacity

4. Self-confidence

5. Self-pride

Self-starters are winners, plain and simple. They need very little guidance and generally are the salespeople who are the first to try to sell a new, unproven product. This alone does not necessarily guarantee that they'll be the most successful on the sales team, but it is one of the two traits common to *all* tremendously successful salespeople. Self-starters are great at beginning new relationships and thus starting new sales cycles. They take initiative on their own because they want to satisfy that internal competitiveness. You can't win the sales race unless you are a self-starter. Self-starters are simply people who don't have to be told to "go out there and win." They do it naturally.

The second trait that internal competitiveness creates in *all* enormously successful salespeople is aggressiveness. From my experience, if a salesperson is aggressive, he is also a sales cycle starter. This person usually generates a huge prospect list. He does not wait for the customer to call back. He is usually on the telephone moving the sale to the next stage in the sales cycle. The aggressive salesperson is always trying to find a way to close the sale or move it to the next stage in the sales cycle. There is a fine line between being aggressive and being pushy. Aggressive salespeople are sales race winners. Pushy salespeople are just plain losers. I must inject a word of caution at this point. I have seen way too many unassertive sales race losers who use the pushy perception as an excuse for losing. These people have actually convinced themselves that they would be better off avoiding calling a customer back than running the risk of being perceived as pushy. This behavior manifests itself in a form of call reluctance. Call reluctance has one result: a long sales cycle. If you have this problem, and more do than don't, you need to change your perspective of taking control of the sales cycle. Chapter 16 addresses that exact subject. It's your job to take control! If you can't do that, then I suggest a career in customer service or marketing. You can still have abundant customer contact, but you won't be put in a position of being perceived, at least from your standpoint, as being pushy.

Tenacity is perhaps my favorite word in the English language. To me it describes the essence of what separates the Short Cycle sellers worldwide from the rest of the pack. Internal competitiveness creates a certain drive within the top 2 percent of salespeople to do whatever it takes, ethically, to win the sales race. This may mean jumping on a red-eye flight to be at your customer's doorstep when the lights go on in the morning. It may mean rewriting a rejected proposal at 11:00 p.m. in the evening in your hotel room so that it can be presented to the board the next morning at 7:00 a.m. Your internal competitive spirit drives your tenacity.

In all my years around successful salespeople, I've never met a top producer who doesn't have that quiet confidence, not cockiness, about his ability to outperform the competition. This self-assuredness comes from many successful experiences at overcoming internal and external competitors. Self-confidence feeds the hunger of your internal competitiveness through continued sales success after sales success. For salespeople in the top 2 percent, this phenomenon creates more internal competition that, in turn, is fed by continued sales success.

I've never heard a top sales producer ever stutter when answering the question, "What do you do for a living?" Whether they are selling banking services or used automobiles, the top guns in their field always exhibit self-pride. This pride is an outward manifestation of self-confidence and internal competitiveness. The self-satisfaction of delivering some fulfillment to the internal competitor is the creation of self-pride. I've never met a salesperson in the top 2 percent who didn't have pride in what he was doing.

Stop here, go back six paragraphs, and reread this entire section on internal competition. Then candidly ask yourself, "How do I measure up against those five personality traits? From what I've learned here, which of those traits do I lack?" Be extremely candid with yourself. *Be assured, though, that the internal competitor within you plays a huge role in your ability to shorten your sales cycle and win the sales race.*

EXTERNAL COMPETITION

External competition receives abundantly more attention from sales management than does internal competition. In my opinion, the two reasons for this are quite apparent.

1. External competition is real. It has a name, a face, a product or service, and it is susceptible to blame. In other words, when we fail to compress our sales cycle and we lose to a competitor, it would be unacceptable to say that it was primarily due to a lack in our internal motivation. We blame it on someone else—namely, the competitor. The competitor's price was better. The competitor had more features. The customer preferred the competitor's services to ours. Indeed, in many cases this can all be true, but in just as many cases the external competitor becomes a scapegoat for our own lack of action.

2. Only the strongest of sales managers understands how to recognize, foster, and reward the force of internal competition.

The irony of the whole situation is that, as salespeople, we spend a significant amount of time learning about the competition's products and services, but very little time analyzing the actual competitor. Most sales professionals insist on isolating the competitive battle on product or service quality, features, benefits, and price. They try to out benefit, better feature, out service, or underprice the competition. The biggest problem that exists with this way of thinking is that salespeople tend to view this from their perception of what is better about them than their competitors. They do not try to discover how their customer perceives the competition. You see, no matter how desperately you want it to be so, your perceptions of the competition do not really matter. Your customers' perceptions are the reality in a sales situation. Do you want to beat your competitors through the sales cycle and win the sales race? Learn how your customers feel about your competitors, not what your sales trainers or sales managers feel about them. Once you understand your customers' perceptions, it will then be easier to affect or change those perceptions and that is what you are paid to do as a sales professional—change customer perception.

COMPRESSION CONCEPT: COMPETITIVE ANALYSIS BASED ON YOUR CUSTOMERS' PERCEPTIONS

In many of our client workshops I ask the participants how they determine their customers' perceptions about competitors. Even though many of these client companies have large marketing departments, we find that specific competitive analysis does not exist. For those clients who do utilize competitive analysis, most base the analysis on product superiority or feature differentiation from their own points of view. Their internal marketing departments prepare most of these comparisons using what they feel are the competitive factors in their marketplaces. It is most likely this comparison data, based on these self-appointed factors, that is presented in a summary or market segment overview format. I'm not downplaying the importance of these forms of marketing department studies, but I am pointing out that rarely will one of these analyses provide specific data about what's important to, for example, XYZ Company in Rocky Mount, North Carolina. So, if you want to shorten your sales cycle and win the sales race to a particular customer, you are left with no alternative but to ask that prospect or customer how you are viewed in relation to your competitors. I guarantee that it is simple, quick, and quite enlightening. The results will yield significant insight into how this customer wants to be sold to, and that, in turn, will tell you how to shorten your sales cycle with them.

There are six quick steps to developing a *customer specific competitive analysis*. They are all focused around customer perceptions and the resulting competitive matrix that you will develop to help identify sales opportunities.

Step 1: Competitive Forces

The very first thing you will need to do in preparing your competitive analysis is to arrange a 30-minute interview with your customer or prospect. During this interview one discovery should be which of your rivals are viewed as viable competitors to you. The best way to ask this is, "Mr. Customer, I need your help. Our company is conducting a market study and we value your input into this study. Knowing what you know about our marketplace, who would you consider, besides us, as the four or five most reputable suppliers?" By asking the question in this manner, you will obviously include yourself, but you do not come right out and say, "Who are my three or four best competitors?" One word of caution: You shouldn't take this answer for granted or assume you already know it. More than one time, I've been unbelievably surprised by what prospects and clients have told me.

Step 2: Competitive Factors

The next area you will want to explore with your prospect or customer is the criteria that he used to identify your competitors in step 1. The best way to approach this subject is to ask, "Mr. Customer, if you had to identify six or seven key areas, besides price, that are important to you in choosing suppliers, what would they be?" My experience tells me that, depending on the nature of your products or services, many of the following will be on the list:

Order process	Customer service support
Delivery time	Billing terms
Location	Industry knowledge
Quality	New product development
Features	Size

After you have compiled this list, ask your prospect or customer to prioritize the items in order of importance to his buying decision-making process. Leave price out of the discussion for now. If your customer brings it up, then tell him that you were certainly going to include price, but you want to look at these other factors first. After he has completed the prioritization, then ask him to fit price into its proper place on the list. When you have concluded this exercise, review the priority list with your customer to confirm any changes or additions to the list. Thank your customer or prospect for his input and assure him that he has been very helpful. Be aware that many times customers have asked me if they could see the results of the market study. I always tell them that they can. I want them to see the results in order to validate my perceptions and to inform me of any market changes that may have occurred that I'm not privy to.

Step 3: Matrix Development

At this time, you have the key information that you need to construct a rather elementary, yet effective, competitive analysis matrix. The purpose of this matrix is to rate your firm, against the competitors from step 1, in all the competitive factors that your customer has identified in step 2. Here are the uncomplicated instructions on how to construct the matrix.

1. On the x axis of the matrix on the top row, list your competitors' names leaving the furthest left cell open.

	ABC Co.	EFG Co.	XYZ Co.	JKL Co.	NOP Co.

2. On the y axis of the matrix, list the competitive factors that your customer identified in order of priority in his decision-making process, in descending order starting with the most important in the second cell of the first column on the left.

	ABC Co.	EFG Co.	XYZ Co.	JKL Co.	NOP Co.
Quality					
Service					
Delivery					
Price					
Features					
Billing terms					
New products					

3. The matrix is complete except for the competitive comparison. This consists quite simply of comparing your perceptions of your strengths and weaknesses against those of your competitors. In order for this to be accurate, you must be very forthright with yourself. If you are honest with yourself, you will identify many opportunities to help you win the sales race. If you are not, you will be contributing to the lengthening of your sales cycle. So here's my simple rating system:

B = better than me   E = equal to me   I = inferior to me

Now, go down each competitor's column and rate each of the competitive factors according to how you perceive their ranking compared to your performance in that category. Note that a rating of "B" for pricing means that the competitor offers better pricing to the customer. A rating of "I" for pricing means that the respective competitor has pricing higher than yours. Here is an example of the completed matrix.

	ABC Co.	EFG Co.	XYZ Co.	JKL Co.	NOP Co.
Quality	B	I	B	E	I
Service	I	E	B	B	E
Delivery	I	E	E	B	E
Price	B	B	I	E	B
Features	B	I	I	E	I
Billing terms	I	B	E	I	E
New products	E	I	B	E	B

4. After you have developed the matrix, e-mail it to your customer and have him conduct the same rating that you did. Do not send him a copy of your completed ratings. Be sure to explain the pricing rating so that both of you are comparing "apples to apples." Have your customer e-mail or fax back his completed rating to you as soon as possible.

5. Now go to both of the matrices and shade those cells that contain an "E" or "I." This will highlight all the competitive factors, by competitor, that are equal or inferior to you. Do not skip this step because within your customer's matrix lies your opportunities based upon his perception. He has just told you in what areas you have a competitive advantage over your competition. Be sure to compare his matrix against your viewpoint. Here is an example of the two shade matrices:

My Competitive Matrix

	ABC Co.	EFG Co.	XYZ Co.	JKL Co.	NOP Co.
Quality	B	I	B	E	I
Service	I	E	B	B	E
Delivery	I	E	E	B	E
Price	B	B	I	E	B
Features	B	I	I	E	I
Billing terms	I	B	E	I	E
New products	E	I	B	E	B

Customer's Competitive Matrix

	ABC Co.	EFG Co.	XYZ Co.	JKL Co.	NOP Co.
Quality	B	I	E	E	I
Service	B	E	B	B	B
Delivery	I	B	E	B	E
Price	B	B	I	E	B
Features	B	I	I	I	I
Billing terms	I	B	E	E	E
New products	E	I	B	E	B

Step 4: Matrix Interpretation and Opportunity Analysis

By comparing your customer's competitive matrix against your own, you are able to validate both matrices. Certainly your customer will have greater insight into some of the competitive factors and vice versa from your position. Carefully evaluate both matrices, keeping in mind that your customer has just told you how he buys and why he buys from your competitors. By doing this quick exercise, your customer has just told you what he thinks of you compared to your competitors.

Again, any shaded cell in either matrix identifies a sales opportunity for you. If you are perceived as equal, you have a chance to change your customer's perception of you through testimonials or actions. If you are perceived as superior in some aspects, then you will want to leverage these strengths through proposal generation or additional benefits to your customer. In either case, by focusing your efforts on these shaded areas, you will be able to practice compression selling, or the application of such, in shortening your sales cycle.

SALES RACE WRAP-UP

There are two forms of competition: internal and external. Internal competitiveness is the force within us that drives us to be the best we can be. It outwardly manifests itself in five personality traits: self-starter, aggressiveness, tenacity, self-confidence, and self-pride.

External competition can be assessed using the competitive matrix. You must collect the names of your five most worthy competitors and the competitive factors upon which your customers make their buying decisions. This matrix will reveal to you sales opportunities that exist in areas in which you are equal or superior to your competitors. The competitive matrix that your prospect or customer completes will tell you the areas in which you need to improve in order to earn your customer's business. Conducting this study will again focus you in the proper direction of compressing your sales cycle while your competitors are out trying to stumble into the truth.

Computer and e-selling technology, such as sales force automation, customer relationship management software, e-mail, and Web browsers, will help you conduct your competitive analysis more quickly and share the data enterprise-wide within your company.

MASTERING YOUR OWN SALES CYCLE

1. Evaluate your internal competitiveness by candidly classifying yourself against the five personality traits discussed in this chapter. Using the evaluation scale provided, place your self-evaluation score on the line after each personality trait. After you have completed this, ask your sales manager to rank you.

   1 = in top 2 percent of all sales professionals I know

   2 = in top 10 percent of all sales professionals I know

   3 = in top 20 percent of all sales professionals I know

   4 = in top 30 percent of all sales professionals I know

   5 = in top 50 percent of all sales professionals I know

   Self-starter _____

   Aggressiveness _____

   Tenacity _____

   Self-confidence _____

   Self-pride _____

2. Using the given matrices, ask a valued customer to help you conduct a market study. Complete the competitive matrices; and write down the opportunities you've discovered.

Customer's Competitive Matrix

My Competitive Matrix

Opportunities for me:

_____

_____

_____

3. Write down what you will do to capitalize on these opportunities.

_____

_____

_____

CHAPTER THREE

TARGET SELLING

Plan Your Sales Race

For every hour you spend conducting research and identifying customer targets, you will save 6 to 8 hours in your actual sales process.

What is *target selling* and how does it benefit you? What is market *segmentation*? What is their relationship with compressing your sales cycle and edging out your competitors? And, most importantly, will any of this really help you make more money in a shorter period of time? *You can bet it will help you make more money faster!*

Market segmentation can be likened to viewing New York City through one of the observation telescopes on the top of the Empire State Building. Without the telescopes, you have a grandiose view of a massive city. Much like New York City, your marketplace looks huge and overwhelming. There appears to be so much opportunity. To get a more precise view of New York City, you drop some coins into one of the observation telescopes. Now you are able to focus all your attention on a smaller, more specific area of the city. You may even be able to determine what activities are taking place in that specific area. Actually, you have the ability to zero in on a specific target such as the famous Statue of Liberty. Using the telescope in this manner can be likened to *target selling*. Your goal is to identify a specific target within your market for further analysis.

The concepts of target selling and market segmentation concern narrowing the focus of your selling efforts. When you examine specific smaller parts (*segments*) of your market, you will gain a better understanding of the market characteristics (*dimensions*) and buying behavior of those precise market segments.

Market characteristics include, but are not limited to,

Market size

Number of competitors

Profitability

Life cycle

Geographic locations

Buying behavior includes such actions as

Frequency of purchase

Brand loyalty

Urgency

Motivation

Price importance

Quality perception

The number one complaint that I hear from customers about salespeople that call on them is, "They don't understand my needs or my business." By conducting the exercise of market segmentation, segment examination, and target identification, you will have a stronger understanding of the needs that drive the buying behavior of the customers within that segment. Once you have completed this exercise, your prospects and customers will not be able to say that you don't understand their needs or business. Once you grasp the segment buying motivation, you will be able to design a marketing mix and sales plan that will enable you to reach this market segment much quicker than your competitors. In other words, you can reduce your sales cycle significantly.

If you are an experienced sales veteran within an industry, this entire process of market segmentation and target identification takes just a little longer than the time you are allotted on one of those telescopes on the Empire State Building. If you are a rookie salesperson or new to your industry, it will only require a little more effort, patience, and persistence to segment your market and identify your target prospects than it takes a veteran. Most of the information you will be seeking is readily available by utilizing your sales manager, key suppliers, strategic customers, or trade journals.

The market segmentation and target identification exercise can literally be completed in less than an hour, and the top benefit is that you will be the one who will shorten her sales cycle. You will be the winner of the sales race because

1. You will stop spinning your wheels by trying to "swallow the elephant whole." Instead of attacking the market, you will be tackling one segment at a time and will know exactly what the needs and wants are in that segment.

2. Time is money, and by segmenting your market you will be saving yourself significant blocks of time. In lieu of jumping from industry to industry in search of new business, you will be more focused if you apply the same strategic and tactical plans to many similar accounts within the same industry.

3. Your understanding of specific segment buying behavior will be a powerful tool because you will walk into a customer's place of business able to speak with employees using their language and able to understand the customer's business environment.

4. You will gain many referrals due to segment knowledge.

5. Segmentation will allow you to stop trying to be everything to everyone and concentrate on a specific market area. You will become known as a specialist within that market segment, and to top it off, specialists are paid more money for what they know and do.

6. Prospects and customers will seek you out because you are the noted authority in that market segment.

THE BENEFITS OF SPECIALIZATION WITHIN MARKET SEGMENTS CASE

Industrial Chemical of Arizona (ICA) is a much smaller company than Southwest Airlines, but certainly more profitable as measured by percent of sales. A wholesale janitorial distribution firm located in Tucson, Arizona, ICA has become a specialist in the floor coating business. Instead of competing with every other janitorial supply company in Arizona, owner Don Wine identified a market segment that was woefully underserved. Mr. Wine became a self-proclaimed (he positioned himself) expert in the coating and maintenance of Mexican tile floors. Soon he was recognized from Texas to southern California as the Mexican tile guru. ICA's sales per sales representative are triple industry averages, and its gross profit is at least 15 points higher than his competitors. Like Southwest Airlines, Don found a market segment that was underserved, large enough to grow profitably, and in need of a specialist. When a potential customer has a Mexican tile problem, she will seek out Don Wine. It's easy to see that Don's efforts to position himself as a specialist in this market segment has significantly shortened his sales cycle.

COMPRESSION CONCEPT: THE MARKET SEGMENTATION AND TARGET PROCESS

There are seven steps to quickly segment your market and identify targets within those segments. For purposes of example and simplicity, let's assume that you own a small high-end luggage manufacturing company. Your products are manufactured from the finest Corinthian leather and are designed to carry enough clothes for an overnight stay. You think the commercial passenger travel market is your segment. The following is the segmenting process that you should follow for your product or service.

Step 1

Identify your overall market and assign a name to it. The overall market for this example will be called the *commercial passenger travel market*. The exhibit illustrates this overall market.

Overall Commercial Passenger Travel Market

Step 2

Divide your overall commercial passenger travel market into submarkets (segments) by the predominant area of buying pattern and similar behavior. The commercial passenger travel market can be divided into several smaller segments.

Air	Bus	Taxi	Ship	Train

List as many submarkets as you can think of.

Step 3

From carefully examining the market segments given in step 2, we realize that the biggest segment of the commercial passenger travel market is in air travel. Let's select the air travel market segment to explore in more detail. Next we need to further break down the commercial passenger air travel market into even smaller groups of homogeneous submarkets with similar market characteristics and buying habits. We will assign a name to each of those submarkets.

Business	Leisure	International	Domestic
Commuter	First Class	Economy	Coach

Step 4

Now we need to estimate the size of each target segment to determine if it will be big enough to be worth our time to sell to it. It is important to remember that if your final market segment is too small, it will not pay for you to specialize and sell to that group. From our observation and personal knowledge, we deduced that combining the first-class, domestic, and business air travel submarkets would provide us with the biggest market segment for our fine Corinthian leather luggage.

Step 5

Assign a name to the market that you have identified.

First-class, domestic, business air commercial passenger travel

Step 6

Now, list the luggage needs and wants of the market segment called *first-class, domestic, business air commercial passenger travel.*

- Carry-on for speed of boarding and deplaning
- Durable baggage
- Fit in overhead compartment or small airplane clothing closets
- Good appearance (identification with success)
- Lightweight
- Compartment for laptop computer and peripherals

Step 7

Classify and list the potential customer categories within the final submarket. In our example, you would probably find the following types of professionals regularly flying first class on domestic business trips:

Successful salespeople	Executives	Doctors	Consultants	Successful lawyers

We now have identified the targets most likely to buy our rich Corinthian leather baggage. You can do the same exercise with your market. In fact, it is a great activity to stimulate thought on new business sources, and I guarantee that your competitors' sales forces have done it. The importance in segmenting your market cannot be overemphasized. To prove this point, Heiman and Sanchez have added it to their best-selling book, *The New Strategic Selling*. They refer to it as "narrowing the universe," but the concept is actually market segmentation and target selling.

COMPRESSION CONCEPT: DO YOUR HOMEWORK BEFORE YOU CALL

Your segmentation process is over. You have identified the largest prof-itable segment within your market, the needs of that segment, and the customer categories. It is now time to identify your specific customer targets and conduct research on each. Again, this is fundamental work that needs to be done in order to compress your sales cycle. There is no use wasting your time calling on deadbeats who can't pay their bills or calling on the wrong person within that organization. Just think, while your competitors are out being rejected by everyone under the sun and talking to the wrong people, you will be prepared to discuss business with the decision maker. For every hour you spend conducting research and identifying targets within your segments, you will save hours upon hours in your actual sales process.

The types of information that you need to accumulate on each target customer can be classified best into four basic categories:

1. Recent financial performance

2. Personal information on the top officers

3. Plans for business expansion or new markets

4. Any problems or issues that open an opportunity door for you

The absolute best place to start to gather your intelligence data is with the Internet. Many different search engines exist that can help you find data on a firm. Lycos.com is a good place to start. The process is rather easy.

1. Go to a search engine such as Lycos.com, Google.com, Excite.com, or Yahoo.com.

2. Type in the company name, and click on Search or press Enter on your keyboard.

3. Either several entries using this company's name will be displayed, or it will read that there is "no match."

4. If there is no match, be sure that you have spelled the company's name correctly. Also, it is a great idea to call your prospect and ask for her Web site address. That act alone may save you significant time. If your prospect doesn't have a Web page, ask for the financial officer and request an annual report.

5. If there are several entries listed by the search engine, read the brief description and look for the company's home page or main site.

6. Once you reach that site, you will more than likely see icons that read: About Us, Our Officers/Management, Investor Information, Our Client List, and Job Postings. What more could a professional salesperson ask for? I have learned a lot about a company by printing and studying all these pages. Use your newfound data in your first telephone call or in your first contact letter to attract the prospect's attention. Remember that despite common sales ideology, customers are human and want to talk about themselves.

Many private companies will not send out annual reports to anyone, so then you need to retreat to the Internet and search for any articles from trade journals, industry associations, or competitive companies. If you cannot get information on a specific target, get information on the industry and competitors.

COMPRESSION CONCEPT: DEVELOP A UNIQUE SELLING PROPOSITION

Answer these two questions in the spaces provided:

1. If you were one of your target customers, would you buy from you? Yes or no. _____

2. Why? List as many reasons as possible.

_____

_____

_____

Now go back through your answers to the second question and scratch out the following words and phrases if you have listed them:

> *best, largest, strongest, product knowledge, honest, helpful, sincere, quickest, understanding, responsible, timely, responsive, caring, customer service oriented, accessible, quality, innovative, factual, direct, good delivery times, trust, trustworthy, best deal, best price, variety*

In fact, go through your answers and cross out anything that any one of your competitors can also claim, regardless of whether you consider it truthful. Now, how small is your list of reasons for your target customer to buy from you? I suspect that if you have a list at all, it is very small.

The reality of the situation is that your competitors are giving the target market the exact same reasons to buy from them that you are for buying from you. The lesson in this exercise is that in order to compress your sales cycle, you must differentiate yourself from your competitors and give customers a unique reason to do business with you.

In order to differentiate yourself from your competitors, you must first conceive what the late Victor Kiam of Remington Razor called a *Unique Selling Proposition (USP)*. Your USP gives your customer or prospect the best reason she should buy from you rather than your competitors. It is something that you, and only you, can legitimately and solely claim. The best way to begin developing your USP is to make a list of the things that make your firm the *first*, *original*, or *only*. This can be accomplished by completing the following phrases:

We were the first to _____

_____

We were the original ones to _____

_____

We originated the _____

_____

We are the only to _____

_____

Secondly, you must realize that unless you tell the customer or prospect what your USP means to her, you might as well be talking to the walls in your office. Every one of us wants to know, "What's in it for me?" Your customers are no different. So, after you have composed your USPs, you must then relate them to your customers. This is achieved by using the following expression: "And, what that means to you, Ms. Customer, is . . ."

If your USP is that your company was the first in the industry to offer 180-day billing, then the benefit statement to your customer may look like this: "And, what the 180-day billing means to you, Ms. Customer, is that not only are you able to get started with us, but you are able to earn significant interest on that money by investing it for those 6 months."

Finally, each market segment, or submarket within a segment, has its own selfish interest in your USP. This means that you need to adjust your USP to each segment. In fact, you probably will need to go a step further and customize it for each individual customer you see.

SALES RACE WRAP-UP

Market segmentation is the process of breaking your market into submarkets of homogeneous dimensions or characteristics. Some of these characteristics are market size, number of competitors, profitability, product life cycle, and geographic location. Prospects and customers within each market segment have their own distinct and common characteristics. They tend to exhibit the same *buying behavior,* such as frequency of purchase, brand loyalty, urgency, motivation, quality perception, and price significance. There is a seven-step process to break your market into submarkets or segments. In the personal development activities that follow, you will conduct an activity that walks through these seven steps.

36

When conducting the seven-step segmentation process, you must remember that segment size is important. In other words, you need to ask yourself if the market segment contains enough potential sales to warrant your investment in mass and personal selling efforts. Is the segment large enough to be profitable or provide an acceptable return on your investment?

Once you have identified the market segments that you find most lucrative, it is time to begin your *target selling*. Target selling consists of using due diligence to learn about each prospect within the market segment and identifying target accounts that you wish to become your customers. Do not practice the shotgun method of selling by trying to be everything to all market segment members. Identify your specific targets, learn as much as you can about them, and be their sales cycle guide.

Having identified your market segment targets, the absolute most effective way to differentiate yourself from your competitors that operate within that market segment is to develop a *Unique Selling Proposition*. The USP is characterized as a series of factors that your competitors cannot claim for themselves. Your USP is derived from your uniqueness. The best method to determine your uniqueness is to ask yourself the following questions:

What were we the first to do in the market?

What were we the originals at?

What are we the only ones to do?

These questions apply to both you and the organization you represent.

Finally, ground your USPs with your customers by telling them why this uniqueness is a benefit to them. Many years of experience have clearly shown me that you cannot take this part for granted. You cannot assume that your customers automatically can make the leap from your USP to a benefit for them. I've seen too many veteran sales professionals make this fatal assumption and walk away empty-handed.

Remember that the sales winners today are very organized and make good use of the most advanced techniques in sales force automation and customer relationship management software.

MASTERING YOUR OWN SALES CYCLE

Using the segmentation model provided in this chapter, take a market where you have been less successful than you planned and segment it down into target accounts.

Step 1. Identify your overall market and assign a name to it.

_____

Step 2. Divide the overall market into submarkets and name them.

_____

_____

_____

_____

Step 3. Break down the submarkets named in step 2 further into homogeneous submarkets and assign a name to each submarket.

_____

_____

_____

_____

Step 4. Estimate the size of each submarket in step 3 in total sales dollars and rank by size.

_____

_____

_____

_____

Step 5. Based on step 4, give a specific name to the market that you have identified and write its name on the line below:

_____

Step 6. Pick a submarket from step 3 and list the specific needs and wants of that submarket segment.

_____

_____

_____

_____

Step 7. Classify and list the names and the potential customers within the final submarket listed.

_____

_____

_____

_____

Write a Unique Selling Proposition for that submarket and tailor it to one of the prospect accounts you have listed in step 7. Don't forget to list the benefit of the USP.

USP: _____

_____

_____

And what that means to you, Ms. Customer is . . . _____

_____

_____

_____

CHAPTER FOUR

GET NEW BUSINESS MORE QUICKLY

Race on the Fastest Course

It's a quick race to your customer! Are you participating?

The most commonly accepted definition of *new business* is one of the following sales:

1. Sale to a new account
2. Sale to an account that has been inactive for a year or more
3. Sale of a new product or service to a current account

It is no secret that the best way to compress your sales cycle is to sell new goods and services to current accounts, but how many of us have gotten absolutely the most from our current accounts? From my experience, with many companies within several varied industries, the answer to this question is less than 30 percent. Why? There are five simple reasons.

1. Traditionally, sales management has been focused on new account development, not necessarily on new business development. There is a distinct difference.

2. Sales management has a more difficult time measuring the amount of new products or services sold to a current account than the amount of new account numbers.

3. Salespeople fail to identify opportunities within their current accounts. Many fall short in penetrating the entire account.

4. The prevalent perception is that you should not push the customers and should be happy with what they have given you.

5. Sales management does not want salespeople to put all their eggs in one basket. If you have one large account, what will happen to your volume if you lose it?

Let me help you overcome these obstacles so that you may increase your income quickly. Let me begin with the first issue. Sales management, whether this describes you or not, is paid to do one thing—increase sales at a profitable level. The quicker management does this, the better. It is all based on doing more in the same amount of, or less, time. In all my years of sales and sales management, I have never seen a company terminate a top-producing salesperson for increasing business from within his current account base. In fact, the smart sales executives encourage it.

Secondly, with the advent of sales force automation software, sales managers are able to track new sales to current accounts. It is as simple as pulling up or printing a report.

Third, the best place to find opportunities to expand your business is from within a friendly environment. The reasons for this are numerous:

- You face less rejection because you are a known and proven entity.

- It is easier to network due to the fact that your current contact can take you around and introduce you to other key people within that account.

- You know the company's business. (You better know it.)

- The company's culture is familiar to you.

- You already have an understanding of purchasing procedures.

- Supposedly, you know who are the decision makers and influencers.

- Your current contacts will support you. If they don't, they are saying that they made a bad buying decision and no one will own up to that.

41

- You will face less competition. When you do face competition, it will be easier to get data on them.

All of the above means one thing…you'll sell more in a shorter time!

Sometimes our current account relationships are taken for granted. Not only can you network within your accounts, but you can also compress your sales cycle by asking a current account, "Who else supplies you who could use *our services*?" Your contact has a certain amount of clout over other vendors, channel partners, and key suppliers. Get them to exert that clout for you. Remember that it is a race between you and your competitors to sell more new business.

Fourthly, I have worked with an abundance of professional sales people who feel that they should be happy with the business that a customer has given them. Let's get this straight right now! You have earned that business (they haven't given it to you) and the right to ask for more. Do you want to sell more, increase your income, and experience unlimited success? Then don't let the customer control the sales cycle. That's *your* job! Don't fear that you are pushing your account if you ask for more business. The only time that you ought to fear that is if you haven't met expectations when servicing the account. Always, I repeat, always ask the account for more business.

A very wise sales manager once told me, "Don't ever buy for your customer from your own pocket." In other words, don't assume your customer views things the way you would if you were in his shoes. Don't prejudge or make decisions for your customer. Don't assume that your customer is not interested, considers the price to be too high, or won't give you a referral or exert some pressure on another supplier for you. Let your customer be the one to tell you, "Not right now." As I once advised my then teenage son about dating, "Let the young lady decide for herself if she wants to go out with you. Don't make the decision for her by not asking. You just might be surprised."

Finally, as I stated previously, if the numbers add up to a win at month or quarter end, then you've done your job. Your sales manager may be absolutely correct in urging you not to put all your eggs into one or two large baskets. There are many uncontrollable variables in these types of relationships; however, I will tell you that if the deal is structured properly to ensure a long-term contract and you maintain a strong relationship, you just might be okay. It is up to you to penetrate that account to become indispensable. One word of caution: Beware of the new faces on your customer's organizational chart.

COMPRESSION CONCEPT:
CUSTOMER INTERNAL OPPORTUNITY ANALYSIS

By conducting a brief customer internal opportunity analysis, you will discover just how much more time you should invest in that particular customer. Along with maximizing your time investment, this short exercise will assure that you have earned all the business before your competitors stumble into that customer. Listed here are some key questions that will provide you with the answers in identifying additional opportunities that exist within that account.

- How satisfied have you been with our service or product so far?

Remember that this question is only asked when you are sure of the answer, and the response had better be positive. Once you have received the positive reply, then the next words out of your mouth should be the following questions. If you feel an answer is going to be negative, then you had better focus on cleaning up your act before you look for more problems.

- Within your company (division), who do you know that could possibly use our service or product?
- Within your company (division), who do you know that currently uses a service or product similar to ours?
- How could I meet with your counterpart in the other division? Or, how could we arrange to meet your counterpart in the other division?
- How could I get on the agenda for your next management meeting to show what we've accomplished together using our service or product?
- I'd like to write a letter to your chief executive officer (CEO) telling him or her about the tremendous results that you've realized using our service or product. What is that e-mail address?
- Who are some of your other (noncompetitive to you) strategic suppliers who might be able to use our service or product?

43

- Which customers of yours would you feel good about referring me to?
- What are some of the other programs your company is developing that we might be able to help you with?
- If budget weren't a concern, what would be on your wish list for the next 2 years?
- What are your firm's top initiatives for the next 2 years?
- Who is on your board of directors? How would I be able to contact them?

It is a well-known fact that many of your accounts have boards of directors to advise your customers' managements on their respective areas of expertise. For instance, most boards of directors have an attorney, a financial expert, an operations guru, a technical person, and possibly a sales and marketing authority. It is also a well-known fact that these directors usually serve on multiple boards or are highly placed within their own organizations. Many directors hold large blocks of stock of the companies on whose boards they serve. They have a vested interest in what you can do to help the companies on whose boards they sit. Again, it's a race to the sale. Why not run on the fastest track to that business? Instead of cold calling on a buyer in XYZ Company, wouldn't it be quicker to have a member of the board of directors refer you to the right people within the prospect?

It is imperative to get answers to all the listed questions. They will help you win the sales race and trim down your sales cycle because of your predisposition within that account. You no longer need to build credibility or rapport. It's already done. How much time will that save you? Who will get there first?

SALES RACE RULE 1

Short Cycle sellers know that there is no substitute for a good account management plan.

COMPRESSION CONCEPT: ACCOUNT MANAGEMENT PLAN

Once you have identified the opportunities for new business within your current accounts, thereby compressing your sales cycle, you will need to develop an account management plan that you can use to guide your customer through your sales cycle. The act of writing an account management plan in itself will not condense your sales cycle or keep your competitors out. Rather, it is how you use the account management plan to sell more to those respective accounts that will condense your sales cycle. By writing a plan for your strategic accounts, you are taking responsibility for your successes within those accounts and that will force you to take control of your sales cycle. When you control the sales cycle, you control the accounts. That means that you establish the buying plan for all your accounts.

Among many other things, the account plan shows how you think you can help improve your customer's business. In other words, based upon the customer's needs, the plan shows what you intend to sell to that particular account within your next fiscal year. Once you have identified this information, what is the best way to use this data to speed through your sales cycle?

The best method to accomplish this is to guide the account at a year-end meeting. Namely, you hold a strategic account-planning meeting with your customer. The objective of this meeting is to show how you can help your customer grow his bottom line and/or sales in the next year. Together, you determine his goals, sync them with your plans, lay out a time line, and obtain a *tentative* commitment from your client. The best way to illustrate this is to cite a plan used by Vectra Bank's private bank senior vice president, Jeana Chisholm, and vice president, Russell Anderson.

THE VECTRA/ZIONS BANCORP CASE

In their 2000 annual report, the Zions Bancorporation of Salt Lake City listed over 370 banking locations throughout the western and southwestern United States. Until recently, their Vectra Bank group did not have a particularly strong private banking division. Private banking refers to the services and products that banks sell to individuals, mostly those with significant wealth. These services and products can range from investments and retirement planning to trust services. In an effort to bolster their private banking efforts, Vectra recruited and hired both Ms. Jeana Chisholm and Mr. Russell Anderson. Immediately, Mr. Anderson began working with the few Vectra private bankers already on staff. Knowing that cross-selling new products to already existing private bank customers was the quickest way to shorten his private banker's sales cycle, Mr. Anderson began an analysis of each private banking client's portfolio. From this examination, he was able to determine which existing private banking customers were good candidates to cross-sell new products. Then he met with each private banker and developed an account plan for each of their respective private banking clients. Within each *account plan* is a list of products each customer currently uses and goals and strategies to sell these customers products they are not presently using.

Mr. Anderson then instructed his private bankers to set up a meeting with each of their private banking customers to lay out a plan for increasing that customer's personal wealth for the next year. These private bankers were trained to approach their clients by saying, "After several discussions with you and a careful analysis of your private banking needs, I would recommend these financial products to help you build and protect your personal assets for next year. Here is what each one will do to enhance your situation. . . . Just for planning reasons, ideally what would be the best timetable to do each of these?" Big benefits were realized very quickly. Of course, what this actually did was put the bankers back in control of their sales cycle and allowed them to become more consultative by having a plan to "guide" their customers to the next sale.

Mr. Anderson found that by soliciting a tentative or "just for planning reasons" time line commitment on each financial product, his bank indeed received

1. An assurance from its client that he was interested in the financial products or services being proposed

2. The approximate time that the client would like to implement such programs

If the banker runs into some resistance, he handles it by saying, "I understand your concerns about making a commitment, but this information is just for planning purposes and would illustrate the *ideal* situation. In order for me to help you grow your assets, we need to lay out several different scenarios. If the opportunity arises, we will be prepared to capitalize on the situation. Now what were those tentative dates?"

Next the banker prepares a written account plan and gives a copy to his client so that both parties are "on the same page." Remember that if it is in writing, it is much more likely to happen. The banker then marks his client calendar or palm device to remind him when the first proposals are due. The result is more sales to his current relationships within a shorter period of time.

SALES RACE RULE 2

The absolute #1 QUICKEST way to beat your competitors through the sales cycle is to ask your current accounts for help.

COMPRESSION CONCEPT: YOUR CUSTOMERS WANT TO HELP YOU

Believe this! It's true. Your customers want to help you be successful. They want to help you win the sales race. Besides buying more from you, the best way they can help you compress your sales cycle is by providing you with names of prospects, but you must ask them first. You know this already! I know that you do, so then why don't you ask for referrals? Over 70 percent of all the salespeople that I observe on calls never ask their good customers for a referral. Never! Is it that you expect them to greet you at the door with a new list of prospects every time that you visit them? What is it that keeps you from asking? Four of the most common reasons that salespeople don't ask current customers for referrals are

1. Salespeople don't really understand the significant compression or shortening impact that a referral has on their sales cycles.

2. Many salespeople know how to ask for the order, but don't know how to ask customers for help in the form of a referral.

3. The prospects you are referred to are really suspects, and you end up wasting your time chasing around after someone who is not going to buy. Remember that a true prospect for your product or service has

   Control over budget

   The authority to make a buying decision

   Need or want for your service or product

   If your so-called prospect is missing one of these criteria, he is a suspect, not a prospect. Stop wasting your time and prolonging your sales cycle. Tell your customer that you would prefer referrals that meet the criteria for a prospect.

4. You often encounter "referral reluctance" because you feel it is awkward or you don't want to pressure your customers. If you want to shorten your sales cycle, you'll need to get over it. Once you try asking current customers for help finding new business, you will see just how dedicated they become to your success.

All four of these are symptoms of either not training your customers to give you quality and consistent help finding new prospects or not knowing how to train them. Most importantly, if you are not precise in specifying what type of prospect help you are seeking, you will get lists and lists of suspects. Remember that if your accounts receivable department can train your customers to pay their bills on time, you can train your customers to automatically give you unending help finding new business. Training them to give referrals certainly has to be easier than training customers to pay their bills in a timely manner.

The best place to have a customer start looking for new business for you is in their *realm*. The pools of people that surround your customers in their everyday lives are frequently referred to as their realm. Their realm typically includes:

Friends

Neighbors

Family

Doctor

Dentist

Minister

Lawyer

Insurance agent

Suppliers

Trade association members

Fellow employees

Current customers

Past customers

These are the people that your customer knows the best. Each member of your customer's realm has his own realm with just as many, if not more, people than your customer does and so on and so on. It is a self-perpetuating stream of information and referrals. The key is to be disciplined enough to teach your customers to promote your business within their own realm.

The benefits to you for doing so are major. Let's take a quick look at the spoils of diligent referral practice:

- A steady stream of prospects not suspects.
- A shortened sales cycle because you already have credibility with these people.
- A condensed prospecting stage, in your sales cycle, due to the fact that you do not have to spend as much time searching out prospects.
- A higher close ratio due to the fact that you are selling to prospects, not suspects.
- You win the sales race.

COMPRESSION CONCEPT:
THE FIVE STEPS TO TAKE TO TRAIN YOUR
CUSTOMERS TO SHORTEN YOUR SALES CYCLE

How do you train your customers to find and refer prospects from their realm, thereby shortening your sales cycle considerably?

Reciprocate. Be proactive in giving your customers solid referrals for their business. The best payback is to help your customer find more business. Once you begin reciprocity, you will be perpetuating a strong referral relationship.

Enumerate. Keep a list of referrals that each customer sends your way, and let that customer know you appreciate it. The best way to accomplish this is to develop a spreadsheet on your computer for each customer. List the referrals the customer has given you and the outcomes.

Formulate. Develop a strategy with a series of handwritten letters that informs your customer of his referral outcome, good or bad. The first letter should be a quick thank you note for the referral and assurance that you will call on the referred party immediately. The second letter should be notice that you've just met with the referred party and any outcomes. The third letter should be the final letter to your customer telling him what happened as a result of his referral.

Educate. Be specific about the type of prospect that you work with best.

Reward. Be sure to reward the customers who help you the most. Appropriate rewards include lunches, dinners, gift certificates, plants, or a solid referral for them. Remember that you will get more of the type of behavior that you reward. It's human nature!

I frequently hear clients ask this question, "How many times should we call a prospect and experience zero response before we give up on them? Since my customer has given me this name, I feel an obligation to make every last effort." My first response is that regardless of where you obtained the lead, you should feel obligated to make every effort. My second retort is that if you are continuously prospecting and asking for referrals, no one prospect will make or break your sales year.

There is no predetermined number of times that you should continue to call a prospect without response. You must weigh three facts:

1. The size of the sale or potential of the account.
2. The probability of making the sale.
3. The amount of time you are spending that could be used looking for other prospects with higher closing probabilities.

A great way that I've found to test your nonresponsive prospect's intent is to send a quick e-mail saying, "Mr. Prospect, I've been given your name by Joe Soandso. I'm a person who might be able to help improve your bottom line. I have been leaving voice mail messages for you, but I thought that e-mail might be a more expeditious way of communication. On a scale of 1 to 5, 5 being very interested and 1 being not interested, how interested would you be in arranging a brief appointment to visit with me? Please let me know what you think." I will tell you from personal experience that many times I have been surprised and received an almost instant message back from them. You see, it's better to get a response of "1" and move on than to keep on trying to no avail to reach this person.

Don't be afraid to walk away because, if you don't walk, you might be extending your sales cycle and wasting your money. Let your competitors call on suspects.

Finally, do not be apprehensive about what your customer will say if the referral doesn't work out. He was just trying to help, and if you phrase it properly, you will continue to earn his help in finding new business. The best way to position this statement is, "Mr. Customer, thanks so much for referring me to Neil Down. We were unable to connect (or we played telephone tag), so I will put him in my database and I'll try back in a few days."

SALES RACE WRAP-UP

Sales management is universally focused on performance. In reality, it doesn't matter where the numbers come from, whether it is new accounts or referrals from current customers. Management wants you to win the sales race against your competitors. The safest and fastest place to gain new business is from leads that are generated from current satisfied customers. Most of these opportunities will be from sources external to your customer, but many possibilities exist within the customer himself. As a professional salesperson who is in training to become a Short Cycle seller, you must practice the five steps that will train your customers to give you referrals. These steps are

Reciprocate. Be proactive in giving your customers solid referrals for their business.

Enumerate. Keep a list of referrals that each customer sends your way and let the customer know you appreciate it.

Formulate. Develop a strategy with a series of handwritten letters that informs your customer of his referral outcome, good or bad.

Educate. Be specific about the type of prospect that you work with best.

Reward. Be sure to reward the customers who help you the most.

In order to enhance the probability of success, you must be well versed in utilizing *opportunity analysis* determination. This comes from practicing the usage of specific questioning techniques discussed in this chapter.

An account management plan assures you that you are running the sales race on the fastest track. By implementing an account plan for your customers, you are taking back control of your sales cycle. By taking control of your sales cycle, you are accomplishing two major goals toward beating your competitors through the sales cycle:

1. You, as the professional consultative salesperson, are determining the speed at which the account will develop.

2. Presenting an account plan to your customer's top management will provide you significant leverage throughout the entire organization. It will keep your competitors running the sales race in their street shoes.

MASTERING YOUR OWN SALES CYCLE

Write a referral profile of the type of customer you like dealing with. Be sure to include location, size of business, type of business, position titles, technical orientation, financial position, the prospect's customer base, and anything that you consider to be important to your success. Use the given form to complete your profile. After you have done this, fax, e-mail, mail, or hand carry it to five of your customers. Attach a nice letter thanking the customer in advance for his cooperation. Be sure to print this on your letterhead and include your business card.

Date: _____

Characteristics:

1. _____

2. _____

3. _____

4. _____

5. _____

6. _____

7. _____

8. _____

9. _____

10. _____

Who does this remind you of?

Name: _____

Title: _____

Company: _____

Phone: _____

How do you know them? _____

Name: _____

Title: _____

Company: _____

Phone: _____

How do you know them? _____

Name: _____

Title: _____

Company: _____

Phone: _____

How do you know them? _____

CHAPTER FIVE

A.R.E.B.A.!

The Quickest Track to the
First Appointment

As in all races, when the starter's gun sounds, the first step is the most crucial.

As we alluded to in Chapter 4, sometimes the roughest thing to do in your sales cycle is to get the prospect or customer to return your messages or voice mail. This is a place where you spend an inordinate amount of time, probably too much time. Hence, this is an ideal stage to concentrate on squeezing your sales cycle. It is an ideal opportunity to gain a step on your competitors.

With the advent of the consultative salesperson, the only real selling you need to do is getting the initial appointment. This is no easy task in today's world of the wonderful voice mail feature; however, our experience shows that the absolute quickest way to get a response and sell the appointment is to use a model we call *A.R.E.B.A.* It is an acronym for **A**pproach, **R**eason, **E**xplain, **B**enefit, and **A**sk. It was designed with one thing in mind—to shorten your sales cycle.

Remember that your goals are

1. To get your prospect customer to grant you an appointment with as few telephone calls to her as possible.

2. Get in front of the prospect or customer before your competitors do.

THE A.R.E.B.A. MODEL

The A.R.E.B.A. concept is a five-step system that, when strictly adhered to, will help you compress your sales cycle time and blow the doors off your competitors.

Approach. Introduce yourself and your firm, ask about timing, and present your Unique Selling Proposition (USP).

Reason. Tell the prospect the reason for your call.

Explain. Explain to the prospect what you normally do at the interview. This will get her past the uncertainty or threat stage.

Benefit. What benefit will the prospect derive by visiting with you? Her time is very valuable so what will her payback be? Remember that everyone is interested in what's in it for them.

Ask. Ask for the appointment!

Next, let's examine each component of the model and develop possible scripts. Again, our goals are to sell the appointment with as few telephone calls as possible and get in front of the prospect or customer before your competitors do. You will probably face one of the following four basic scenarios of initial prospect contact when using this model:

Cold call. First contact ever.

Two-letter introductory series. Warm call due to prior correspondence.

Networking chance meeting. Met at the chamber and she said, "Call me."

Referral. From another client.

For purposes of examination, let's use the toughest scenario, the cold call. If you can handle this situation, you will certainly be able to adapt to the other three.

COLD CALL: FIRST CONTACT EVER

Approach

This may seem foolish to many of you, but over the years I have observed several salespeople, veterans and rookies, who actually have a difficult time making a halfway professional telephone approach to a person they do not know. Consequently, they procrastinate and build significant delay into their sales cycles. Meanwhile, their competitors are down the street selling initial appointments to the same prospects like it's going out of style.

Many times I've heard the first words out of a veteran salesperson's mouth be, "Ms. Smith, you don't know me, but I'm so and so with ABC Corporation." Right away Ms. Smith is on the defensive because you're right, she doesn't know you and she's not so sure she wants to know you. She has enough business contacts in her life. Some sales professionals advise you to start with the "You don't know me, but . . ." My particular experience is that this begins the conversation on a negative note.

The strongest prospect approach method in the A.R.E.B.A. model would sound like this: "Ms. Smith, my name is Stan Tall and I am your account manager with ABC Corporation. We are the original manufacturers of Artificial Water Products. Is this a convenient time for me to take a brief moment to introduce myself?"

Take note that Stan Tall mentioned his USP in the first two sentences. Also, take note that he did not go into much about his USP. Stan has set the stage to repeat his USP later in the *reason* and *benefit* steps of the A.R.E.B.A. model.

Once you have agreed upon a time of mutual convenience or you have been given the green light on the first call, move quickly to the reason for your call.

Reason

The reason for your call is to get an interview appointment with the prospect or client as soon as she can see you. It is delivered as a statement and can be phrased in many different ways. Remember that your only objective at this point is to sell an appointment and get off the telephone. There are two rules, Sales Race Rules 3 and 4, for delivering your reason for the call.

SALES RACE RULE 3

Keep it brief. The more you talk, the more chance you have of prompting an objection.

YOUR REASON: The reason for my call is to see how I can get on your calendar for a few moments to show you how we have helped other large companies like yours improve their bottom line through the use of artificial water. (Be quiet at this time! Wait for a response. Do not talk before the prospect speaks!)

You have just asked an open-ended question that requires an explanation from your prospect on *how* you can get on her calendar. You didn't ask *if* you could get on her calendar. Always assume you can get on her calendar. Now find out how.

Explain

The explanation stage of the model refers to the process of telling the prospect what will transpire at the appointment. It is stated carefully in a way that eliminates any tension or threat perceived by the prospect or customer. Any hint of a hard sell at this point will definitely make your sales cycle longer because the prospect or customer will find a way to stall you. Therefore, it is imperative to word the explanation in a way that makes it apparent to the prospect that you are just looking for information (that is exactly what you should be doing). Try this wording of your explanation (of what will occur at the customer appointment): "Let me suggest that we set aside a few moments next Wednesday morning to meet. That would allow both of us to ask a few questions of each other to determine if there is any interest. The benefit to you of doing so is . . ."

You have just put the prospect or customer at ease and told her that you are going to ask a few questions and she can ask a few questions. It's an interview! Not a sales call!

Benefit

Do you want to cut your sales cycle time in selling the initial appointment? Give the prospect a real benefit for seeing you!

SALES RACE RULE 4

More than likely your prospect or customer will not give you the appointment unless you give her a benefit for seeing you.

Everyone wants to know, "What's in it for me? What will be my payback? What can I gain from spending some time with you? How can my organization benefit? How will this meeting eventually help me look good in the eyes of my boss and employees?" Keep these questions in mind when you state the *benefit* to your prospect for allowing you an appointment.

The benefit can be stated in two ways: directly or implied. If your style is to be more direct, then use the word *benefit* in your statement. Your Direct Benefit Statement will sound like the following: "The benefit to you for seeing me is that I can show you how we have added 2 percent to your competitors' bottom lines and improved employee morale."

If your style is to be subtler, then use the Implied Benefit Statement. It implies that the prospect will infer the benefit from your statement. An Implied Benefit Statement will sound something like the following: "As I mentioned earlier, I can show you how we have helped add 2 percent or more to other large companies' bottom lines and not at the expense of employee morale."

Ask

The final and easiest step in the model is to ask for the appointment. As someone once said, "They are expecting you to ask. Don't let them down." This is called *closing the appointment.* It may be accomplished in a couple of different ways.

1. OEQ Close (open-ended question close)

2. Consultative Close (suggestive or recommendation)

YOUR OEQ CLOSE: When would be a good time for you next Wednesday?

OPTIONAL OEQ CLOSE: How could I get on your calendar for next Wednesday?

YOUR CONSULTATIVE CLOSE: Let me recommend that we get together next Wednesday for a few moments to discuss this.

YOUR OPTIONAL CONSULTATIVE CLOSE: I normally suggest that the best way to find out more about each other is that we get together for a few minutes. How does next Wednesday look for you?

Because today's selling environment is changing so rapidly, you may be an inside salesperson who is trying to make the next appointment for a teleconference or a Web conference. If that is your situation, then A.R.E.B.A. will work very nicely for you. Just don't forget to find out whom else in their organization you should contact for the conference. Also, many times inside sales professionals will encounter a prospect who will want to talk right now. Be prepared for the interview. If she wants to do it now, do it!

If you are an outside salesperson and your prospect starts to ask questions about your product or service, very politely say, "That is an excellent question. I'll take note of that, and we can discuss it in more detail next Wednesday." Resist the temptation to talk. I've seen too many salespeople talk on and lose the appointment to an objection that they were unprepared for.

The entire dialogue for selling the appointment looks like this:

YOU: Ms. Smith, my name is Stan Tall and I am your account manager with ABC Corporation. We are the original manufacturers of Artificial Water Products. Is this a convenient time for me to take a brief moment to introduce myself?

PROSPECT: How much time will this take?

YOUR OPTIONAL REPLY: Just a couple minutes.

YOUR REASON: The reason for my call is to see how I can get on your calendar for a few moments to show you how we have helped other large companies like yours improve their bottom line through the use of artificial water.

YOUR EXPLANATION: Let me suggest that *we* set aside a few moments next week to meet. That would allow *both of us* to ask a few questions of each other to determine if there is any interest.

YOUR BENEFIT STATEMENT: The benefit to you for seeing me is that I can show you how we have added 2 percent to your competitors' bottom lines and improved employee morale.

YOUR OEQ CLOSE: How could I get on your calendar for next Wednesday?

THE SPECTRANETICS CASE

One of the most progressive fields in America's healthcare industry is that of cardiac care. Spectranetics Corporation is the most innovative manufacturer of excimer lasers used to vaporize coronary blockages in cardiac arteries and remove faulty electrical leads on heart pacemakers. The unique selling propositions for Spectranetics are that their laser procedure has much longer lasting results for the patient than that of the traditional angioplasty and takes much less time than the conventional procedure of removing faulty pacemaker leads. The benefit for the cardiologists (heart specialists) using the excimer laser is that actual time to perform each operation is drastically reduced. The benefit for the patient is a shorter time on the table in the cardiac catheter laboratory, safer conditions, and better results. The equipment costs of over $250,000 forced cardiologists to rely on the hospitals where they practice to purchase it.

The ultimate end user is the cardiologist. However Spectranetics' sales people must call on hospital CEOs and chief financial officers (CFOs) because they are the ones who provide the funding to put a laser into their hospitals. If a significant number of different cardiologists practicing at a hospital want a piece of equipment badly enough and the CEO or CFO feels that the equipment will generate a sufficient number of procedures to be profitable, a purchase order is placed.

For those of you who sell medical equipment, supplies, or pharmaceuticals, you know how difficult it is to get medical doctors to grant you an initial appointment. For those of you who don't sell to this market, we can liken it to a task more difficult than Dorothy, the Tin Man, the Scarecrow, and the Lion trying to get into see the Wizard of Oz. The typical Spectranetics' sales representative was having difficulty gaining entrance into the doctor's office because of the new technology of excimer lasers and some bad publicity from a few years ago. The way that they would make a doctor's acquaintance was to wait outside the cardiac catheter lab (the place the cardiologists perform these procedures) until a procedure was over and then talk with them on their way to another patient. Generally, they were given very little time by the doctors and had difficulty explaining their USP.

Spectranetics then trained their representatives on the A.R.E.B.A. model. At first it took a few weeks of practice to develop the proper approach and benefit, but once the Spectranetics' sales staff started using it, their number of initial appointments soared. What they quickly discovered was that the cardiologists were very interested in the *benefit* of being able to do more procedures in less time (more income to them) and that the patients would actually be more comfortable with less risk and longer lasting affects.

The A.R.E.B.A. model helped Spectranetics cut its sales cycle time drastically because now the salepeople were able to visit with the cardiologists in their offices and consult on various cardiac cases. Just recently they posted record sales and earnings.

A question that consistently is posed to us is, "Can A.R.E.B.A. be used in person or is it designed to be used only over the telephone?" The answer is that A.R.E.B.A. can definitely be used in person. It is very effective when used at networking events, trade shows, or trade association meetings. Regardless of whether you are on the telephone or in person, the fact remains that in order to cut your sales cycle time, you must sell the appointment as soon as possible. A.R.E.B.A. helps you get in front of the prospect more quickly than your competitors so that you can start your consultative sales process before your competitors sell their first appointment.

Now imagine that you are attending an industry trade show and you run into one of your top prospects at breakfast. Your initial effort should be to secure an appointment on the spot using the exact same A.R.E.B.A. system. You can use the same approach: explain to them what will happen at the interview, give them the same benefit as you would over the telephone, and ask for the appointment.

E-TECHNOLOGY WILL SAVE YOU THOUSANDS IN LITERATURE COSTS AND SALES CYCLE TIME

The greatest boon to paper conservation and elimination of paper waste due to uninterested prospects dumping your literature is your Web site. While you cannot force a prospect or customer to read your Web site, you can successfully sell yourself faster and easier through Web site promotion. I have not had a marketing brochure for my company for over 6 years, and I can honestly say that it has not hurt our growth or sales effort one bit. Yes, I do use a two-letter introductory series to prospects and, yes I do e-mail our Web site to prospects, but my primary goal is to drive prospects to my Web site.

Many times prospects will ask me to send them a brochure, and I respond to them by saying that they can get up-to-date information on our firm by visiting our Web site. Quite frequently, when prospects or referrals call me and ask for literature, I ask them if they have Web access near them at that very moment. I'd estimate that 85 percent of the time they do. I then give them my URL (Web site address) and ask them to go there right at that time. I take about 5 or 10 minutes to help them navigate the site, and during that time I begin to qualify them with open-ended questions.

Recently, our firm invested several thousand dollars in updating our Web site. Experts say that it should be renewed every 2 or 3 years, so don't expect that you will save thousands and thousands by eliminating your product brochures and putting them online. If you are marketing properly, that money will be spent on Web site enhancements and updating. The sweetest thing about putting all your products and services on your Web site is that if you change or improve a product feature, your customers and prospects will know quickly, not a month or 6 weeks later due to printing and graphic arts design time. Talk about an advantage in winning the sales race. That's a big one.

SALES RACE WRAP-UP

The two goals of the A.R.E.B.A. model are to

1. Sell the appointment with as few telephone calls as possible
2. Get in front of the prospect or customer before your competitors do

The reason that your current efforts to sell the initial appointment may be taking so long is that you may not be giving the prospect a benefit for spending time with you. Everyone is interested in "what's in it for me." So, tell them what's in it for them. Give them a reason to see you.

MASTERING YOUR OWN SALES CYCLE

Write the name of the market segment that you have not had as much success with as you had hoped on the line.

Market segment: _____

Identify a target prospect within this segment and write their name on the line.

Target prospect: _____

Then going back, review the Unique Selling Proposition for that segment. Write it in the lines provided.

Unique Selling Proposition: _____

_____

_____

Now using the information you have provided, write your A.R.E.B.A. steps for the initial call on the target prospect you have listed.

Approach: _____

_____

Reason: _____

_____

Explain: _____

_____

Benefit: _____

_____

Ask: _____

_____

COMPRESSION OBJECTIVES

A Big Key to Winning the Sales Race

The most tenacious competitor will win hands down.

If indeed there is one specific key to compressing your sales cycle and beating your competitors, it is your ability to get the prospect or current customer to do exactly what is required to move to the next stage in your sales cycle at *your will*. This sounds like a magic trick performed with smoke and mirrors, doesn't it? In all actuality, you only need three criteria that I've previously discussed to accomplish this sorcery-like job:

1. *A true prospect or customer*. Remember, without a want or need, a budget, and the ability to make a decision, you have a suspect, not a prospect.

2. *Knowledge of your sales cycles*. We thoroughly examined the racecourse, your own sales cycle. In fact, by conducting the personal development exercises in Chapter 1, you will have intimate knowledge of your sales cycle.

3. *Desire to close the transaction*. Motivate yourself and want to get the business at darn near all costs.

Then what's the big deal? Where is the hidden factor that allows us to shorten the time it takes to get from prospect to close? What is a *Compression Objective,* and what part does it play in our sales race strategy?

Most professional salespeople, veterans and rookies alike, make two costly, time consuming mistakes in their sales cycles:

1. They focus on the wrong sales objectives.

2. They concede control of the sales cycle to their customer.

FOCUSING ON THE WRONG SALES OBJECTIVE

Sales management forces us to focus on many differing and some-times conflicting sales objectives. Generally in the profession of sales, we start from zero sales every month and our goal never decreases from year to year; it only increases. Management wants us to attain ob-jectives like

Increase volume

Increase margin

Find more strategic accounts

Obtain more referrals

Do more cross-selling of product lines

Reduce sales expenses

Increase the number in our account base

Reactivate old accounts

Increase call activity

Reduce sales cycle time

While these are admittedly excellent objectives for every sales force in the world, sales management doesn't address the one real objective that will shorten your sales cycle, thereby allowing you to easily reach all the above. That one objective is referred to as the *Compression Objective*, which we will discuss in the next section.

CONCEDING CONTROL OF THE SALES CYCLE TO THE CUSTOMER

In many contemporary sales training programs, participants are bombarded with the concepts of customer-centered or customer-focused philosophies. This curriculum is excellent, but misleads you into believing that unless you concede control of the sales cycle to the customer or prospect, you will be viewed as not having the customer's or prospect's best interests at heart. It is vital to be customer-centered and -focused, but nothing gets sold to those valued customers if you let them take control of your sales process. Being customer-centered and -focused really means that you understand enough about your customers' businesses that you are selling them what they want and need to make their businesses profit and grow. It means that you have a thorough understanding of why they buy, what they buy, when they buy, and how they buy. In other words, it means that you know your sales cycle better than they do. It does not mean that you relinquish control of that sales cycle to them.

COMPRESSION CONCEPT: THE COMPRESSION OBJECTIVE

The concept of the Compression Objective can best be explained as making the number one objective of a sales appointment, interview, or call the attainment of the next stage in your sales cycle. I have worked with many companies who have taught their veteran and rookie salespeople that once in front of the customer or prospect, their first and primary priority is to gain as much information as possible in order to be able to identify and solve the customer's problem. Most recently this has been referred to as the act of *profiling* the customer. While obviously this is very important to keep the sales cycle operating, our clients have found that by making "fact and feeling" discovery a secondary objective and the Compression Objective the principal goal, their salespeople reach the close stage faster, thereby beating their competitors through the sales cycle.

To effectively illustrate Compression Objectives, Exhibit 6-1 returns us to the generic sales cycle that we offered in Chapter 1.

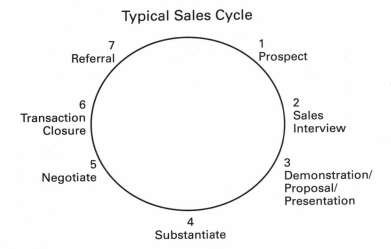

Typical Sales Cycle

7 Referral

1 Prospect

6 Transaction Closure

2 Sales Interview

5 Negotiate

3 Demonstration/ Proposal/ Presentation

4 Substantiate

Exhibit 6-1

While this may or may not resemble your particular sales cycle, we will use it for purely representative purposes. In this particular sales cycle, stage 1 is customer or prospect penetration. This is the stage where we make the initial call, whether it's the very first contact with a prospect or the first call to an incumbent customer on a new product or service. This is also the stage in which you need to "sell the appointment." This is not the stage in which you determine if you have a prospect or suspect. That should have been determined in a prior segmentation analysis conducted long before this initial call. Your Compression Objective in stage 1 is to get the customer to agree to stage 2 in your sales cycle, the sales interview. Once you have reached that goal, you need to stop talking and politely hang up the telephone.

SALES RACE RULE 5

You, as the professional salesperson, set the Compression Objective for each customer or prospect.

In stage 2, you have engaged the customer or prospect in a sales interview. Your only real objective, vis-à-vis the Compression Objective, is to secure stage 3, the demonstration/proposal/presentation. Yes, you do need to collect, discover, or profile your customer's needs, wants, and problems, but your ultimate objective is to guide the customer to agree to stage 3 before you leave the interview. That is the benchmark that you should measure the success or failure of your interview against. Do not leave the customer interview without an appointment or commitment from your customer or prospect for stage 3. Later in this chapter I will show you the best way to ask or suggest that commitment.

The same philosophy goes for stage 3 in the sales cycle of Exhibit 6-1. It is very important to make a positive and effective demonstration or proposal presentation. It is also vital that you address all your customer's or prospect's questions, objections, and stalls. However, during stage 3, your primary responsibility is to reach your Compression Objective. In this particular instance, your Compression Objective is to procure your customer's or prospect's agreement to substantiate you and your business proposition. In other words, you want your customer or prospect to agree to check your references within a particular time frame. It is imperative that you establish an agreed-upon time frame to check references and that *you* guide and enforce that time frame.

SALES RACE RULE 6

It is not necessary to follow all the stages in a sales cycle if your customer or prospect is ready to buy. Go to the close, but don't forget that after the close is the referral stage of your sales cycle.

After the customer or prospect has completed the substantiation stage, set your sights on stage 5, negotiation. The best way to make the transition from stage 4 (substantiate) to stage 5 (negotiate) is to suggest to the customer or prospect that if all your references check out to his satisfaction, you should meet again to discuss how to proceed. You already know how you want to proceed before you make this suggestion, don't you? You want to close the sale or engage the customer or prospect in some form of negotiations, so set a *tentative* date to meet after the substantiation activity. My experience from working with thousands of sales professionals in many fields tells me that the faster you reach the negotiation stage in your sales cycle, the better your chances of closing the sale. I have found that your probability of closing the transaction reaches 85 percent or better when you arrive at the negotiation stage. Does this mean that you can skip the other stages in your sales cycle and set negotiations as your Compression Objective during the initial "sell the appointment" telephone call? Yes and no! All customers have a need to feel in control of the sales cycle for their own psychological comfort. What you must do is be sensitive to that feeling, but also retain total control of *your* sales cycle. That is what you are paid to do. Since you are the one guiding the sales cycle by determining the Compression Objectives, you automatically have control of it.

Let me give you some pointers from personal experience that will make this work every time for you:

1. Always review your Compression Objectives before you ever pick up a telephone to call a customer or step into a prospect's premises.

2. Always know where you want the discussion to go before you open your mouth. Then take it there.

3. Always know the next stage in your sales cycle for that particular customer or prospect.

SALES RACE RULE 7

By establishing Compression Objectives for each stage of your sales cycle, you, not the customer, control the sales cycle.

COMPRESSION CONCEPT: THE CUSTOMER MUST TAKE SOME FORM OF ACTION

The concept of every customer visit or interview having a Compression Objective is counter to the philosophy of making *goodwill* customer calls. A "goodwill" call is a poor excuse for visiting your customer. In your mind you may have rationalized that goodwill calls are productive and in some way it helps the customer buy from you. You probably have told yourself that people buy from people they like, so I'd better drop in and spread some love. While it's true that people do buy from people they like, a *goodwill* call neither spreads love nor builds credibility. It shows the customer that you have nothing else to do, but waste their time. By utilizing Compression Objectives, you no longer need an excuse to make a customer call. In other words, I'm saying if the only reason you are calling on a customer is to build goodwill or courtesy, save your time and money and write them a polite thank you note or e-mail message to spread your love.

Put quite simply, and perhaps harshly, your only job is to get the customer to take some form of action or make a commitment to move the sale to the next stage in the sales cycle. That can be done politely, and that by itself will build goodwill. That form of customer action or commitment can manifest itself in many patterns. The customer can

Grant another appointment

Agree to allow you to meet with decision influencers

Introduce you to the real decision maker

Make a counteroffer on your proposal

Place the order

Provide you with three referrals

Check your professional references

Consent to a demonstration

Arrange for a formal presentation

Present your proposition to business partners

All the above examples are action- or commitment-based activities performed by your customer or prospect. They all require the customer to take some form of action on your behalf to move the sales cycle to the next stage. Your job is to identify what that action is and *ask* for it. Without your guidance, through asking, the customer will take control of *your* sales cycle because he'll have to guess what is next, take no action, make no commitment, or stall you.

The best ways to ask your customer for your Compression Objective are consultative in character. You need to take on the consultant's role. What is the primary job of a consultant? A consultant recommends and makes suggestions based on his expertise and specialized area of knowledge. Here are some ways of speaking to consultatively guide your customer to the next stage in your sales cycle.

May I suggest that we set up the next appointment now?

What we normally do at this point is meet with all of those who have input into the decision.

Let me recommend that we conduct a formal presentation.

Normally, at this point, we like to *recommend* a demonstration.

What my other clients have found that helps them is a face-to-face appointment.

What would we have to do to arrange a demonstration?

How could you help me get in front of the committee?

Let's pencil in a tentative date so that we will at least have it on our calendars.

Of course, like any good sales question or closing statement, these are all followed by silence. Remember that he who speaks first comes in last. Notice that these all have the feel of a consultative or counselor approach. Remember that you must *guide* customers to the next stage in *your* sales cycle.

THE "I DIDN'T STUDY ENGINEERING AND CHEMISTRY IN ORDER TO SELL" CASE

One of our most interesting cases involves a company that for years manufactured a pharmacological drug using very sophisticated manufacturing methods. Because of changes in the marketplace, this company eventually lost the contract to sell this drug. Revenues that the company derived from this contract were over 50 percent of its annual income. Other services such as material testing and chemical analysis earned the other 50 percent.

At the time, the organizational structure of this specialized firm did not lend itself to the extensive usage of an outside sales force. Because of the highly technical nature of its products and services, the company utilized its project managers and departmental managers for the actual sales function. This group of people, as you can well imagine, consisted primarily of very highly educated scientists and engineers. Many of them held doctorates and other advanced degrees in their respective fields. In fact, there was more brainpower in one of their training sessions than most companies have in their entire worldwide operations. These were people who did not go to school to become sales executives or account managers. In fact, they abhorred the word *sales* and anything that might be construed as even slightly associated with it.

Since their reputation was quite strong, leads were not a problem. As much as they didn't want to admit it, their sales efforts consisted only of responding to Requests for Proposals (RFPs) and not giving themselves much of an opportunity to actually sell their services or products or close the leads that they were getting. Exhibit 6-2 illustrates what they thought their sales cycle looked like.

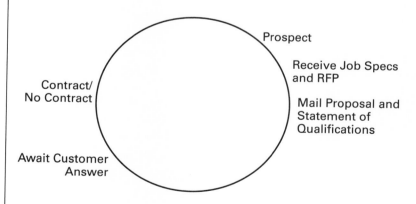

Exhibit 6-2

The problem with this sales cycle was that the prospect or customer had complete control of the process. The customers mailed a RFP, and the engineers and chemists responded. If the price or methodology was not satisfactory to the customer, then the company didn't get the job. If it was satisfactory to the customer, then the contract was signed. There was no information exchanged in the form of customer interviews. If the company was unsuccessful in winning a bid from a prospect, then so be it. If the company was unsuccessful in gaining a job from a current client, then it just waited for the next RFP from that client. If the company was awarded a job, after completion of that job, it waited for the next job RFP.

Gradually these scientists and engineers began to recognize that they did not understand their own sales cycle, and, therefore, they were losing a lot of work from current clients and they were at their clients' mercy. The very first thing that they did was to establish their real sales cycle by doing what chemists and engineers do best—analysis and process development. Once this was completed, they began to realize how they could take control of the sales process back from their customers.

The next step was to have the scientists and engineers realize that they had to identify Compression Objectives and procure some form of action from the client to reach that objective. In order to stimulate client action, they had to learn to become consultative. They found it much easier to suggest or recommend action than outright ask for it. Remember that these are the professionals who went to school not to learn how to sell, but to solve scientific and mechanical problems through equations and formulas and procedural analysis.

Breaking the mystique of selling into a logical sequential process of events was the first step to success. Then, I showed them that in order to reach the next logical stage in their sales process, they had to consultatively suggest or recommend some form of action to the customer. This was nonthreatening to them, and they found it to be a very professional approach. The genuine success came when they were able to gain control of the process and land more business. These non-sales types began to uncover opportunities within current clients that they thought never existed, and they also stopped waiting around for the business to be granted to them.

E-SELLING AND COMPRESSION OBJECTIVES

One of the biggest advantages to owning sales force automation or customer relationship management software is the capability these systems have to automate your Compression Objectives. Many CRM and SFA programs will allow you to input your sales cycle stages and then track your progress through that sales cycle by providing you with friendly little reminders that it's time to sell the first appointment or ask for the order or get a referral. Every morning that you log on to the system, it lists your Compression Objectives for countless prospects and customers.

The latest e-selling tool in attaining your Compression Objectives is Web conferencing. Several companies offer services that actually allow you to put your sales presentation online and combine that presentation with a telephone conference. Talk about shortening your sales cycle and winning the sales race through technology. Again, in The Resource Center at the back of the book, I list two such companies that can help you present to many customers or prospects with multiple decision makers at one time anywhere in the world. It is considered a virtual-reality meeting room. They stay at their respective desks and view your presentation while being able to ask questions at any time. This is ideal for long-distance relationships. The benefits to prospects and customers are phenomenal. They don't need to host an out-of-town guest, sit through a 2-hour meeting, dress up, or even be in their offices to participate in your sales presentation. They can even be in Asia and attend. My experience is that they truly enjoy the adventure. The benefits to you of Web conferencing are

1. You can conduct a presentation instantly to an interested prospect—beating your competitor and reaching them while they are interested.

2. There is no time lag while your arrange a trip in your busy schedule for travel to visit the prospect.

3. You eliminate travel expenses.

4. You can qualify your prospect without visiting them and eventually finding out that they are really suspects, not prospects.

5. Once you have qualified them as a true prospect, then you can use the trip to solidify the deal. This absolutely strengthens your return on your travel-dollar investment.

6. You can ask for the Compression Objective much more quickly than your competitor.

Many Web-conferencing companies offer free trials with their products. I urge you to give one of them a try. It will only take once, and you'll see what a tremendous aid this is in beating your competitors in the sales race.

SALES RACE WRAP-UP

The keys to successfully applying Compression Objectives are to

- Know the stages of your sales cycle.
- Guide your customers to that next stage by setting a Compression Objective for your next call. You will find that if you practice establishing Compression Objectives for each customer contact, guiding the customer will be easy.
- Gain some form of commitment or action from your customer at each stage. By taking the action that moves you to the next stage in your sales cycle, the customer has allowed your guidance.
- Maintain control of the sales process by utilizing Compression Objectives.
- Be consultative. Recommend or suggest to the customer that the next step is to move forward in the sales process.

If the customer is ready to buy, your next Compression Objective is to close the sale and ask for a referral. You do not need to follow your entire sales cycle if the customer wants to short-circuit it for you.

MASTERING YOUR OWN SALES CYCLE

List four customers or prospects with which you are currently working on a sale.

1. _____

2. _____

3. _____

4. _____

For each of the customers or prospects you listed, write down which stage of your sales cycle each is in currently?

1. _____

2. _____

3. _____

4. _____

Write your next Compression Objective for each customer or prospect.

1. _____

2. _____

3. _____

4. _____

CHAPTER SEVEN

LET THE CUSTOMER TELL YOU HOW TO WIN

It's Her Job!

No one knows more about what the customer needs and wants than the customer.

This precept holds true for buyers, customers, and prospects. They know their jobs and how they affect their business better than anyone else does. They know what will make them look good to their bosses and make their companies money. That's exactly why they can tell you how to be successful in dealing with them. They know the way to the sale. They possess the map to the end of the sales race. All you need to do is stop telling, start listening, take copious notes, and tell them what they've told you.

SALES RACE RULE 8

Let the customers tell you what to tell them in your proposal or presentation.

The entire customer interview process can be likened to driving down Main Street in an unfamiliar city. You are driving a car down a very busy main street in a city you've never visited before. Since you are driving, you are in control of the vehicle's speed and direction. Your destination is known, but you have no idea what the directions are to get there (your car does not have a global positioning device). There are many side streets that branch off of Main Street, and you know that eventually you will need to make a turn, but you don't know where or what direction.

Behold! You are not alone. Sitting in the other seat is your passenger clutching the city map, but she is unwilling to *volunteer* directions. Not only does she know the destination, but also she knows the quickest way there. At every street corner and intersection you look at her and ask, "Do I turn here?" She replies, "no!" The next street intersection approaches rapidly and you ask, "Is this the turn?" "No," she retorts. This goes on for several minutes, and soon you begin to simmer with frustration. You realize that you are getting nowhere fast, and deep down you recognize that time is slipping away. You've seen many other cars pass you, so finally you ask, "This is the street, isn't it?" and she replies, "yes!" You pull into the left turn lane and quickly complete the turn. As you hurry down the street, your intuition tells you to find out if you turned the correct direction. You ask, "Was I supposed to turn left back there?" She replies, "no!" Out of desperation you blurt, "What is the fastest way there from here?" Exactly!

In this analogy, the driver is the professional salesperson and the passenger is her customer, client, or prospect. As the driver, the salesperson must realize that she is in control of the car's speed and direction. This is parallel to what professional salespeople experience in their sales cycle. The cars passing her are her competitors, and from what you've just read, they know exactly where they are going. What could have saved this sales professional a significant amount of time in her journey? If you answered this question by saying the salesperson should have immediately asked the customer the fastest way there before she even turned on the engine, you are correct. By doing so she would have known the proper route and been able to reconfirm the directions as she proceeded. This is much like what the sales professional must do with every sales opportunity that she encounters. She must know the directions she wants to take according to each respective customer's situation.

So, what is the fastest path to the sales race finish line from where you are? It is the one shown to you by your customer, client, or prospect. Remember that it is your job to solicit these directions rather than wait for them to be volunteered. What is the best methodology to conduct this solicitation? The most concise and proven means to accomplish this is to follow the Sales Racer's Winning Discovery Strategy. Before we discuss this strategy, you must understand that the whole premise of this approach is based on disclosure and response. You must allow the customer to disclose key feelings and facts and respond accordingly. In a nutshell, you must be prepared for just about anything. Let's take a look at just how this is accomplished.

COMPRESSION CONCEPT: THE RACE WINNING DISCOVERY STRATEGY

All world-class sprinters and distance runners will tell you that no matter what the length of the race, they always, always, have an overall race strategy. That strategy is intended to produce a winner. Included in that scheme are conditioning, repetitive practice, biofeedback, diet, visualization, and a plan. Take note that all components of the strategy deal specifically with race preparation. As famous National Football League (NFL) coach and television commentator, Iron Mike Ditka, is attributed with saying, "Champions are made in the off-season." That is, champions are made through preparation. All the time and energy expended in preparation pays off in a few short moments of truth known as *The Race*.

As a world-class salesperson, you too need a race winning strategy that encompasses a strong preparation facet and focuses on your few short moments of truth known as the customer encounter or sales interview. From my observations and mistakes over nearly 25 years of selling, I also have developed a Sales Race Winning Discovery Strategy that has provided great returns for my clients and me many times over. It is heavy on preparation, listening, questioning, and diagnostics. Its main objective is to produce the sales race winner.

PREPARATION PHASE: USING INTERNET TECHNOLOGY

With the daily improvements and usage of Web sites, there is absolutely no excuse for the lack of preinterview planning. In fact, there is no excuse for not having some data on hand before you call to sell the initial appointment. As I've mentioned before, it's all out there. All you need to do is retrieve it. The time that it takes to do fundamental research on a customer or prospect is insignificant in the overall time of your sales cycle. I mentioned before that proper research time will compress your sales process over seven or eight times its value.

What resources do you have available to uncover data during your research? Not too long ago, I preached to salespeople to call public companies for their annual or 10K reports. Also, I told them to go to the library and see if those documents are on file there. If you've ever done that, you'll find that it takes about 10 days to 2 weeks to get the records that you've requested or you've found that the possibility of your library having them on file is remote.

The resources of the Internet will allow you to cut your sales cycle in half. Most company Web sites are designed to sell or attract investors. Therefore, they are usually abundant with information, if not even boastful. I have found that the data that I need to collect about prospects or customers is easily found on their Web sites. Even privately held companies seem to disclose a good portion of information that you need to prepare for the initial telephone call, initial visit, or tailoring your two-letter introductory series.

Most of the facts that you'll want to have at your fingertips during the interview can be found on the customer's Web site. If they're not, I've discovered that a customer's receptionist, telephone operator, administrative assistant, and even customer service department are great sources for that information. Try something right now. If you're reading this during traditional daytime working hours, put down the book, pick up the telephone, call a prospective customer's number, and ask for the customer service department. When they answer, say something like this. "Good afternoon, this is Jane Doe from ABC Company, how is the customer service business at XYZ Company today? (Pause for answer)

That's great (or that's too bad). Well, I have a very simple question for you and I'm not sure how I found my way to customer service, but I am sure you can help me." Then you ask the question for which you are seeking the answer. I've personally had great luck with this, and I'm sure it's because people in customer service are trained to help.

What type of data do you need before you enter the all-important interview stage of your sales cycle? It's best to be armed with an information base that includes recent financial history; current state of the industry; up-to-date company news such as acquisitions, mergers, key personnel changes; strategic customer list; new product offerings; chief competitors; branch or plant locations; and, of course, what the prospect's business is.

How important is it to have data in hand before or during the sales interview? Many times I have sat down with a prospect and the first thing she asks me is, "Well, Jim, how much do you know about our company?" Or, she may ask, "Jim, what have you read recently about what's going on in our industry?" I've also had many prospects say, "I suppose you know what's going on in our business?"

I remember once when I was trying to reach a senior vice president of sales for a $300 million electronics equipment manufacturer in quest of an initial appointment. I left numerous voice mails in his mailbox and messages with his administrative assistant, but I never received the courtesy of a reply. Since one of my best personality traits is tenacity, this went on for several weeks. Finally, one Friday evening about 6:00 p.m., I reached this gentleman in his office. He acknowledged that he had received my multitude of calls and proceeded to let me go through my A.R.E.B.A. steps. When it came to the moment to ask for the appointment, he said, "I'm sure that if you're calling on me to do business, you're current on the industry trends, aren't you?" He caught me cold. I had no idea about the industry trends or even his financial position. I had read, in the *Rocky Mountain News*, that he was the newly appointed senior vice president of sales and assumed that this was a good time to make inroads with him. Wrong! He certainly was the freshly anointed senior vice president of sales, but had I spent just a few minutes on the Web, I would have discovered that his industry was in the toilet. He went on to say, "Because our industry is so flat right now we can't even think about spending money, even on entertaining our largest customers. I tell you what though, why don't you call me back in a year and that should give you sufficient time to study up on our industry." Needless to say, I have never made another call without first either having someone in my office go online to get the necessary data or sitting down on a Saturday morning and researching it myself.

Since that embarrassing moment, information gathering has become a way of life around here. Because of that attitude, I have had many prospects tell me that they are very impressed by the knowledge I have accumulated about their businesses. I can personally attest that it gives you an inside track and definitely improves your chances of winning the sales race. By the way, I did call that senior vice president of sales back 1 year to the day. From reading press releases on his Web site, I knew that his business was much better. He granted me an appointment upon his return from a lengthy trip to Asia. The appointment never became a reality because upon his return, he mysteriously resigned, and I am now working on selling the initial appointment to his successor.

SCENARIO PLANNING

The second major aspect of the discovery process is referred to as scenario planning. If you've never tried this, you'll find it very helpful in your preparation for a sales interview. Scenario planning is a sales cycle shortening technique that can be used in the approach, interview, proposal, presentation, or negotiation stages of your sales cycle. It is another time-saving instrument in your sales toolbox that deals with preparation. It can best be characterized as a rehearsal mechanism that addresses your preparation for the unknown. Scenario planning is best described by the example of, "If she (customer or prospect) says this, then what do I say or how do I respond?" The objective of scenario planning is to identify all the possible outcomes, responses, or questions that your customer may have and prepare a proper response to each. This includes preparing for potential objections, stalls, and questions.

The most effective implementation of scenario planning is performed with your sales manager, if you have confidence in her abilities as a top salesperson. I don't say that as a disparaging remark, but out of actual concern for your sales success. If your sales manager does not have a strong track record in the field, this is one activity that you are better off doing with one of your other thriving sales colleagues.

The best place to scenario plan is in a conference room with a white board or an easel and pad. Scenario planning is great for both veteran salespeople and rookies. The scenario planning sessions that I've been involved with take anywhere from 30 to 45 minutes and are well worth the minimal time invested. They generally are conducted before the very first appointment with that strategic prospect or before an important presentation or the closing appointment, if your sales cycle includes those stages. These sessions are very helpful when you are trying to displace a competitor's line in one of your current accounts. I have, however, participated in scenario planning sessions that are held before that first telephone call is even made.

To begin the scenario planning session, list on the easel or white board all the questions you anticipate that your customer or prospect will ask you. Leave plenty of space between the questions so that you will be able to write your reply to each specific question right under it. Now list all the negative comments that you expect the customer to make, leaving space below each of them to write your response. These skeptical comments can come in the form of an objection, stall, or negotiating ploy.

Once you have all the likely questions and comments listed, go back and collaboratively develop several responses for each, taking into consideration the customer's behavioral style (Chapter 8). Write those responses in the space you left under each comment or question.

Next, review all your responses with your sales manager to be sure that you are comfortable with the wording. If the verbiage makes you uneasy and doesn't sound natural to you, then spend some time figuring out a more natural way to express yourself.

Finally, role play with your sales manager. Set the scenario, and then allow your sales manager to play the part of the customer. Be sure to spend several minutes rehearsing your answers. Firmly embed your replies into your memory, and visualize a positive outcome to your sales interview.

THE USA.NET CASE

Mr. Bob Moroni, former senior vice president of sales for USA.NET, the world's first and largest provider of Internet e-mail service, is a huge proponent of scenario planning. Mr. Moroni remembers one occasion where his sales team used this preparation tool on a large international telecommunications prospect. As Mr. Moroni told us, the telecommunications prospect drove a particularly hard bargain. They were firmly entrenched with an e-mail system that they had used for years, backed with a strong corporate relationship at the top management level with their current e-mail provider. The account potential was huge, and the telecommunications company's direct sales organization was interested in USA.NET's e-mail services over its existing provider. The time had come to close the deal, and Mr. Moroni's team set some time aside to scenario plan before they approached the close stage of their company's sales cycle. After a few hours of thorough brainstorming, the team members felt prepared. The next day Mr. Moroni's team went into the appointment fully primed.

According to Mr. Moroni, the results were amazing. They promptly addressed, with complete confidence, every obstacle, negotiating tactic, and stall that the telecommunications firm's executives threw out. Mr. Moroni said that his sales team estimated that about 90 percent of the conversation had been anticipated and prepared for during the scenario planning session. The result was the opening of a new relationship between the major international telecommunications firm and USA.NET. Good work! That's the way to Short Cycle Sell. The lesson so far in this chapter is simple. Precall preparation, via scenario planning, will assure that you are on the way to winning your sales race.

SALES RACE RULE 9

Seventy percent of the sales appointment should be spent listening, 20 percent should be spent questioning, and 10 percent should be spent addressing only the specific things customers tell you that they need to know.

One of the biggest mistakes that I continually see sales professionals make, rookies and veterans alike, is the penchant to tell and not sell. Successful sales trainers worldwide will tell you four things to ensure victorious sales appointments:

1. Only tell customers or prospects what they need to know to make their decision and never volunteer more than they want to know.
2. The more you tell customers that does not relate specifically to what they want to know, the more you expose yourself to the possibility of an objection.
3. If you are talking during a sales interview, you are not listening and diagnosing.
4. Never impulsively answer a customer's question without trying to uncover the logic behind that question.

This means that in every sense of the expression, the "sales call" has now evolved into a "sales interview." By that I mean the sales call should now be a discovery process typified by questioning and listening, not a monologue based on the facts that you want to disseminate. This is such an important concept in compressing your sales cycle that I need to be sure you fully appreciate its significance. I've seen way too many sales veterans decide what and how much information they are going to tell the customer before they even find out what the customer wants to know. My estimate is that about 70 percent of it is not germane to the customer's decision-making process and will result in the customer mentally drifting away or finding something that she doesn't like.

This is an easy trap to fall into, so beware when the prospect says, "Well, Mary, tell us what Artificial Water does?" or "Welcome, Mary. Tell me about Artificial Water." At this point, resist the tendency to barge in with all the facts, figures, dates, features, and company history. I mean stop right there! Don't engage your mouth without engaging your brain. This is the perfect moment for you to reply, "You know, Fred, I do intend to cover that, but may I ask you some quick questions first?" That, my friend, is how you take control of the situation and start the interview process. Never, and I mean never in over 20 years of selling, have I ever had a customer or prospect say, "No. I don't want to answer questions! You talk first!" People want to talk first, especially if it's about them and their business.

THE SALES INTERVIEW

The ideal model for a sales interview begins with rapport building, includes a number of different questioning techniques, and concludes with attainment of your Compression Objective. We covered Compression Objectives in Chapter 6, and we will examine rapport building in Chapter 8, so let's concentrate on questioning technique.

During your sales interview, you will focus on discovering wants and needs. Disclosure is the *predominant activity* in this stage of your sales cycle (Chapter 1). There is a difference between needs and wants, and in order to build a strong foundation of discovery you'll need to appreciate this distinction. Needs are fundamental and fact-based. You need transportation to visit your customers. On the other hand, wants are desires and always more than a need. You need transportation to visit your customers. A Geo would satisfy the need, but you want a Mercedes or Volvo. Wants are the emotional side of any sale. Needs are the factual side of any sale. A more practical example would be your customer *needs* your highest-quality product delivered on time for the lowest price. She *wants* to look good to her boss by getting the best deal for her company. See if this doesn't make good sense: The best way to Short Cycle Sell is to sell to your customers' needs and close to their wants.

I don't intend to dwell on the concept of open-ended questions. You probably have had plenty of that in other training, but it is imperative to briefly review them because they are the fastest way to determine a customer's wants and needs. Also, open-ended questions are the principal way to guide and control the sales interview and it is your job to take control of your own sales cycle.

As you may recall, open-ended questions (OEQs) always begin with who, what, when, where, why, how, tell me about (explain to me), and your feelings are. Many times I've observed very successful veteran salespeople begin a question with *do*, or *can*, or *should*. Suddenly, they realize that they have not asked an OEQ, and they say, "Excuse me, let me rephrase that question. How…" If the predominant activity in the interview stage is to discover wants and needs, you had better focus on getting the customer to talk, not answer a question with "yes" or "no." Emulate successful salespeople by redirecting your questions as OEQs; it will make you a winner.

COMPRESSION CONCEPT: THE FIVE QUESTIONS THAT CUT TO THE ESSENCE OF THE SALES PROCESS

In all my personal adventures in selling with, training, and field coaching salespeople with various levels of experience, I have found that there are five questions that help me cut right to the chase in a sales cycle. I refer to them as the *Compression Questions*. Here they are:

1. What is your role in the decision-making process?
2. Of your top five priorities, where does this project (purchase) rank?
3. On a scale of 1 to 10, with 10 being very convinced that we can provide you with what you are looking for and 1 being that you are still looking elsewhere, where do we rank?
4. What would it take to move us up your scale to a 9 or 10?
5. What would happen if you did not get this order (project) completed as you wish it to be?

Of course, you still will need to ask all the proper profiling and rapport-building questions, for example,

What quantities do you buy?

How often do you intend to purchase?

How long have you been buying from Competitor ABC?

What do you like best about Competitor ABC?

What kind of budget have you allotted for this project?

Those rapport-building questions are great questions, and they need to be asked, but you also need to know how to accelerate the decision-making process. I have found that the answers to the Compression Questions have provided me with the clues to expediting the purchase process. I refer to them as Compression Questions because they have such a significant impact on compressing your sales cycle time. Let's review why these particular questions are so strategic in your ability to win the sales race.

Compression Question 1

What is your role in the decision-making process? or *Explain your decision-making process to me.*

This is one of the first questions I ask after building rapport. The answer to this question will tell me the following:

1. Who the influencers are in the decision-making process or who else I need to see

2. If I am speaking to the ultimate decision maker

3. The possible time line involved

4. Internal processes (paperwork committees, etc.) that need to be considered

After the customer answers the question, I generally act a little naive and say, "You'll have to excuse me, but I'm a visual person. Let me sketch this out to be sure that I have the correct understanding of your decision-making process." I then draw out a diagram similar to the one in Exhibit 7-1. (*Note*: In real life, I do *not* put the word *influencer* next to the names in my diagrams.) This whole process takes less than a minute, but will save you countless hours of grief. After I sketch the diagram, I ask the customer to scrutinize it. If it is incorrect, I ask her to correct it. Also, I ask, "What have I left out?" I don't ask, "Have I left anything out?" If the customer tells me that my drawing is correct, I then ask her, "*How* can I arrange to speak with the influencers?" Notice that I do not ask her *if* I can speak to the influencers. I just assume that I can. It is very important to keep this decision-making layout in your notes or your SFA or CRM software programs because as time progresses, I have found that this process will change. As organizations change, "right size," reengineer, lay off employees, or whatever, influencers will be added or deleted, or there may be another whole layer of approval involved. It is vital to the success of your sales cycle compression that you review this periodically with your customers. Trust me, I've learned the hard way.

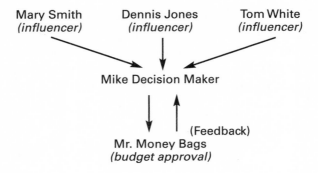

Exhibit 7-1

Compression Question 2

Of your top five priorities, where does this project (purchase) rank?

In essence, what you've asked your customer is to tell you how much time you should dedicate to her right now. You are also discovering if this customer is just shopping or if she is serious about buying. If the customer tells you that the project is ranked number one or two, you know what to do. Get a proposal in her hands as fast as you can type one. If she tells you that it's ranked number three, four, or five, then follow-up with this question, "What is your time table for the other priorities?"

Again, understand that in larger companies, priorities change like the wind or at the whim of a top executive or board of directors. So let this be a lesson to you that you must constantly be checking for changing priorities. Again, learn from my mistakes. Many times in the past I have neglected to ask about changing priorities, and I have either lost the sale race due to an escalation of a priority or I have spent way too many hours on a sale that is no longer important to the customer. By always assuming that the only constant in a sale is change, you will rarely find yourself in my shoes.

Compression Question 3

On a scale of 1 to 10, with 10 being very convinced that we can provide you with what you are looking for and 1 being that you are still looking elsewhere, where do we rank?

Why beat around the bush? I've seen so many sales professionals who have kidded themselves into believing that their customer is still interested while the customer is placing the order with a competitor. If these sales-people had just been upfront about asking this question, they would have known their position and the choice on how to proceed would have been up to them, not the customer. You need to realize that by asking these types of questions, you are taking control of the sales cycle.

If your customer tells you that you rank a 9 or 10, ask for the order! If your customer ranks you at 8 or below, then ask them Compression Question 4.

Compression Question 4

What would it take to move us up your scale to a 9 or 10?

You have now just asked the customer to tell you the secrets to making the sale. The key to using this technique is to reaffirm this question in the buyer's mind after she has given you the action or steps required to move you to 9 or 10. In other words, after the customer has rendered her answer, your response should be, "Just so I understand what you are saying, Ms. Customer, I want to repeat this back to you. It is my understanding that if this and that take place, we will move from a 6 on your scale to a 9. Is that correct?" If that is correct, then you have just been told what to do to close this sale or what to tell the customer in your proposal. In other words, your customer has just told you what to tell them. *You win!*

Compression Question 5

What would happen if you did not get this order (project) completed as you wish it to be?

This question provides a reality check for your customer; hence, I refer to it as the *reality check technique*. It is to be used only on a customer that exhibits a propensity to stall. If the customer has ranked this purchase as one of her top priorities, then you need to test the water by helping her realize what would take place if the purchase was not consummated in a timely and efficient manner. In this case, the customer has professional and personal risks to weigh.

If your customer responds to this question by indicating that nothing of negative consequence would occur, then either she misunderstood the situation internally, deliberately mislead you, or something has changed. Then it's time to go back to Compression Question 1, 2, or 3 and ask it again. Remember that there is a huge difference between being patient in the sale and losing control of the sales cycle. If the customer's buying style is slow and deliberate, I can respect that; however, if her buying style is to play games, let your competitors deal with her. You have other sales races to win!

COMPRESSION CONCEPT: DISCOVER THE MOTIVATION BEHIND YOUR CUSTOMERS' QUESTIONS

It never ceases to amaze me that so many "heavy hitters" fail to use perhaps the best discovery technique available to our profession. That is the use of the *question-the-question* method. Conceivably the reason that it is used so sparingly is that it does take about an hour of practice to perfect. Some of us have fooled ourselves into thinking that 1 hour is too much time to spend improving ourselves, so we end up finishing second in the sales race. Second place doesn't pay very well. I guarantee you that it will take 1 hour or less to become proficient enough in the question-the-question method to uncover more of your customers' motivations, hidden agendas, and buying signs.

Let's analyze the fundamentals of the question-the-question technique. You need to realize that sometimes customers have hidden agendas or ulterior motives for asking certain questions of you. Give one wrong answer and you've just created another objection or disqualified yourself from the sales race. That's why I so vehemently advocate this approach. In order to avert disaster, you should answer many of your customers' questions with your own open-ended questions designed specifically to reveal the customers' motivations behind their solicitations. Note that I said open-ended questions, because you want the customers to explain to you what it is that they are trying to determine. In other words, you are trying to get the customers to tell you what to tell them. Let's take a look at a classic example:

CUSTOMER'S QUESTION: When can I expect your delivery?

YOUR NORMAL ANSWER: Well, it takes a minimum of 10 days for a new customer. We have to get your credit checked, order processed, and product shipped.

92

CUSTOMER'S REPLY: Too bad. I need it in three days. I'll have to keep searching.

Wouldn't it have saved a lot of time and grief to determine what time frame the customer required instead of hurriedly providing the wrong answer? I know what you're thinking. It's not the wrong answer; it is a realistic picture of what it takes to get the customer's first order out. If that is your thought process, you are viewing this from an inwardly focused point of view. It's not what the customer wanted to hear. The result is, unless you do some fast-talking, you've been disqualified. Let's try addressing this same customer's question by answering with a question.

CUSTOMER'S QUESTION: When can I expect your delivery?

YOUR QUESTION-THE-QUESTION ANSWER: What is your required time frame?

CUSTOMER REPLY: To be honest with you, we need the shipment in 3 days.

YOUR REPLY: What is the reasoning behind your urgent need?

CUSTOMER REPLY: Our current supplier has backordered this to us, and we need the order to keep our assembly lines running. I didn't want to pay a premium for your materials, so I didn't tell you that up front.

(The customer has just told you what to tell her.)

At first, the buyer's question about delivery seems quite standard. This is probably one of the most common questions we've all been asked. By not taking this customer's question for granted and by answering a question with a question, you have now put yourself back in control of the sales interview and the sales cycle. It is now up to you, not the customer, to decide how badly you want to do business. Besides, you have uncovered a superb opportunity to be a hero. Take note that the customer is telling you to tell her that you can save her hide and make her look good to her manager. In order to capitalize on this particular situation, you will need to continue the conversation this way:

YOUR RESPONSE: Oh, I wasn't aware of that circumstance. Well, I'm not positive I can have it here in 3 days because of all the hoops I will have to jump through back at my office. If I can pull this off for you, what do you suppose the possibility would be of getting more of your business?

CUSTOMER'S ANSWER: If you can bail me out this time, you can have the next order. How's that?

YOU: Great! Let's fill out this credit application while I call the office to do some checking on inventory.

Here are some suggested question-the-question answers to other customer questions that I'm sure you've been asked. It is important for you to pay special attention to the manner in which I utilize open-ended questions in the answers.

CUSTOMER QUESTION: Why is your price so high?

YOUR ANSWER: What are you comparing my price against? or Why do you think my price is high? or What makes you say that my price is high?

CUSTOMER QUESTION: Why should I buy from you?

YOUR ANSWER: Who are you buying from now? or How important is it to get better results than you are currently experiencing?

CUSTOMER QUESTION: Why should I switch suppliers now? I've been with XYZ Company for 5 years?

YOUR ANSWER: Tell me a little more about why you agreed to see me today. or How familiar are you with our guaranteed contract pricing? or Tell me what XYZ has done to increase your bottom line lately.

At the end of this chapter, you will be asked to complete an exercise using the question-the-question technique. It is very important that you give this exercise some deep thought. Your answers must be presented to your customers in a way that they perceive as sincere and nonchallenging.

COMPRESSION CONCEPT: ASKING FOR YOUR COMPRESSION OBJECTIVE

Never leave the sales interview without asking for your Compression Objective for that specific customer. If you truly want to shorten your sales cycle, ask for the commitment in stages. Regardless of how you do it, be certain to move the customer to the next stage in your sales cycle before you leave her premises or hang up from the phone call. I have found that there are a few ways to do so without creating excessive tension for your customer or prospect. They all create the perception of a consultative approach on your behalf. Be sure to review Chapter 6 to reaffirm this skill.

SALES RACE RULE 10

After you have recommended, suggested, or asked for any form of customer commitment, never be the first one to talk. Always let the customer or prospect answer, even if it takes several seconds.

The long-taught dictum that I subscribe to is that the person who talks first, after you have asked for or suggested that the customer consider some form of commitment, is the loser. It's a simple rule to understand, but a tough one for many salespeople to follow. Many of us are so tempted to fill the silence with words, but if the customer doesn't answer immediately, don't further explain your question, answer your own question for your customer, or ask another question. You must be patient and let her think about the answer without any babbling in the background. If you do, you will be very happy with the outcome and well on your way to winning the sales race.

SALES RACE WRAP-UP

The concept is no longer to make a sales call on a customer or prospect. The image of the salesperson popping in the door with the latest and greatest product or service is passé. Enter the new professional consultative salesperson who conducts interviews to determine customer wants and needs. As this contemporary sales hero, you have done your homework on the Internet and collected much of the available data in preparation for the prospect interview. You have been very tenacious in gathering this information and are ready to uncover the customer's factual and emotional aspects of buying.

As our diligent Short Cycle Selling champion, you have conducted a scenario planning session with your sales manager and are prepared to respond to many customer questions and objections. You fully realize that 70 percent of the sales interview will be spent listening, 20 percent will be spent questioning, and 10 percent will be spent addressing only the specific items that the customer has concerns about. You know that by volunteering additional information you are willingly trying to disqualify yourself from the sales race.

Your plan is to let the customer or prospect tell you what to tell her. You will accomplish this through five proven sales interview success strategies.

1. Use open-ended questions like:

Who?	Why?
What?	How?
When?	Tell me about . . .
Where?	What are your feelings about . . . ?

2. Always asking the five Compression Questions:

    What is your role in the decision-making process?

    Of your top five priorities, where does this project (purchase) rank?

    On a scale of 1 to 10, with 10 being very convinced that we can provide you with what you are looking for and 1 being that you are still looking elsewhere, where do we rank?

    What would it take to move us up your scale to a 9 or 10?

    What would happen if you did not get this order (project) completed as you wish it to be?

3. Answering the customer's questions with the question-the-question technique.

4. Concentrating on controlling your urge to talk first after you recommend some form of customer commitment—*observing silence.*

5. Never leaving without asking for the next stage in the sales cycle.

By following this prescription for sales interview success, I know one thing for sure: you are going to do very well against other runners in the race to the finish. My money is on you!

MASTERING YOUR OWN SALES CYCLE

Using the following words to begin your questions, devise three questions that will help you uncover your customer's needs and wants.

Who

Q1 _____

Q2 _____

Q3 _____

What

Q1 _____

Q2 _____

Q3 _____

When

Q1 _____

Q2 _____

Q3 _____

Where

Q1 _____

Q2 _____

Q3 _____

Why

Q1 _____

Q2 _____

Q3 _____

How

Q1 _____

Q2 _____

Q3 _____

Tell me about . . .

Q1 _____

Q2 _____

Q3 _____

What are your feelings about . . .

Q1 _____

Q2 _____

Q3 _____

On the lines entitled CQ, list the five most common questions that customers and prospects ask you. Then on the lines designated as QTQ, develop open-ended questions that you can use to question the question.

CQ 1 _____

QTQ _____

CQ 2 _____

QTQ _____

CQ 3 _____

QTQ _____

CQ 4 _____

QTQ _____

CQ 5 _____

QTQ _____

CHAPTER EIGHT

FAMILIARITY BREEDS SALES RACE WINNERS

Ever heard this one before? It's not only what you know, but also what you know about who you know that will make you the sales race winner.

Let's begin this chapter by conducting a very special exercise that I use in many sales training workshops. Exhibit 8-1 shows a drawing that I want you to study carefully. Take a couple of minutes and think about what is going on in this scene. Then on the lines below the drawing, write what you think is going on. Be specific on your thoughts. Among the things I want you to tell me are where they are, what is being said, what caused this situation, and what is their relationship, if any. Be as descriptive as possible.

In order to make this more interesting, take this to your spouse, significant other, partner, or associates, and ask them to do the same. Don't tip your hand on what you have written. This is a classic exercise with which you can have some great fun!

This is known as a *projection technique*. It is used by thousands of consumer marketers from international motorcycle manufacturers to the major automakers to consumer goods companies. It is used primarily to determine what the consumer's perception is of a package, product design, or product use. Marketers usually discover many perspectives

anne lukas ©2001

Exhibit 8-1

about their packages, labels, product names, and product colors that they could never, ever imagine on their own. By using projection technique they learn what consumers see or perceive in their object of study. Marketers assemble the data collected from projection studies and look for trends in perception, whether they are favorable or not.

You have just projected into the situation in Exhibit 8-1 what you perceive is happening. Now let me tell you what some of your colleagues across the world have seen in this depiction.

1. A married couple having a spat at a dinner party.

2. A man at a bar trying to pick up a woman. He uses an old pickup line and she reacts adversely.

3. A woman reacting to a feminist comment by a fellow worker at an office party.

4. The boss (woman) reacting to a drunken subordinate's comment at an office Christmas party.

5. A drunken husband trying to switch drinks with his sober wife.

These are just five of the literally thousands of responses that we have collected while administering this projection technique. Yet, the number of novel responses that I hear every time never fails to amaze me. The most important lesson from this is that everyone is looking at exactly the same picture, but reading different meanings into what they see. Your projection or opinion of what you think is occurring is a product of your perception. All of us have different perceptions or see a slightly different angle to the environment around us. Our perceptions are the result of our upbringing, education, ethnicity, outside influences, and spiritual preparation. Some of our sales colleagues with comparable backgrounds may view events in a similar light, but if you dig a little below the surface, you'll find out that family influences and work experiences will cause differentiation in perception.

So, what does all this have to do with shortening your sales cycle and winning the sales race to the customer's budget, wallet, or checkbook?

SALES RACE RULE 11

As a professional salesperson, it is your job to favorably affect your customer's perception of you, your company, and your products or services.

If you adhere to Sales Race Rule 11, you will be the sales race winner! It is your job as a professional salesperson to reinforce, influence, or sway your customers' perceptions. The advent of the information age has complicated this challenge for many of us because our customers are more aware of choices available to them. As a result, our customers are overwhelmed. The line of differentiation between our competitors and us becomes blurred in the mind of the customer. Therefore, it is up to us to bring focus to this situation by favorably affecting the customer's perception of our position in the marketplace.

COMPRESSION CONCEPT: UNDERSTANDING YOUR CUSTOMER'S PERCEPTION IS A KEY TO AFFECTING IT

Now, before you go rushing out and start spreading your message, take time to find out what message you *need* to spread. Here are four truths that you must grasp before you get carried away with changing any perceptions:

1. Your customers' perceptions are their reality. What your customers think of you, right or wrong, is fact to them. It affects how they will make their decision on your business proposal, unless otherwise influenced.

2. In order to affect your customers' perceptions, thereby changing their reality, you first must know their perceptions. Since it is your job to change perception, the first duty you have is to discover what those perceptions are. This is accomplished through the open-ended questioning technique. Use such questions as

   What are your feelings about . . . ?

   What are your thoughts about . . . ?

   What is your understanding of . . . ?

   What do you know about our . . . ?

   Why do you feel that way?

   What experience have you had with . . . ?

3. No two customers or prospects are going to perceive you or your business proposal identically. That is due to how their perceptions have been molded over their lives and past experiences with salespeople or business in general. What one customer views a "definite buy" will be seen by others with a "caution flag." To compound matters, many of your customer companies have resorted to purchasing by committee. Suppose for a minute that you find yourself cast into this situation. You will be the salesperson who determines each committee member's perceptions in order to sell the U.S. Congress better chairs for the House of Representatives' chamber. In this case,

many issues exist, such as party lines, gender, seniority, diversity, tradition, fabric color, and comfort (notice I didn't mention budget). Your job is to determine each congressperson's perception on these issues and try to *affect this perception* so that you can build a consensus. Failure to do so will assure you second place in the sales race.

4. Your customers each have distinct behavioral and personality types, which drive their judgment of your business offering. Let's examine the two basic personality types and their affect on your job of shortening your sales cycle.

COMPRESSION CONCEPT: THE TWO BASIC BUYER PERSONALITY TYPES— BOTTOM LINER AND TOP LINER

Those practicing the field of sales psychology have written much about basic behavioral types. These styles go by different names depending on the authors, but many sales training programs have incorporated great detail on them in their respective training materials. You may recognize them as the

Driver/dominant director

Analyst/cautious thinker

Friend/steady relater

Artist/interactive socializer

(To read more about these, see Jim Cathcart's *Relationship Selling*.)

Now please understand that my academic preparation in psychology consisted of one undergraduate class, therefore, I needed to find a more simplified method to classify common behavioral traits in customers. After years of selling, it finally dawned on me that there are two basic classifications of behavioral styles in which I can categorize a vast majority of my customers. This revelation exposed that my customers showed either a propensity to be very focused on the outcome of my business proposition, the bottom line, or they exhibited strong tendencies toward the sales event and personal aspects of the proposition. I equated these behaviors to generally accepted accounting principles for making a profit and loss statement. Those principles state that the top line on a profit and loss statement is always the Sales figure. The bottom line (Profit or Loss figure) is the outcome of all business dealings. My customers who focused on the outcome or bottom line of the sale were called *Bottom Liners* and those customers who focused more on the sales event or personal aspect first were branded as *Top Liners*. To me it is such a simple explanation of predominant buyer behavior that when I apply these labels to my customers' behaviors, selling becomes much less challenging. Let's examine the Bottom Liner and Top Liner customer behavior patterns and how they relate to you winning the sales race. Exhibit 8-2 illustrates the comparison between the two behavioral styles.

	Bottom Liner	**Top Liner**
Substyles	Logical, Achiever	Idea Person, Cooperator
Motivation	Factual Driven	Emotional Driven
Behavioral Traits	Numbers oriented	People oriented
	Deliberate	Impulsive
	Decisions based on facts	Buy from "who I like"
	Conducts endless search and evaluates all alternatives	Little search and evaluation of alternatives
	Develops loyalty based on "good deal"	Loyalty = personality
	Makes "sense" to me	It "feels" right to me
	"I'll look good"	"We'll look good"
	Few influencers involved	Committee involvement
	Shorter sales cycle/decisive	Drags on - indecisive

Exhibit 8-2 Comparison of the Two Basic Customer Behavioral Styles

It is vital to take note that facts, numbers, and quantitative analysis primarily drive the Bottom Liner customers. They take a no-nonsense approach to buying, and, in a way, their sales cycle can be much shorter, but much more brutal. They may ask you to jump through more hoops than the Top Liner customer, but if that is the case, it's generally for more facts to help them justify buying from you. The Bottom Liner behavioral style is classified into two substyles: logical and achiever. Logical Bottom Liner buyers are certainly motivated by facts, but the facts tend to be quantitative in nature. They use the quantitative facts to justify an impartial "numbers don't lie" purchasing action. Achiever Bottom Liner buyers are also motivated by facts, but they use these facts as a "power" tool to push their decisions on both superiors and subordinates. In order to better understand the concepts of Logical and Achiever Bottom Liner buyers, Exhibit 8-3 compares the types of titles that each typically holds within all organizations.

Logical	Achiever
Accountant, CFO, CEO, engineer, chemist, MIS manager, analyst, quality assurance, finance vice president, marketing manager, controller	CEO, chief operating officer, vice president of operations, plant manager, president, general manager, chairperson

Exhibit 8-3 Typical Job Titles of Bottom Liner Substyles

From Exhibit 8-3, you will notice that the Logical Bottom Liner primary behavioral style finds its way into job positions that can be classified as requiring logical or analytical skills. These are commonly referred to as the number crunchers, data manipulators, or design people. The key to remember about these people is that they like to follow a *process* in everything they do. A process provides them with structure, and, honestly, they don't do very well in an unstructured environment. They feel that a process gives them control over any event they face. The process consists of very logical steps that lead from chaos to completion. This process provides uniformity in their lives. They are very likely to follow the same process in their buying habits from work to personal necessities. Needless to say, they are very organized and facts play a huge part in how they react to various circumstances.

For those of you who remember the classic 1950s television show *Dragnet*, actor Jack Webb played a character named Detective Sergeant Joe Friday. Both Joe Friday and Jack Webb will be remembered for the classic line, "Facts, Ma'am, just the facts." Joe Friday would utter those words when, during one of his investigations, the witness would stray off the line of questioning and start babbling about other unrelated happenings. Joe had a set method (process) to his investigations and he focused on obtaining all the facts. Joe Friday had a Logical Bottom Liner behavioral style.

To the Logical Bottom Liner, the correlation between facts and processes is quite simple. The process is the framework within which the facts belong. The process is the machine that takes the facts and produces an outcome. Their process cannot operate without facts or data. Remember this when you encounter a Logical Bottom Liner person in your next sales interview.

Accountants have a process, also known as a procedure, that they follow to crunch the numbers into sales reports, income statements, and balance sheets. These procedures have been in existence for years, and day in, day out accountants follow these same processes. Engineers, chemists, and quality assurance people all follow established procedures to do their jobs. They know that if they follow the procedure, the results will be consistent every time. They put the facts (numbers) into the process (machine), and they derive an expected outcome. From the outcome, they attempt to produce an analysis. These customers want strong proposals that are filled with facts to support a logical buying decision.

What if the Logical Bottom Liner encounters a situation that does not have a pre-ordained process? Quite simply, they use their experiences in similar past conditions to make one up as rapidly as possible.

One question that is constantly posed to me is, "Why do you classify the marketing managers as having a Logical Bottom Liner behavioral style?" Many people are under the false assumption that the titles marketing manager and sales manager are synonymous. This just isn't the case. The skill sets required for these two positions couldn't be further apart. Marketing managers are definitely researching for facts and data to plug into their marketing models to measure customer appeal, satisfaction, and preferences. In all reality, the sales and product design functions are driven by market research and the data derived from it. Truly educated and trained marketing people are empirically oriented.

Going back to Exhibit 8-3, the Achiever Bottom Liner can be found in top management jobs. *Warning*: Not every top manager, CEO, president, or general manager can be classified primarily as an Achiever Bottom Liner. You can, however, expect this behavioral style in most of these people. While it is true that this behavioral type is factually oriented, it is even more significant that they are driven to be in charge. An excellent example of this type of behavioral style came out of the tragic attempted assassination of former President Ronald Reagan. With President Reagan lying in an emergency operating room clinging to life, his Secretary of State, Alexander Haig, blurted out during a press conference, "I'm in charge!"

Achiever Bottom Liner behaviors do not use the facts to process a result, rather they use the facts to confirm a conclusion, influence others, and then take action. These people seek out the top responsibilities and always feel they can do it better than someone else can. Good or bad, they are seen as the leaders, or heir apparents (Alexander Haig in our example) to the leaders, within any organization. Generally speaking, they will want *all the facts* before making a decision. A key to selling to them is to understand that they are always careful to consider how a decision will make them look to their superiors. They will not always make a purely objective decision based on the facts alone. Their own career path may be more important than the facts. Their buying decisions are influenced heavily by what their perceptions are of the impact that specific decision will have on their future career.

Achiever Bottom Liner people are always very busy. My experience with them shows that they thrive on activity and flourish in an emergency. Chaos, not disorganization, can be a stimulant to them. They are always ready to respond by quickly analyzing the facts for themselves and formulating an impromptu action plan. Achiever Bottom Liner people rarely seek advice from influencers. If they do seek input, their own analyses will generally play an overriding role in the decision process.

Going back to Exhibit 8-2, you will notice that the right side of the exhibit shows the *emotionally driven* behaviors or the *Top Liner* style. Top Liner people are influenced much more by feelings than facts. They take a more subjective approach to their buying decisions in that they rely more on their "gut feel" than on empirical analysis. Top Liner buyers speak frequently of past relationships and want you to establish rapport before you interview them. They can be best described as a "people person." Again, my personal lengthy sales experience shows that there are two basic substyles to the Top Liner customer: Idea Person and Cooperator. They both use emotion and relationship as a basis to make decisions. Be aware that because they do bank so heavily on the emotional aspects of making a decision, their sales cycle can be much longer than that of Bottom Liner buyers. Their sales cycles will be extended because

1. They will seek opinions of others (influencers) and are concerned with how the influencers feel about the situation.

2. Emotions are difficult to counter. You can generally argue against facts with facts, but emotions and feelings are very difficult to affect.

3. Inasmuch as decision making is an emotional event, they may procrastinate, postponing the decision until they feel good about it or they feel the timing is proper.

4. Relationships can sometimes produce procrastination because Top Liners do not want to place a strong relationship at risk by hurting someone through the decision-making process. They have a difficult time saying, "no," or telling someone that they were unsuccessful in selling them. There is an old adage that goes, "The easiest sale to make is to a salesperson." My selling wisdom acquired from years of practice tells me this is true, not because salespeople have empathy for other salespeople, although they do, but because most salespeople are cut from the same behavioral cloth. They understand their own behavioral style and know how to manipulate it best.

Exhibit 8-4 illustrates the job titles and positions that are most commonly held by the two substyles of the Top Liner behavioral type. These jobs generally require a skill set that is best characterized as people-oriented and creative.

Idea Person	Cooperator
Graphic designer, director of advertising, product development manager, public relations, consultant, trainer, sales representative, architect, human resources director, entrepreneur	Sales manager, sales vice president, business development manager, customer service manager, human resources director, CEO

Exhibit 8-4 Typical Job Titles of Top Liner Substyles

The Top Liner Idea Person behavioral style is based on creativity and a feeling for what will be acceptable. This buyer views a buying decision as a creative process rather than an end result to that process. The Top Liner Idea Person customer sees the advantages of making the buying decision, but is not very interested in the process. These individuals are *visually* oriented and appreciate a strong visual presentation packed with animation. They appreciate a proposal that looks professional regardless of content. You will find that due to their feelings orientation, they do not like conflict. Because of their aversion to conflict, they may not tell you what is really on their minds. Typically, when you ask them to express what they envision, the answers are explicit, detailed, and lengthy. It's important to be the first salesperson to present to the Top Liner Idea Person because my experience has been that they are impulsive and will buy when they see what they like. This type of buyer loves to build rapport through discussing ideas and visualizing. They want to see what clever ideas you have used to solve other customers' problems.

The Top Liner Cooperator behavioral style is again embedded in the emotional or people side of a buying decision. This person wants to be seen as a friend to all and tries to avoid conflict whenever possible. An individual with this behavioral style is considered to be very social in nature and is usually most comfortable around groups of people. Do you remember the last time that a prospect or client set up an initial appointment with you and when you arrived there was a committee there to greet you? Chances are that the person with whom you had set the appointment is either a Top Liner Cooperator or a Bottom Liner Achiever. If he is a Top Liner Cooperator, he invited a group of coworkers because they are all influencers and he feels better getting everyone's opinion. If he is a Bottom Liner Achiever, then he issued invitations to the initial meeting because he is probably going to delegate it off due to his perceived menial nature of your business proposition.

The problem with both the Idea Person and the Cooperator is that their sales cycles can be lengthy. They both exhibit *sales staller* type behaviors. You may not be able to get a firm answer one way or the other from them. They may not tell you what is really going on in hopes that you will eventually go away. That would save them the uncomfortable task of telling you that you didn't get the deal. This way they avoid conflict and still hope they are viewed as a good person.

There is absolutely nothing wrong with either subtype of the Bottom Liner or Top Liner behavior styles, but you do need to know the idiosyncrasies of each predominant type and how to deal with them. Before you can understand how to deal with them, you must first identify which behavior you are dealing with. There are three key areas that will tip you off to a person's behavior patterns. They are

Vocabulary

Office environment

Background information

Bottom Liner		Top Liner	
Logical	**Achiever**	**Idea Person**	**Cooperator**
Logical	Goals	Visualize	I *feel* . . .
Makes *sense*	Objectives	I *see* . . .	Check with *our team*
Figures/numbers	Time line	Ideas	*Our* decision
Systematic	Workload	Ideally	*Let's* do . . .
Rationale	Payback	Clever	Support

Exhibit 8-5

110

You will notice that members of each behavioral style use distinct patterns of specific words when you are interviewing them. Exhibit 8-5 depicts the words and expressions spoken by your prospect or customer that will tip you off to his behavioral style.

A sure tip-off to a customer's behavioral style is the environment in which he works. Specifically, his own office decor, organization, and activity level reflect his behavioral style. Exhibit 8-6 characterizes each behavioral kind by what his respective office surroundings look like.

Bottom Liner		Top Liner	
Logical	**Achiever**	**Idea Person**	**Cooperator**
Organized	Organized	Disorganized	Disorganized
Quiet	Lots of interruptions	Music playing	Phone ringing
No personal effects	Personal tributes to "me"	Personal pictures	Lots of personal effects
Clean desk syndrome	Items of personal interest	Eclectic decor	High-energy feel
Sterile	Fairly sterile	Cluttered desk	Cluttered desk

Exhibit 8-6

In Chapter 7, I told you to let customers or prospects tell you what to tell them. This same rule applies to quickly identifying your prospects' or customers' behavioral types. Question them, and listen carefully to their replies. The best questions to ask a prospect or customer that will aid in detecting his behavioral style are

1. *Tell me about your favorite job duties.*

   Logical Bottom Liners will focus on process activities.

   Achiever Bottom Liners will answer this question by alluding to being in charge.

Idea Person Top Liners will intimate the creative aspects of their job or new ideas.

Cooperator Top Liners will make reference to working with people.

2. *What is your educational background and what were your favorite subjects in school?* Interestingly enough, the answers to this question may vary significantly due to the rapidly expanding fields of study and Internet courses. The real telling fact is, if they have a degree, what their field of study was. Most Bottom Liners will have studied computer science, finance, mathematics, economics, engineering, accounting, or some science field. Most Top Liners will have studied the social sciences like political science, sociology, psychology, business administration, history, physical education, or theater arts.

3. *What did you do before you took this job?* This is a great question to determine your customer's behavior type. You may see a pattern in the employment history of those holding Bottom Liner type positions. The real surprise occurs when you observe a Bottom Liner person in a Top Liner job. Then you will absolutely need to go further in the interview. Many times while dealing with high-technology clients, I've encountered operations, technology, or financial people in Top Liner jobs. They've either been the only candidates and, due to loyalty to their employer, they've been moved into that position, or they've decided to make a complete career change. My experience is that this rarely, if ever, is a long-term situation. If you are still confused about your customer's behavioral style, then ask question 4 to really clarify things.

4. *Tell me about your hobbies and outside interests.* Now, what type of hobbies or outside activities do you suppose the Achiever Bottom Liner has? If you thought "very few," you are correct. Most of these people have little outside interests dealing specifically with relaxation or self-actualization. Anything they do outside of their job is strictly for self-advancement. You may find Achiever Bottom Liners that play sports or ski, but the difference in them is that they play to win or improve their game. Logical Bottom Liners may have some very interesting hobbies such as automobile maintenance, managing investments, home improvement, coin collecting, stamp collecting, or music collections

played on their favorite electronic toys. The Cooperator Top Liners will generally be club members. They play golf at the country club, cards at the bridge club, and eat with the dinner club. The Idea Person Top Liner will be an artist or painter or writer. He will like to spend his spare time creating or traveling to see new, exciting things.

COMPRESSION CONCEPT: SELL TO THE BEHAVIORAL STYLE THAT YOU IDENTIFY

Once you have identified the behavioral style of your prospect or customer, you will be able to shorten your sales cycle by adapting your selling style to his buying style. Your buyer's behavioral type dictates his buying style, which will have a profound effect on your sales cycle. The best way to compress your sales cycle with each of these behavioral patterns is to approach them in a manner with which they feel most comfortable. This requires that you make certain adjustments in your own behavioral style in the different stages of your sales cycle in order to relate better to theirs. My experience shows that people buy from people they like, and they generally like people who act like them. Exhibit 8-7 shows the sales cycle from Exhibit 1-1 and tips on how you need to approach both forms of Bottom Liner behavior in each stage.

	Bottom Liner	
Sales Cycle Stage	**Logical**	**Achiever**
Prospect	Give logical reason to meet	Be quick on the phone, feed their ego
Sales Interview	Keep it structured and pointed	Control with questions; be direct
Demonstration/ Proposal/Presentation	Stress the details and process	Concentrate on outcome for them
Substantiate	Focus on similar customers who have like applications and processes	They don't care who else has used your services or products

113

	Bottom Liner	
Sales Cycle Stage	**Logical**	**Achiever**
Negotiate (Chapter 10)	Keep very focused and orderly. Don't jump around. Appeal to logic	Play HARDBALL. Have several straw issues to give. Always get, when you give
Transaction Closure (Chapter 12)	Use the words: *makes sense, it's a logical conclusion, it all adds up, better bottom line*	Use the words: *successful, powerful results, better bottom line, make you look good*
Referral	Use the words: *next logical step, prospects with your background, prospects with your understanding*	Use the words: *looking for client like you, your caliber, your level of sophistication*

Exhibit 8-7

Exhibit 8-8 shows the sales cycle from Exhibit 1-1 and tips on the best way to approach both forms of Top Liner behavior in each stage.

	Top Liner	
Sales Cycle Stage	**Ideal Person**	**Cooperator**
Prospect	Approach in an unconventional and creative manner	Spend time building rapport
Sales Interview	Ask for visions, ideas, concepts	Focus on how they feel and their team's ideas
Demonstration/ Proposal/Presentation	Talk about the concepts behind your product or service; ask them to visualize how they can use it	Engage them

	Top Liner	
Sales Cycle Stage	Ideal Person	Cooperator
Substantiate	Mention your customers who have used your product or service to solve similar conceptual problems	Drop names of current customers who are well known
Negotiate (Chapter 10)	Be considerate of their self-esteem; talk in conceptual terms	Stick to the issues; do not allow them to sidetrack you with small talk
Transaction Closure (Chapter 12)	Use the words: conceptual, ideal, theoretical, visualize, conceive	Use the words: us, we, team, help, let's
Referral	Use the words: Who do you know that views this the same way you do?	Use the words: Which of your business or personal friends could we help with our service or product?

Exhibit 8-8

THE FARMER'S INSURANCE GROUP CASE

Mr. Tom Black, CIC, LUTCF, has a reputation of being one of the finest insurance specialists for the Farmer's Insurance Group. Tom has well over 25 years' experience selling and handling claims, both property and casualty and life insurance, for his clients. Tom's biggest challenge appears when he deals with couples where each partner exhibits differing, and sometimes conflicting, behavioral patterns. He may encounter one partner who is a Top Liner Cooperator (much like Tom himself) and the other partner may be a Bottom Liner Logical. According to Tom, this occurs more frequently than you would imagine. In this situation, the formidable task is presenting a proposal that not only satisfies the nitty-gritty details and logical conclusion for one partner, but also makes the other partner feel good about the purchase.

Recently, Tom had the opportunity to submit a proposal on long-term health care to a couple in their mid-fifties who had been married for 30 years. Tom identified the wife as a classic Bottom Liner Logical and the husband as an archetypal Top Liner Cooperator. By asking key questions he discovered that the wife was a controller for her employer. The husband was a successful lifelong salesperson (he can't be all bad). Most of Tom's proposals are standard computer-generated forms that focus on the numbers aspect of this purchase, reflecting the main concern of the wife. Nevertheless, Tom knew that he had to also appeal to the husband, whose primary concern was spending his twilight years in a facility that would give the best care possible. Tom quickly realized that both the husband's and wife's primary considerations were at odds with each other. Again, the wife was interested in low cost and the husband was absorbed with high-quality care.

To solve this dilemma and get the sale, Tom recommended a long-term care policy that contained a benefits inflation escalation clause that would assure the best care 20 to 30 years from now, when the couple was likely to need the policy. At the same time, in order to please the wife, Tom offered monthly automatic withdrawal premiums from their checking account. After a short negotiation between the husband and wife, common ground was agreed upon and the policy was written.

Selling to couples and committees whose members have differing behavioral styles can be your biggest challenge. Tom Black was able to overcome this obstacle by identifying the differing demeanors, addressing them separately, and then providing benefits for all in some form.

SALES RACE WRAP-UP

While your customers may exhibit traits of all the differing behavioral styles, there are two primary types of behavioral styles of customers: Bottom Liner and Top Liner. Each classification is refined into two subcategories.

Bottom Liner	Top Liner
Logical	Ideal Person
Achiever	Cooperator

Successful salespeople have favorably affected their customers' perceptions of them, their company, and their products. In order to accomplish this, they must first be able to identify the types of behavior they are dealing with. There are three basic areas that will help you identify your customer's primary behavioral style:

Vocabulary

Office environment

Background information

In order to further assure that you have correctly identified your customer's behavior, there are five basic questions that will provide revealing answers. They are

1. What do you like best about your job?

2. What is your educational background?

3. What were some of your favorite subjects in school?

4. What did you do before you took this job?

5. Tell me about your hobbies and outside interests.

Both Bottom Liner and Top Liner customers need to be sold to in different fashions. By tailoring your approach, proposal, presentation, and closing statement to the differing behavioral styles, you will experience a significant reduction in your sales cycle times. You will be able to relate to them in their world and reap the financial benefits of a better relationship and understanding.

Finally, it is vital to communicate to your key staff the differing primary behaviors of your various customers. By doing this, you will assure a stronger bond between your valued customers and your organization.

MASTERING YOUR OWN SALES CYCLE

1. By using the exhibits in Chapter 8, identify your primary behavioral style.

   _____

2. List the name of the principal contact person at your top five accounts.

   Account 1: _____

   Account 2: _____

   Account 3: _____

   Account 4: _____

   Account 5: _____

3. Utilizing the exhibits in Chapter 8, go back to question 2 and identify the primary behavioral classifications for each of the contacts.

4. In the respective spaces provided, write a brief narrative on how to treat each of these five contact people in order to relate to them better.

Account 1 contact name:

Primary behavior type: _____

Best way to relate to them: _____

Best words to use: _____

Account 2 contact name:

Primary behavior type: _____

Best way to relate to them: _____

Best words to use: _____

Account 3 contact name:

Primary behavior type: _____

Best way to relate to them: _____

Best words to use: _____

Account 4 contact name:

Primary behavior type: _____

Best way to relate to them: _____

Best words to use: _____

Account 5 contact name:

Primary behavior type: _____

Best way to relate to them: _____

Best words to use: _____

5. E-mail or fax this information to anyone in your firm that has contact with these people on a regular basis.

CHAPTER NINE

SHORTEN YOUR SALES CYCLE

Using Strong Sales Presentations, Demonstrations, and Proposals

The customer will make her purchase decision at the point of presentation, demonstration, or proposal.

Never underestimate the importance of your presentation, demonstration, or proposal in your customer's decision-making process. Your customer may or may not give her approval after your presentation, demonstration, or proposal, but be aware that she has largely made her buying decision at this point in time. Even if the customer denies that she has made up her mind, be assured that she has decided to either include or exclude you from the set of choices she will select from. It's just that simple.

Now consider these realities. You have worked very hard to find this prospect or customer and you have sold her on an interview. During the interview, you've gathered copious relevant notes that are significant in preparing a presentation, demonstration, or proposal. Also, you have suggested and been granted permission to move to the next stage in the sales cycle: the presentation, demonstration, or proposal.

Soon it will be your turn in "the barrel." You've spent several hours getting to this juncture. Now it's time to move your game into transition from information gatherer to problem solver. Keeping in mind that the customer or prospect will generally either select or eliminate you at this event, and that you get only one shot at this stage in your sales cycle, make the most of it. What do you do first to ensure your success?

SALES RACE RULE 12

Make your customer play an active role in your presentation, demonstration, or proposal before, during, and after the event.

COMPRESSION CONCEPT: CUSTOMER INVOLVEMENT CUTS TIME FROM YOUR SALES CYCLE

As a long-time facilitator of adult learning and an associate professor of marketing for an adult undergraduate program, I've witnessed firsthand that people learn much better by doing and participating. If you put an adult learner in a traditional undergraduate introductory classroom where the format is pure lecture, that learner will not comprehend, retain, or understand as much as if you put her in the exact same subject class formatted around discussion, participation, and small group breakouts. Even though the same professor may teach the same subject in both of the classes, the professor will find that her participative class will understand the material much better than her lecture class.

Presentation Secret 1: Enthusiasm

Picture yourself in one of those all-day personal development seminars on improving your closing skills. The typical program is usually held in a moderate to high-end hotel ballroom or conference facility. Each table is covered with a white linen tablecloth, and a pitcher of water and several water glasses are strategically positioned in front of your chair.

Next to the water pitcher sits a plastic bowl full of the usual hard pep-
permint candy wrapped in the plastic that makes that horrible crackling
sound when you open it. Your instructor stands behind a podium several tables in front of you. Behind her is the roll-down projection screen
reflecting the first transparency overhead of the day. The glare from the
screen is distracting and causes your eyes some discomfort because the
instructor is using the traditional transparency projector. She begins to
speak and change transparencies on a regular rhythm. Occasionally a
hand will go up in the crowd, and the instructor encourages the inquisi-
tive participant to hold her questions until the time designated for questions and answers. Hours drag on for you as the instructor roams
through countless personal anecdotes and strays from the subject matter.
Finally lunchtime rolls around, and as you stand up to leave for lunch,
you make a decision. "This is not worth the $169 I've paid. I've better
things to do with my time, so I'm leaving! I haven't learned a thing!"
Why haven't you learned a thing? Because you didn't have any interaction or participation in the learning process.

A month later, you have registered for one of these motivational seminar programs that feature several nationally renowned sports and political personalities. You saw it advertised in your local newspaper and
the registration is regularly $139 for the day, but if you preregister, you
can get in for $49. You plop down your hard-earned $49 and buy a
ticket. The day of the program you show up at your local movie theater
with 500 other Top Liner adults eager to learn the secrets of life. The
first speaker is a retired hometown sports hero from the NFL or NBA,
and he addresses self-discipline. His message is quick and filled with
energy. He uses no podium, but paces back in forth on the stage for an
hour, frequently relaying humorous locker-room anecdotes to prove his
point. Just before he concludes, he plugs his audiotapes for sale on the
tables out in the theater lobby. When he concludes, there is thunderous
applause and you hear several people seated around say, "Boy, he was
good. That hour went fast. We need to get out to the lobby and get his
tapes before they're sold out."

After a quick break, you return to your seat for the rest of the morning's program. You hear a retired politician talk about ethics, a former
high-ranking military officer discuss strategic career planning, a Hol-

lywood movie star speak on taking risk, and an international personal development guru give a rousing discourse on self-motivation. They are all excellent speakers, and as each finishes you feel yourself growing more and more confident and eager to start anew the very first thing the next morning. You are pumped up!

As the week after the motivational seminar wears on, your energy level begins to dissipate quickly. You start having trouble recalling each expert's respective message, but you still remember the "high" that you felt as your drove home after the program that particular day.

Remember how you felt that day? Well, that's the way you want your customers and prospects to feel after your presentation. You want them pumped up! The difference between the first seminar you attended and the motivational seminar is the energy you felt when you left the room. The distinction between the two formats points to one of the secrets of making a strong presentation or demonstration and that secret is spelled E-N-T-H-U-S-I-A-S-M. You cannot expect your customers to get pumped up if you aren't. Trust me! Enthusiasm is very contagious and it will shorten your sales cycle. People want to be happy and feel positive momentum. I've seen professional salespeople make enthusiastic presentations on products that they had little or less knowledge about than the prospects they were addressing. When these meetings were over, the prospects were very excited about the salesperson and her product.

Presentation Secret 2: Participation

While enthusiasm can carry you a long way, your ultimate Compression Objective must be to move your customer or prospect to the next stage in your sales cycle. Enthusiasm alone cannot accomplish this. Your customer must have developed an appreciation for your business proposition and see the benefits to her of buying from you, but it must be presented in an enthusiastic manner. Your predominant activities in the presentation stage of your sales cycle must be to

1. Teach the customer or prospect about the benefits of doing business with you so that she retains the information in a favorable light.

2. Convince the customer or prospect of the validity of your business proposition.

3. Position yourself into the customer's or prospect's evoked set (final two viable purchase options—you and a competitor—from which your customer or prospect will choose the winner).

Taking what I've learned from my classroom experiences as a professor of marketing, I have found that the most effective manner to achieve this high level of customer interest, retention, and understanding is to totally involve the customer in the participative sales presentation model. The *participative sales presentation* is truly outcome based. It is focused on earning the most favorable outcome in the selling process—the sale. The participative sales presentation is best illustrated by the flow diagram in Exhibit 9-1. The exhibit shows the natural progression that takes place *within the buyer* during this presentation model if you have successfully fulfilled your obligation as a participative presenter.

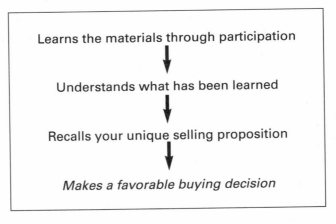

Exhibit 9-1

From Exhibit 9-1 you can see that in order for your customer or prospect to make a favorable buying decision on your behalf, she must be able to *recall* your Unique Selling Proposition. In order to accurately recall the benefits of your Unique Selling Proposition, she must have a firm *understanding* of them. This understanding is *learned* through your ability to engage her using your participative facilitation and presentation skills.

The participative sales presentation model contains three phases of customer involvement:

Pre-presentation Involvement

Presentation Engagement

Post-presentation Connection

Each phase has its own unique activities that will assure the optimum level of customer learning and retention when it comes to your product or service benefits to her. These activities, if conducted properly, will provide you greater influence over your customer's or prospect's decision-making process than your competitors will ever have. Because of that greater influence, they indeed will act as a stronger force to compress your sales cycle. Let's examine each of these three phases individually.

PHASE I: PRE-PRESENTATION INVOLVEMENT

The Pre-presentation Involvement phase can be best described as engaging your customer in presentation planning so that you get her buy-in and commitment. One of the many things that I've learned over all my years of making presentations is that it's very difficult for a customer to react any way but favorably if she helps with the presentation planning and preparation. It doesn't guarantee the order, but it does usually mean three things:

1. You'll be among that customer's or prospect's final choices.

2. You will have established customer buy-in and stronger rapport.

3. Your sales cycle will be shortened.

What is the best process for getting the customer or prospect involved in your presentation? During the interview stage of your sales cycle, or the stage just prior to your presentation, your Compression Objective is to *sell* the presentation, demonstration, or proposal stage. Once you have successfully completed selling this stage, your job is to solicit your customer's or prospect's ideas on what she'd like to learn from the presentation and the best method to accomplish that task. Here are some questions you can ask to achieve this:

In order to better prepare for our presentation, what are the top five areas you want me to address?

In order to make the best use of the presentation time, let's make a list of the topics you would like to cover.

What do you visualize the presentation looking like? (Include location, audiovisual equipment, samples, demonstration.)

Who, besides you, will be in attendance? (Get names, titles, positions, role in decision-making process.)

What do you think the other attendees would like to see me cover?

What is the best way to get in touch with them, so that I may ask them if there are any other specific topics they'd like to see me cover? (This assures the other participants' attendance and buy-in.)

By seeking the answers to these questions you will realize four huge benefits for yourself.

1. You will confirm who is in the decision-making process and what their roles are.

2. By involving multiple members of your customer's or prospect's team in the Pre-presentation Involvement phase, you will be able to uncover many concerns and issues that otherwise would have taken you by surprise during your presentation. Once you are apprised of these matters, you actually can tailor your presentation to each one of them. I have been in the situation before when my main contact person has overlooked a concern of a decision-making influencer, and after my presentation I had to get back to that person to specifically address her concerns. As a result, my sales cycle was delayed 4 weeks.

3. This process will allow you to validate the information given to you by other members of the customer's or prospect's team. There have been many times that I've been thankful that I had followed my own advice and involved many people before my presentation. Either I had misunderstood what my contact person was trying to tell me or her perception of the situation was not totally correct. In either case, by involving the others, I was able to refocus my presentation to the proper issues.

4. You will significantly compress your sales cycle by making your presentation both proactive and participative.

Remember, you are trying to project a consultative approach to your customer's problems, and the best way to realize that is to involve the customer in each step of your sales cycle and her sales cycle. It is a tremendous rapport opportunity.

PHASE II: PRESENTATION ENGAGEMENT

It's show time! If we follow the proven educational model discussed earlier in this chapter, our presentation becomes facilitation. The traditional presentation is more of a one-way street, with you doing all the telling or talking followed by a question-and-answer session. In the participative sales presentation model, you make a transition from lecturer to *facilitator*. The entire session is a question-and-answer forum. Your role changes from informer to helper. Your predominant activities will remain the same, but your methodology transforms from telling to assisting the customer in discovering how your proposition will solve her problems. Remember our previous discussion on the most successful classroom-learning model for adults? Participation! How do we incorporate that proven model into a results-oriented sales presentation that will incite action by your customer? You can do it in four ways:

1. Tell your customer what she told you she wants to know. Focus your presentation only on what the customer or the customer's team has told you is a concern. Do not volunteer anything more unless you are asked or are certain that it will receive universal acceptance from all the presentation attendees. If you continue to talk, all you are accomplishing is setting yourself up for more objections and a longer sales cycle. Trust me on this one! Tell them only what they think is important.

2. Make a list of the issues and concerns of the people you have interviewed, and either present them in a formal written agenda or post them on a easel just before you begin.

3. Be sure to involve the customer by stimulating as many of her human senses and activities as possible. There are many noteworthy methods to achieve this:

a. The use of a dynamic electronic slide show with animation (visual) and occasional sound (auditory) that will achieve your goal of leaving a lasting impression. Like the successful classroom environment, you are seeking to have your customer retain the information you are presenting.

b. Placing samples on a table in the back of the room can arouse the tactile and visual senses. Use those samples to illustrate key points in your presentation.

c. Varying your voice tone and volume (auditory) will keep attendees attention level up.

SALES RACE RULE 13

The best way to engage your customer is to conduct a presentation that is 50 percent customer interactive and 50 percent relaying your business proposition (telling).

4. Engage your customers or prospect in the presentation itself through various methods of participation. I have used this so effectively with groups that it almost appears the contact person is selling my ideas for me. The most powerful techniques are

a. Ask your prospect contact person to conduct your introduction and explain why you are there (credentials, expertise, validation) to address them. In many cases, I've had to write up a summary for my prospect to use, but it doesn't matter as long as you are introduced in a favorable light.

b. Begin your presentation by having attendees go around the room and introduce themselves and what they see as their role in the decision-making process and their main interest in your presentation. Jot those items down on a notepad for future reference. This is crucial information in order for you to shorten your sales cycle.

c. Before you begin your presentation, illustrate that you've done your homework by citing your client's latest news release, current market conditions, recent product introductions, or pertinent personal data on certain participants. The morning of one of my presentations, I noticed an article in a local paper that said the stock price of my prospect had gone up $3.50 a share the day before. When I congratulated the vice president of sales on this fine accomplishment, he was startled because he had been traveling and hadn't had time to check the company's stock quote. The entire room was pleased that I had knowledge of the stock position, and I used that theme throughout my presentation.

d. Carefully craft a list of questions that will help you guide the participative aspect and stimulate significant interaction on behalf of the attendees. Good examples of these questions are

Tim, when is the last time that you encountered . . . ?

Ellen, what specifically do you find challenging about . . . ?

Sue, how much experience have you had with . . . ?

Fred, how many times have you been in a position where this has happened to you?"

Jeff, in our previous discussions, you mentioned that you were skeptical about this. How do you feel about it now?

Jen, I gathered from our previous conversations that this will work well for your group. Is that still correct? If so, based on your knowledge of Jeff's group, how do you see it helping him?

e. Another creative way to engage customers is to actually have a participant present part of the materials. This is arranged in advance of your presentation and carefully planned so that you know exactly what the attendee is going to say. When you employ this tactic, it will actually appear to the balance of the group as though the presenter is teaming with you to present your business proposition. To the audience, it appears to border on an endorsement of you. I will caution you that sometimes, for various reasons, your prospect may refuse to help you and that's okay. Also, sometimes your prospect may stray from the topic. Remember that you are in control, and you will need to guide the discussion to your desired outcome.

THE BARRIERS TO
PARTICIPANT ENGAGEMENT CASE

About a year ago, I was asked by a client to observe a presentation being made by one of his sales representatives to a relatively large group of customers. This salesperson did not know that I would be observing, so I purposely arrived after the presentation had begun. As I stood in the back of the room, I observed that out of approximately 40 attendees, about 50 percent of them were busy with their noses buried in the presenter's product catalog. This went on for most of the hour-long presentation. Not only did they miss her key points, but also many of them departed before the presentation concluded leaving their catalogs on their chairs. How much interaction do you suppose she got from them? She had thoughtfully left an entire carton of catalogs at the room's entrance so that all participants could grab one on the way into the presentation. To make matters worse, the salesperson didn't roam the room or try to engage the attendees. Not only was her presentation a waste of time, but she failed to accomplish her Compression Objective, which was to schedule interviews with any interested prospects. What she did successfully accomplish was to lengthen her sales cycle because now she will have to address each of these participants individually at a later date in order to qualify suspects from prospects.

This case illustrates three points:

1. Handing out product literature or product catalogs prior to your presentation creates a barrier to participant engagement. You've seen it before. The first thing the attendees will do is open up your catalog and start paging through it. Unless the handouts are an agenda or are actual program materials, keep them until you are done; otherwise handouts will be a detrimental distraction to your presentation. In fact, even during the proposal stage of my sales cycle, I make it a practice to keep the proposal in my possession until I have highlighted the most important points. Then I hand it out to the prospects or clients. The results are astonishing. Their retention and understanding levels go way up. I attribute a good part of my high close ratio to this activity.

   To pass product or parts samples around the room is equally distracting, but sometimes it is a necessity in emphasizing your Unique

Selling Proposition. The best way to successfully make your point and not interrupt attention or participation is to hand out parts or product samples just before a planned break. The participants can then concentrate on the sample and not worry about missing a key point you are making. Try this in your next presentation.

2. Professional salespeople conduct many sales presentations in any given year. Consequently, they have a tendency not to treat each presentation as unique. Routine presentations cause a barrier to participant engagement. How many presentations does a typical successful sales professional facilitate in a year? So many that we can't even give you an answer to that question. Consequently, some salespeople tend not to tailor their presentations to their prospect or customer, and they eventually lose their own enthusiasm. Never forget that you increase the prospect's understanding by tailoring your presentation, and you increase her retention by using enthusiasm.

3. You must set Compression Objectives for every presentation, even those with large open groups. Even these can vary by each participant in a large group because your attendees can quite possibly be in different stages of your sales cycle. Be aware of this, and don't forget to ask for or suggest the commitment that you need in order to move to the next stage in the sales cycle. Remember that even though there are 40 or 50 people in a room, you are still in charge of each one of their respective sales cycles.

Employing these activities are essential to shorten your sales cycle and help you beat your competitors in the sales race.

PHASE III: POST-PRESENTATION CONNECTION

The third and final phase of the participative sales presentation is the Post-presentation Connection to your prospect or customer. Simply put, it is the follow-through that will determine how successful you were at getting your presentation message across to your audience. It is the phase of the presentation that will earn you the sale. This is one step that *must* be performed in order to shorten your sales cycle. It is the critical point where you learn the answers to some very important Short Cycle Selling questions:

1. Was I able to favorably affect my prospect's or customer's perception of my business proposition? What is my prospect's or customer's perception?

2. What could I have done better that I will change in my next presentation?

3. What did I do very well that I would incorporate in all my presentations?

4. Where do I go from here with this particular prospect?

The Post-presentation Connection occurs at two distinct intervals following your presentation: immediate and extended. The immediate Post-presentation Connection takes place minutes after you have concluded. This is the opportune time for you to review each attendee's issues and concerns that you compiled prior to your presentation. The best procedure for this is to ask each participant these questions:

Andy, your primary concerns prior to our presentation were timing and implementation. How do you feel now?

Tim, your primary issues revolved around pricing. On a scale of 1 to 10, 10 being very satisfied, where do you rate your satisfaction now?

Valeria, the issue of prime importance to you was your company's lack of technology. How comfortable are you now with our proposal?

Amy, I can tell from your comments that you are still a little skeptical. On a scale of 1 to 10, 10 being completely convinced, where are you? (Amy answers "7.") What would it take to get you to a 10?

Charlie, you told me that the program must fit the company's vision. How do you feel now?

Todd, what else should we cover before we adjourn?

It is so important to get this immediate Post-presentation Connection completed before anyone leaves the room. It is also vital to ask one more meaningful question before you conclude:

Normally, I follow up with a brief telephone call within the next few days to answer any other questions that might arise. Who has a problem with that?

I have yet to have anyone object at this point. What you have just done is set the stage for your extended Post-presentation Connection. This activity is most effective within 3 to 5 business days after your presentation. The dialogue and questioning is quite brief and simple:

Josey, it's been about 5 days since you participated in my presentation. What questions have arisen since then?

Stacey, do you still feel as positive as before?

Nell, has anything changed since we made our presentation?

Julie, what would prevent us from moving forward at this point?

The extended Post-presentation Connection is your entrée to close. Do it! It will help you avoid delays in your sales cycle.

THE VIRTUAL SALES PRESENTATION

Most of you conduct long-distance business relationships. I know that many times you are forced at the last minute to hop a high-priced red-eye flight to make an emergency presentation. You rush to the airport and buy one of those expensive last-minute tickets. While sitting on a cramped plane you hastily crank out your presentation on your laptop. Once you arrive (assuming your flight wasn't cancelled), you lug your laptop, overhead projector, and overnighter through the destination airport looking for a rental car. You show up at your prospect's business only to find that one of the key players had to leave town to make her own last-minute presentation. Does this sound familiar?

There is good news! There is a quicker, less-expensive way to accomplish this task that will put significantly less stress on you, yet accomplish the same goal. It is called the Virtual Sales Presentation and is manifested through one of the Web conferencing services. A listing of some of these services can be found in The Resource Center at the conclusion of the book.

Picture this. While your competitors are rushing around the country on airplanes, spending tens of thousands of travel dollars, you are sitting in your office conducting a Virtual Sales Presentation with all your prospect's key people, including the person who had to rush out of town to make her own presentation. Sound good? Can you see how this would compress your sales cycle?

The process is so simple. You conduct phase I of the participative sales presentation model. After you obtain the necessary information, you prepare your complete presentation. At that time, you upload your electronic presentation to your Web conference provider (see above), and you are ready to go. Next, you send e-mail agendas to all the attendees with the time of the presentation, the URL (Internet) address of the presentation, and the conference call toll-free number and pass code. Because it is a Virtual Sales Presentation, participants can be anywhere in the world. There is no excuse, like being out of town, for a key player to miss your presentation. At the appointed time of the presentation, you dial into the presenter's screen on the URL site and call the meeting to order via the teleconference call. As the presentation progresses, you control the electronic slide show, answer specific questions, lead discussions via questioning, and conduct the immediate Post-presentation Connection. Meanwhile, your prospects sit in their own offices, watch your electronic presentation on their own computer screens, and participate much like they were actually in the conference room with you.

Within a short period of time, you will find that the fees for these services plus the cost of a teleconference service will save thousands in travel expenses and time. The benefits to you are outstanding:

Shortened sales cycle

Novelty definitely differentiates you

Lower travel costs

More efficient use of your time

More frequent presentations

SALES RACE WRAP-UP

Strong sales presentations are a major factor in compressing your sales cycle. The predominant activities in the presentation stage of your sales cycle are

1. Teach the customer or prospect about the benefits of doing business with you so that she retains the information in a favorable light.

2. Convince the customer or prospect of the validity of your business proposition.

3. Position yourself into the customer's or prospect's evoked set (final two viable purchase options—you and a competitor—from which your customers or prospect will choose the winner).

The Compression Objective of the presentation stage of your sales cycle is to move the customer to the next stage in your sales cycle. It may lead to negotiations or a close, but the ultimate reason to perform a presentation is to get there. Don't forget to ask for that commitment.

Great sales presentations are characterized as participative. The secrets to successful participative sales presentations are twofold:

1. Be enthusiastic! Enthusiasm is contagious and you definitely want your prospects pumped up to buy.

2. Follow the three phases of the participative sales presentation model:

   Pre-presentation Involvement

   Presentation Engagement

   Post-presentation Connection

Remember that your presentation will need to favorably affect the perception of your prospect or customer. In order to do that, your audience or attendees must learn, understand, and recall the benefits of your Unique Selling Proposition.

MASTERING YOUR OWN SALES CYCLE

1. List the date of your next sales presentation:

_____

2. What is the prospect's or customer's name?

_____

3. In the left column, list the names of those who will be attending your sales presentation. In the right column, list
   what their main concerns or issues will be. You will need to
   call or e-mail them.

Names of Attendees   **Concerns or Issues**

_____   _____

_____   _____

_____   _____

_____   _____

_____   _____

_____   _____

4. What will you do to make it participative for each attendee?
   What questions will you ask each of them?

_____

_____

_____

_____

_____

_____

CONDENSE YOUR SALES NEGOTIATIONS

Jockeying for a Better Position Near the Finish Line

Sales negotiating is nothing more than putting a deal together.

For many years, I've listened to banker after banker and salesperson after salesperson complain about how they've had to give up something in order to make the deal happen. Maybe the banker had to give on some service fees or a quarter of a point on interest. The salesperson complains that he had to lower the price, move up a delivery date, or change a packaging array. They lament about how much better a deal they would have been able to "cut" if they had just known some sneaky, yet powerful negotiating ploy to outflank their customer. Almost without exception, they will tell me that their negotiating skills need polishing.

In these instances, I always ask a short sequence of questions.

- Did you get the sale?
- If yes, was the deal acceptable to your organization (boss, price policy, gross margin, etc.)?
- If yes, was the deal satisfactory in your eyes?

- If yes, what are you complaining about?
- If you didn't get the sale, what would you have had to do to get the sale?

Negotiating is not a mystical power that some people possess from birth, nor is it a series of combatlike tactics that involve a shrewd Norman Schwartzkopf-like personality. It is simply guiding your prospect or customer to the negotiation stage of your sales cycle and then recognizing the opportunities to *tactfully* put the deal together.

SALES RACE RULE 14

Regardless of your particular sales cycle, once you have engaged a customer or prospect in negotiations, you have a better than 85 percent chance of closing the sale. If you don't "put the deal together," you must assume full responsibility.

Take a moment and think about Sales Race Rule 14. Eighty-five percent of the sales that you have in progress can be closed if you will just engage your customer or prospect in negotiations: 85 percent! I know what you're thinking right now, "If that's the case, why didn't this deal or that deal close? I certainly engaged both of them in negotiations." Well, there is just one qualifier to this rule. You must *keep them engaged* in the negotiation process!

COMPRESSION CONCEPT: GUIDING YOUR CUSTOMER TO THE NEGOTIATING STAGE

My sales training and consulting business takes me into industries such as business banking, mortgage sales, real estate, medical technology sales, computer peripherals, computer hardware and software, contractor sales, fragrance manufacturing, channel selling, financial services, pharmaceutical sales, and environmental consulting sales. My experience in these diverse industries has proven one thing to me. No matter what business you are in, 85 percent of the sales that get to the negotiating stage should be closed.

If this is the case in your industry, and I bet that it is, you should be quickly guiding your customers and prospects to the negotiating stage of your sales cycle and doing everything to keep them negotiating until you "work a deal." In previous chapters, we have shown you how to shorten your sales cycle through the use of Compression Objectives. While you may not be able to skip directly from prospecting to the negotiation stage of your sales cycle, you now know that by taking control of the sales cycle and guiding your customers to the negotiation stage, you will be able to implement Short Cycle Selling.

Let me share with you three letters that will enable you to engage your customer in negotiations—A-S-K. That's it. It's just that simple. *Ask* them to negotiate. There are many methods that you can employ to accomplish this task. Here are a few that I find work quite well.

1. Ask your customer what he thinks about your business proposition: Mr. Customer, now that we've reviewed the proposal, what are your thoughts?

2. Ask him what the differences are between what you have proposed and what he envisioned or is accustomed to: Mr. Prospect, obviously you had a preconceived idea of what you wanted to see in my proposal. Using that idea as a basis for discussion, what are the differences you see between what I've proposed and what you have envisioned?

3. Ask him what else it would take to get the deal put together: Mr. Customer, what else do you feel you would need in order to proceed with this purchase? Mr. Customer, having just reviewed my proposal, tell me what you feel is missing.

4. Ask him what the differences are between your proposal and your competitor's: Mr. Customer, now that we have reviewed our proposal, what are the major differences that you see between what I've presented and the other proposals you have received?

5. Determine if your customer sees anything in the proposal that would keep the sale from occurring: Mr. Customer, what item(s) do you see in my proposal that would more than likely keep us from doing business?

Many sales professionals fear asking these questions because of the negative response they might receive. My point is that

1. It is better to flush out these perceived issues at this point, rather than wait and learn about them after your customer has awarded the business to someone else.

2. Your chances of obtaining a positive answer are 50 percent. If that occurs, then you have a natural lead into a closing statement. This is what Short Cycle Selling is all about.

Notice that the use of these open-ended questions is intended to elicit a comparative response. In essence, by soliciting this comparative answer, you are asking your customer to identify his principal issues with your proposal. This gives both of you common ground (his issues) on which you will find mutually satisfying solutions. It enables you to negotiate by responding to those issues and further clarifies your prospect's understanding of your position. It keeps you in charge of the sales cycle. Also, this action further clarifies your understanding of your prospect's perceptions and paves the way to a closing statement. Remember that since you have taken the time to conduct an interview and prepare a proposal, your customer owes you a satisfactory reply to that proposal.

COMPRESSION CONCEPT: KEEPING YOUR PROSPECT ENGAGED IN NEGOTIATIONS

Once you've opened the negotiations process as I have shown you, it's up to you to keep the negotiation going until you get the results you're after. Failure to do so will result in a lost sale or even more frustrating, a stall, followed by a lost sale. There are four ways to assure that you will be in control of the negotiation stage and your customer will not end the negotiation's process prematurely, thereby lengthening your sales cycle.

1. Plan your sales negotiation.

2. Have frequent contact.

3. Keep as many issues on the table as possible.

4. Preserve self-esteem by not arguing, insinuating ignorance, or dominating the negotiation.

Plan Your Sales Negotiation

In Chapter 7, you read about scenario planning. This technique is an outstanding application for any sales negotiating situation. Begin your sales negotiation scenario planning by deciding what the *best* (best for all parties involved) and *acceptable* (acceptable limits that you will not go beyond) terms will be in order to close the sale. Then try to list all possible customer concerns that might arise from your acceptable terms. Develop a response to each of those matters that ends with what you feel will be agreeable to both you and your customer. Write this list of customer concerns and your responses down on a notepad and take them with you to the negotiation. This will shorten the negotiation stage of your sales cycle by preparing you to immediately address the customer's concerns rather than delaying the process by having to get back with them. Exhibit 10-1 illustrates examples of how to do scenario planning for your next negotiation. In this example, the acceptable resolutions are listed randomly and not in order of priority.

POSSIBLE ISSUE: Your price is too high.

ACCEPTABLE RESOLUTIONS: Increase order sizes, order more often, offer a true value-added activity like sales training for the customer's sales force.

POSSIBLE ISSUE: Your past reputation is less than desirable.

ACCEPTABLE RESOLUTIONS: Offer a 100 percent money back guarantee; offer a trial purchase and if the customer likes it, he will pay for it and if he doesn't like it, he won't have to pay for it; offer to have your other customers call to validate your competencies.

POSSIBLE ISSUE: Your payment terms of adding freight to the invoice are unacceptable.

ACCEPTABLE RESOLUTIONS: Increase the order size and pay the cost of freight; offer a freight rebate at year-end based on the amount of annual purchases; offer to split the cost of freight if the customer's purchase activity reaches a certain level.

Exhibit 10-1

A very similar planning technique to scenario planning, yet slightly different, is for you to develop a series of trade-offs based on straw issues. *Straw issues* are minor points of concern to your own negotiation position, but may be viewed as major matters to your customer. They are aspects of the deal that you can afford to give away in order to make the sale happen. For instance, in a negotiation, you may identify straw issues that you are willing to give up such as payment terms, delivery date, product color, packaging size, or value-added activities. In Exhibit 10-2, I have listed some typical terms of a sales proposal. Of those terms listed, the ones in italics are my straw issues in this particular negotiation. Below those terms are the trade-off statements that I would use in this particular negotiation. To set the stage, my customer has a problem with my billing terms of net 10 days and wants longer terms, like net 45 days, before he will place the order.

PROPOSAL TERMS: Payment—net 10 days

Freight—prepay and add

Price—full list price, no discounts

Delivery—45 days

Minimum order size—five pallets

TRADE-OFF STATEMENTS: Mr. Customer, our payment terms policy has always been net 10 days. If you can help me by paying net 10 days, I can help you by offering a 2 percent discount for paying within those ten days.

Mr. Customer, if you can pay us net 10, then I will share the freight expense with you 50/50.

Exhibit 10-2

Obviously, my sales objective is to close the deal and my Compression Objective is to get a referral for a new customer. Using a trade-off statement allows me to find a middle ground upon which my customer and I can put the deal together. If I had not completed my negotiations planning process, I would not have been prepared to conclude this deal on the spot. Preparation is what makes sales race winners.

CONDENSE YOUR SALES NEGOTIATIONS

Have Frequent Contact

If your negotiation is conducted long distance via the telephone or e-mail, or if your negotiation is spread out over days or weeks, it is vital to keep your prospect or customer engaged. The old adage that "you should strike while the iron is hot" couldn't be truer than in this situation. It is up to you to keep the iron hot. As your communications frequency wanes, so does the urgency of the matter in the eyes of your customer. By staying in frequent contact, you will compress a normally drawn out sales cycle.

The frequency and content of your communiqués should be planned out. The reason for this is that you may wish to occasionally offer a straw issue as an incentive to push the deal along. My experience has shown me that if I stay in constant contact with a prospect during the negotiation stage of my sales cycle, I will eventually get that sale 85 percent of the time because I have kept him engaged.

Keep As Many Issues on the Table As Possible

Many of my clients tell me that there really isn't much negotiating involved in their sales cycle outside of pricing matters. My first response is one of astonishment. Are they kidding me? It's no wonder that their sales cycles drag on. If you feel that is the case with your business, then you probably are not experiencing an 85 percent close ratio once you get to the negotiating stage. This is because your perception is that the customer's decision will inevitably boil down to one issue—price. When you limit your sales negotiation to one issue, whether it's price or terms or whatever, you automatically cut your chances of making that sale down to 50 percent. You will either win or lose on that one issue. You've left yourself and your customer no other options on which to build a deal. The negotiation process will end prematurely and generally not in a way favorable to your position.

Frequently, my clients tell me they have a tough time finding issues to negotiate that will enable them to keep their customer engaged. After I explore their respective sales cycles and conduct a sales audit, I usually find several points of negotiation. Here is a list of some issues that you might be able to incorporate in your next negotiation.

Delivery time. Special order—order now for later delivery; rush orders.

Payment terms. Delayed billing; split billing; rebate on billing.

Freight expense. Prepaid freight, add freight into unit price, split the freight, rebate freight when your customer hits a certain annual purchase volume.

Accessories. Add optional product features at no charge, offer discount on accessories.

Late fees. Waive late fees.

Offer value-added services such as training. Conduct training for your customer's accounts receivable department on conflict resolution; sales technique training for their sales force; stress management training for their customer service department.

Preserve Self-esteem by Not Arguing, Insinuating Ignorance, or Dominating the Negotiation

The fastest way to lengthen your sales cycle is arguing with your customer instead of negotiating with him, thereby ending the negotiating process. The second fastest way to prolong your sales cycle, by ending the negotiating process, is to attack your customer's self-esteem by insinuating that he is ignorant or stupid. The third fastest way to draw out your sales cycle by ending customer engagement is to dominate the negotiation process by insisting on a one-sided victory—your side. Since these are the fastest ways to *lengthen* your sales cycle by ceasing customer engagement, then the opposite is the quickest way to *shorten* your sales cycle—keeping your customer engaged.

Arguing isn't negotiating. Negotiating is finding common ground on which both you and your customer are satisfied and can put a deal together. Arguing will do nothing but terminate your customer's engagement in the negotiating process, thereby increasing the time it will take to complete the sale. Arguing will more than likely lead to an attack on either you or your customer's self-esteem. Conversely, a successful negotiation will result in the preservation, and possibly the boosting, of your customer's self-esteem. As long as you both get what you want, what damage have you suffered if your customer *feels* like he has the upper hand in the negotiation? Remember that if you attack your customer's self-esteem, either he will never do business with you again or, if he does, he will lay in wait for you and hammer you hard in the next negotiation. Either way, your sales cycle is extended.

COMPRESSION CONCEPT: THE TWO FACETS OF THE NEGOTIATING PROCESS THAT ENCOURAGE SHORT CYCLE SELLING—TIME AND INFORMATION

There are three rules that always apply to compressing the sales negotiation stage of your sales cycle:

1. The person with the most information (best prepared) will always have the upper hand in any negotiation.

2. A majority of the concessions in a negotiation come in the last moments of the negotiating time.

3. The more that time is against you, the more flexible you can become.

Rule 1

This rule is always true because the person who has the most information pertinent to the negotiation is the person who is best prepared. The better-armed party to the negotiation knows all the options available to him. He is in the driver's seat and is able to guide the negotiation outcome to be more beneficial to his position. The more information you have, the more in control you are of your negotiating destiny and cycle time.

Rule 2

To prove Rule 2, let's look at a typical professional athlete negotiating a contract before his respective season begins. Both parties, the athlete and the team owner, want the deal to occur, but at the beginning of the negotiating process they are miles apart on terms such as salary, performance incentives, deferred compensation, promotional events, and endorsements. The season is still months away and both parties make outrageous counteroffers to each other and posture themselves in a positive light with the press. As the season slowly creeps into sight, they begin to negotiate more seriously and more frequently. Suddenly, the season is upon them, and no deal has been struck. As a huge fan of the team, you begin to worry that the season will begin without the franchise player. They appear light-years apart in their demands on each other. You wake up the morning before the season starts, and a deal was reached in the wee hours of that morning. The athlete is signed. Gradually the terms of the contract are leaked out, and you discover that the final agreement contains several concessions on behalf of the team owner and the athlete, but the deal is done.

In this scenario, both the team owner and athlete faced a time constraint. Therefore, as time started winding down toward the season, they both began to make concessions in order to reach a deal. The same applies to your sales negotiations. That is why you must ask your customer or prospect about his purchasing and decision-making time frame. By knowing this one piece of information, you can shorten your sales cycle considerably by letting your customer know that he can get the best deal from you before time becomes a major consideration. On the other hand, if the time pressure is being exerted against you, you will be able to recognize that your customer is going to expect more concessions on your behalf and will drag out the sales cycle until they occur. Once you have recognized that time is being used against you, you will be able to shorten your sales cycle by either stepping up your concessions or employing various cycle-shortening negotiating tactics. This becomes very important at the end of a month or quarter, especially when you are trying to hit a quota or bonus. Don't ever forget that professional buyers are trained to maximize their purchasing efforts and will use time against you to their benefit. They act as if they are in no hurry to conclude the sales cycle. That's why you must take control.

Rule 3

This rule may seem very obvious to you, but I can't count the number of times that I've seen professional salespeople let the sales negotiation drag on for days or months and then abruptly concede on major issues. Why? It's simple. They reached a deadline for a quota or bonus and suddenly recognized that salvaging some of the sale is better than not making the sale at all. It is a fact that as you approach a bonus or quota level deadline you are willing to do more to make a sale happen. Generally, this means that not only has your customer lengthened your sales cycle, but also you will probably have to make a major concession to get the sale. In reality, you have trained your customer to lengthen the sales cycle every time he negotiates with you because he knows that you will make major compromises to get the deal done. The solution is simple. Take care of business before it goes this far.

On the other hand, buyers are frequently against a time deadline. They too will exhibit more flexibility under these circumstances. Let me give you a little advice about this situation. Think twice before you overexploit your customer in this predicament by capitalizing on his lack of time. Someone else may have created his time crisis. Leave his self-esteem intact and allow him to be a hero by negotiating a good deal when his back is against the wall. This act of graciousness will significantly reduce your sales cycle the next time you need some business from him. Good customers never forget when you make them look good.

COMPRESSION CONCEPT: GET SOMETHING EVERY TIME THAT YOU GIVE SOMETHING

It's no secret that it is more blessed to give than to receive—except in negotiating. When negotiating, it is more blessed to shorten your sales cycle by getting something in return for everything you give—every time.

Very often I hear salespeople tell me that they did everything conceivable to negotiate the sale. They gave on price or delivery or packaging or payment terms, but they didn't land the sale. What went wrong? Two things: One, they expected their customer to automatically give back, and, two, they have trained their customers to take without giving anything in return. "How can this happen," you ask? It happens because the sales professional has not proactively asked for anything in return. Why? This is because of

1. *Poor preparation.* Neither planning what concessions to give nor planning what to get in return.

147

2. *Lack of information.* Not armed with the facts.

3. *Fear of rejection.* Afraid that the customer will say "no" if asked for something in return.

4. *Relinquishing control of the sales cycle to the customer.*

SALES RACE RULE 15

Never grant a concession, no matter how insignificant, without getting something in return, no matter how insignificant.

SALES RACE RULE 16

If you are granted a concession, capitulate immediately by giving a concession, regardless of size.

I guarantee that this is one of the secrets to Short Cycle Selling. In the following scenarios, you'll find the proper name of the negotiation statement, such as trade-off statement, followed by a brief explanation of what that really means. The actual wording of the statement is displayed in quotes.

Trade-off. I'll do this, if you'll do that. "Jack, if you will purchase just two more software licenses, I can give you 90 days on your billing."

Meet me in the middle. If neither of us can have our way, can we find a compromise in between? "Lorraine, your budget only allows for $19,000 for this project and my proposal is for $25,000. If I lower my price by $3000, will you meet me there?"

Hook on the back. Oh, I forgot. Even though the deal is done, I still need to get one more item. "Nell, I will agree to those 60-day billing terms. Of course, that means that you will purchase our accounts payable software program, doesn't it?"

You'll need to do better than that. I don't know for sure, but I think you gave me one of your straw issues and I need more than that in order to give something in return. "Stacey, you'll need to do better than that if you want me to throw in the video-streaming feature on your Web site."

In each of the given scenarios, you will notice that the sales professional has asked for something in return after conceding on an issue. This is not done to even the score, but to move you closer to completing the negotiation stage of your sales cycle. With every concession that you receive, you factually and emotionally move closer to the sale. Now, let's take a look at what you should say if you are granted a concession and you need to reciprocate.

Trade-off. Bob, I really appreciate the fact that you're considering paying our terms of net 10 days. If you can pull that off, I'll pay your freight on this order.

Meet me in the middle. Julie, you originally wanted 15 software licenses for that price and my proposal called for 25. Now, you have suggested that we meet in the middle at 20 licenses for that price. I think I can do that if you'll agree to purchase the training section.

Hook on the back. Abby, I appreciate the fact that you'll order if we can meet your installation date of 3 weeks. As I mentioned, our normal installation takes 5 weeks. I'm pretty sure we can accommodate your time frame of 3 weeks, but you will have to pay the price in category 1, not 3.

COMPRESSION CONCEPT: TAKE CONTROL OF YOUR SALES CYCLE BY NEGOTIATING YOUR ISSUES ONE BY ONE, BUT BRING MULTIPLE ISSUES TO THE TABLE

Bringing as many issues to the table as possible will assure you control in the negotiation. The mistake that I see made most frequently, which ultimately lengthens a sales cycle, is that professional salespeople try to address these multiple issues all at one time. This creates mass confusion, you can't resolve anything, and before you know it, time is against you. Start with the simplest issues, such as delivery date, or whatever, and work your way into the more complex issues, such as product or service modifications or customization. Remember to always ask your customer what he is willing to give in return on these single issues. "If I do that for you, Mr. Customer, will you do this for me?"

COMPRESSION CONCEPT: SPEAK TO THE BEHAVIORAL STYLE OF YOUR CUSTOMER DURING SALES NEGOTIATIONS

Whether your negotiation is face to face, over the telephone, or via e-mail, use the words that will appeal to your customer's behavioral style. This will reduce your sales negotiation stage by facilitating comprehension and comfort on behalf of each respective customer.

Use these expressions when negotiating with Bottom Liner customers:

This offer seems *logical,* doesn't it?

My offer *makes sense,* doesn't it?

The *numbers prove* how favorable this would be for you.

I can meet your *time line* if you will . . .

I've designed a very *systematic alternative* to your offer.

This will help you *reach your goals and objectives.*

Use these expressions when negotiating with Top Liner customers:

I have another way to approach that issue. *Visualize* this.

You're going to feel great when you hear what I can do for you.

Let's take another *look at what's best for your team.*

I have a *feeling* that *you're going to love* this idea.

Let's put our heads together to figure out what's *fair for all* involved.

THE COMFORT BATH CASE

Cary, Illinois, is the home to Sage Products, manufacturer of the Comfort Bath, a product used to bathe hospital patients who are unable to get out of bed to take a shower or bath. Comfort Bath is a registered trademark

---

CONDENSE YOUR SALES NEGOTIATIONS

of Sage Products Incorporated. I am personally acquainted with the high quality of this product because it was used on my father during a recent, lengthy hospital stay. Dad was impressed by the product, and it truly made him more comfortable knowing that he was able to maintain a high level of personal hygiene while being confined to bed. To complete its line of patient cleansing and hygiene products, Sage makes hair care, oral care, and perineal care systems.

Sage sells its product line through a distributor network, which in turn sells the products to hospitals in their respective marketplaces. Sage's sales cycle can be classified as rather complex. Not only do the Sage sales people have to sell and service distributors in their respective sales territories, but they also have to conduct direct sales interviews with many different decision-influencers within any given hospital.

Mike Shepard, Sage's northern California sales representative, and Alan McCandless, Sage's western regional sales manager, were working on selling all four Sage products into a major medical center in Santa Clara County in northern California. Sage was currently selling them Comfort Bath, but none of the other three products in the line. Mike Shepard and Alan McCandless's goal was to take that particular medical center's current Sage purchases from $20,000 per year to over $350,000 per year. This is no small task considering the huge number of medical center employees that they needed to interview and negotiate with to get them to buy the Sage line. In this particular instance, the ultimate decision maker was the director of nursing. The key influencers that Mike had to sell were 10 hospital department heads, a nursing committee of 40 people, and the central supply department. As if this wasn't a monumental task already, only 1 of the 10 unit managers was using Comfort Bath.

Sage's sales vice president, Scott Brown, knew Mike's tenacity and negotiation skills were superb. During the numerous sales interviews with all the decision influencers, Mr. Shepard and Mr. McCandless collected much valuable information (and thus were in the position of having the most information) that could be used in the negotiation process. Three pieces of that information would prove to be invaluable when negotiating with the director of nursing.

1. A recent budget cutback forced nursing staff reductions and lower patient-to-nurse ratios.

2. The union was exerting increased pressure on the director of nursing to do something about the workloads resulting from the staff reductions.

3. Trials showed that use of all four of Sage's products saved up to 1 hour per day per patient in patient cleansing time in that particular medical center.

Realizing that he had a solution to lighten the rapidly increasing union tension on the director of nursing (use of time pressure), Mike forged ahead by setting up his final meeting with the director of nursing. The meeting went very well since Mike had solutions to the nursing director's problems and the staff loved the Sage products. However, the director of nursing still made Mike jump through four more hoops before he'd give his blessing. Mike needed to

1. Meet with the patient care committee.

2. Address the local union meeting.

3. Present to the nurse managers' weekly meeting

4. Go through central supply to get the order.

Utilizing Sales Race Rule 15 concerning giving and getting, Mike agreed to all the conditions, if the director of nursing would

1. Eliminate all duplicate (competitive) patient cleansing items immediately.

2. Eliminate the lengthy formal new product evaluation process for all Sage products (talk about using negotiations to shorten a sales cycle).

The director of nursing agreed, and Mike had the sale—almost. He still had to appease the central supply (purchasing) department since the product switches would involve its total cooperation. Up until this point, central supply had been pretty much left out of the process. In order to protect central supply's self-esteem and let it be a hero also, Mike negotiated the free use of the hardware support system for all four of the Sage products. Sold!

The patients, director of nursing, union, nurses, nursing managers, nursing committee, patient care committee, central supply, Sage's local distributor, Sage Products, Scott Brown, Alan McCandless, and, finally, Mike Shepard, all Won!

SALES RACE WRAP-UP

Sales negotiating is nothing more than putting a deal together that is agreeable to both you and your customer. There is no magic to successfully negotiating a sale with your customer. Asking your customer to negotiate, rather than waiting for him to act, and keeping him engaged can shorten the negotiation stage of your sales cycle.

The four best ways to assure that your customer will continue to negotiate and not terminate the process prematurely are

1. Plan your sales negotiation.
2. Make frequent contact with your customer.
3. Keep as many issues on the table as possible.
4. Preserve your customer's self-esteem by not arguing, insinuating ignorance, or dominating the negotiation.

Time and information are the two most important facets of sales negotiating that offer you opportunities to Short Cycle Sell. Generally speaking, the party with the most information and least time constraints will lead the sales negotiation process. The best way to assure continuation and, therefore, quicker resolution, of your sales negotiation is to always ask for something in return when you grant a concession.

MASTERING YOUR OWN SALES CYCLE

1. Write the name of a customer with whom you are currently negotiating or are about to:

   _____

2. What is her or his primary behavioral style?

   _____

3. What expressions and words will you use in your negotiation to address this particular behavioral style?

   _____

   _____

   _____

---

4. List the possible concerns or issues that you anticipate your customer will have. Under each possible issue, develop and write the acceptable resolutions from your standpoint.

Possible issue 1: _____

Acceptable resolutions: _____

_____

_____

_____

Possible issue 2: _____

Acceptable resolutions: _____

_____

_____

_____

Possible issue 3: _____

Acceptable resolutions: _____

_____

_____

_____

Possible issue 4: _____

Acceptable resolutions: _____

_____

_____

_____

5. Itemize all your issues in the current negotiation on the lines below. When you have completed your list, go back and assign a priority number to each.

My Issues:	Priority Number
_____	_____
_____	_____
_____	_____
_____	_____
_____	_____
_____	_____
_____	_____
_____	_____
_____	_____

6. Now go back to question 5 and using a highlighting pen, mark the issues that you consider to be straw issues and are willing to sacrifice as concessions. Write the actual words you will use to get something back when you grant the straw issues in the spaces provided.

Trade-off: _____

_____

_____

Meet me in the middle: _____

_____

_____

Hook on the back: _____

_____

_____

CHAPTER ELEVEN

ELIMINATE ROAD COURSE OBSTACLES

Control the Staller or Objector

Their intentions may differ, but the result is the same— prolonging your sales cycle.

The question that I pose to you is, "Do most customers (buyers) deliberately try to stop the sales cycle process? If so, what does it sound and look like?" The two strategic words in the first part of the question are *most* and *deliberately*. The answer to the first part of the question is "No." Most customers don't deliberately attempt to stop the sales cycle. If you feel otherwise, then it's time for you to start looking for a new career because you must be experiencing tremendous distrust and frustration. I've had a few prospective clients intentionally slow or stop the sales cycle, but it certainly has not been most. Also, I've had clients who have unintentionally tried to stop or slow the sales cycle, this is a common occurrence.

The second part of the question can be answered quite succinctly. Prospects or customers who deliberately try to stop the sales cycle do so in the form of stalling or declining. Those who inadvertently try to stop the sales cycle do so in the form of an objection.

It is important for you to know the difference between a staller and an objector in order for you to fully reap the benefits of Short Cycle Selling. A staller deliberately attempts to slow or stop the sales cycle. She is fully aware that she is stopping the sales process. That is her goal. The *objector* generally isn't giving the sales process a second thought. She is just trying to resolve an issue or question in her mind that somehow may be a concern revolving around the mechanics of the sale. The mechanics of a sale include, but are not limited to

Timing	Geographical considerations
Delivery	Distribution
Pricing	Promotion
Payment terms	Competition
Features	

Regardless of intent, the staller and the objector have the same effect on your sales cycle. You will need to approach both of them in distinctly different manners in order to minimize their effect on your sales cycle. Let's begin by examining the objector.

COMPRESSION CONCEPT: AN OBJECTOR HAS QUESTIONS—JUST QUESTIONS

I detest the word *objection* because of its colloquial nature and its inappropriateness to the contemporary business-to-business sales process. The term objection has historically had such a negative connotation for sales professionals, and maybe rightly so. This negative undertone, coupled with all the original *Perry Mason* court scenes, where the attorneys vehemently objected to something a witness said, has piled years of *rejection perception* upon the word objection. While this scenario is straight from the 1950s, I am embarrassed to say that many companies still sell using their products or services as the center of their business proposition. Today, product selling is out. Product sellers view objections as rejection. Short Cycle sellers view objections as nothing more than the scrutiny that a buyer is allowed before making a commitment. Product selling in today's business climate will prolong your sales cycle. Short Cycle Selling in today's business climate will increase your sales in shorter time. Product sellers still face customer objections and loathe them. Short Cycle sellers view objections as questions and welcome them. Exhibit 11-1 depicts the more fundamental differences between the two styles and their respective perceptions of an objection.

Product Seller	Short Cycle Seller
Rejection	Opportunity
Protest	Hesitation
Reprimand	Uncertainty
Criticism	Reluctance
Denial	Misunderstanding
Disapproval	Indecision

Exhibit 11-1 How Product and Short Cycle Sellers View an Objection

From Exhibit 11-1, you will readily notice the negative nuance that the word *objection* brings to the product seller. If you dwell on those words, it almost becomes a frightening and certainly self-debilitating thought process. The Short Cycle seller views the customer's objection as a normal event in the course of her sales cycle. She can relate to her buyer's position because she too has been a buyer at times and has experienced indecision or uncertainty about a purchase that she has made.

Short Cycle sellers characterize an objection as a

- *Communications issue, not a personal, product, or service obstacle.* Once you get past the fact that an objection is not a personal assault on you or your product, nor is it a deliberate attempt to stop you from selling, you will realize it is merely a lack of proper communications on either the buyer's or your behalf.

- *Form of customer questioning.* Short Cycle sellers realize that objections are nothing more than questions that are generally not phrased in traditional question format. Here are two good examples of this:

CUSTOMER OBJECTION: Your price is 15 percent higher than your competitors!

ACTUAL QUESTION BEING ASKED: Why is your price 15 percent higher than your competitors?

CUSTOMER OBJECTION: Your competitor can get the software installed next week.

ACTUAL QUESTION BEING ASKED: Tell me why you can't get the installation completed sooner.

- *Customer who needs more information to justify his purchase.* Short Cycle sellers know that a customer who is objecting is really one who does not have the proper information to feel comfortable enough to accept the sales proposition. That lack of information may exist for many reasons, such as a competitor misleading the buyer about you or the buyer's lack of knowledge about industry jargon or terminology.

- *Misunderstanding between the salesperson and her customer.* A Short Cycle seller knows that a misunderstanding is another primary cause of an objection. There may be several reasons for this misunderstanding. One of the most prevalent is that the customer was just not paying attention or listening carefully. Another common reason for a misunderstanding is that the salesperson assumed that the buyer had a fundamental basis of knowledge about the product or service that she was buying. Finally, the salesperson did not relate the benefits of her USP to the customer's specific situation. I've had many sales professionals tell me that they've had a customer tell them that she could not make the deal because the price was too high when, in fact, the real reason the customer didn't make the deal was because she misunderstood the pricing proposal.

- *Discrepancy involving her customer's preconceived notions.* Many times bad press, competitors, or rumors will impact the customer's preconceived notion about you. This will come out of the customer in the form of an objection. You may hear, "Hey, I heard that your company is for sale." What the customer really is asking you is, "Why should I buy from you when things are uncertain?" Short Cycle sellers always make discovering the customer's perception a part of their initial interview process. Then they can eliminate these preconceived notions immediately and move on with the sales cycle. This is easily accomplished by asking: "So, Ms. Customer, why don't we begin by you telling me what you already know about our firm?"

- *A temporary hitch in her sales cycle.* The most important aspect of an objection is that it is only a temporary hitch in your sales cycle. Envision an objection as just a single blip on your sales radar screen. I've seen many salespeople who have allowed this blip to completely stall out their sales cycle. Objections are quickly overcome by seeing them for what they actually are, a *short-lived* communications issue.

Short Cycle sales professionals recognize that an objection has utility or usefulness in the sales cycle. By being able to overcome the objection, you will realize three distinct benefits:

1. You will gain credibility with the customer or prospect. Remember that when you overcome an objection, you are answering your customer's questions. Therefore, you are demonstrating and validating your proficiencies in your field of expertise.

2. By validating your competencies, you are building an emotional bridge of confidence to the closing stage of your sale cycle.

3. You move the sale to the next stage in the sales cycle.

COMPRESSION CONCEPT: A STALLER WILL TRY TO END YOUR SALES CYCLE

On the other hand, Short Cycle sellers find that a *stall* is

- *The customer knowingly and deliberately attempting to slow or stop the sales cycle.* Simply put, a stall is a contrived effort on behalf of your customer to prolong your sales cycle. This is not to say that the customer's reasoning is not valid, but valid or not, the effect is the same. You must realize that at best, stallers will slow your sales cycle; at worst, they will take control of the sales cycle from you and stop it at will.

- *A customer's concern about your timetable for the sale.* Many professional buyers will slow the sales cycle down when they have a concern for *your* timetable for the sale. They may feel that you are rushing the sales cycle, or they may resent the fact that you are controlling the sales cycle. Either way, they will deliberately attempt to extend your sales cycle.

- *A referral to a third party or authoritative person.* How many times have customer's told you that they just love your proposal, your products, or your service, *but* they have to run it past their bosses, boards of directors, or executive committees before they can give you the go ahead? A vast majority of stalls result in a third-party referral. If that's the case, three facts exist that you must be aware of in order to get past this situation quickly:

  1. Albeit a deliberate attempt to slow your sales cycles, it may or may not be the truth.

  2. You have not been talking with all the proper people in your customer's decision-making process.

  3. You customer has just made a bid to take control of your sales cycle.

- *More than a blip in your sales cycle.* Unlike an objection that *can be quickly overcome* during a sales interview, a stall may take some time to resolve. Whenever you involve a third party in a stall, your customer automatically lengthens the time it will take for you to close the sale.

- *An opportunity to gain some form of commitment.* Short Cycle sellers see that a stall is nothing more than an opportunity for them to retain control of their sales cycle and gain some form of commitment in order to move their customer to the next stage of their sales cycle. Yes, it may take a little bit longer than anticipated, but the customer will not stop the sales process.

I've spent quite a bit of time differentiating a stall from an objection because if you are going to capitalize on all the principles of Short Cycle Selling, you will need to recognize whether you are being stalled or you are facing an objection. They are settled by applying different methods. If you fail to recognize a stall and try to overcome it by treating it like an objection, you will lengthen your sales cycle. Conversely, if you treat an objection as you would a stall, you will more than likely lose the sale. Having read the differences between a stall and an objection, take a few moments and test yourself by completing Activity 11-1.

Activity 11-1

Put an "s" on the line next to the expressions that you believe are a stall. Mark an "o" on the line next to the expressions that you believe are an objection.

1. _____ My business partner is in Tanzania. I need her approval.

2. _____ There is no way I can pay that price.

3. _____ I've heard some bad things about your post-purchase service agreements.

4. _____ I have no idea where the purchase order is. I sent it upstairs for approval.

5. _____ If I can't get it by the 24th of this month, I don't want it.

The correct answers and the logic behind those answers are listed at the beginning of the Mastering Your Own Sales Cycle section at the end of this chapter. Go there now, and determine how well you did in this exercise by comparing your answers against the ones listed.

COMPRESSION CONCEPT: SIX STEPS TO ISOLATE THE OBJECTION AND MOVE ON

Practitioners of Short Cycle Selling have found that the best way to successfully retain control of the sales cycle and move it to the next stage is to uncover all objections (that is, concerns and questions) up front and dispense with them one at a time. The procedure shown in Exhibit 11-2 is the most proven way to accomplish this Short Cycle Selling task.

Exhibit 11-2

OBJECTION: *I just don't have the budget for this project this year.*

Step 1. *Listen carefully, don't interrupt, but always take notes.* This is a point where you really need to focus all of your attention on what your customer is saying. She will give you a lot of clues on how to compress this stage of your sales cycle. Most importantly, take good notes. Taking good notes will keep you focused, pro-

---

vide you with clues that will help you quickly address the issues, and build credibility for you by showing the customer that you are sincere about answering her questions. Notes are your biggest asset in shortening the sales cycle.

Step 2. *Show understanding, not agreement.* Believe it or not, I have witnessed many salespeople who actually agree with a customer when they express an objection. No kidding, they actually agree because, as I understand it, they feel that the customer will miraculously feel an instant trust and bond. They feel that if they didn't agree, they'd be misleading their customer. In all actuality, all they are literally doing is extending the sales cycle and nothing more. What you are saying to a customer by agreeing with one of her objections is, "You know, you're right. This makes no sense to me either." What customer in her right mind would buy from you then?

Understanding what your customer is saying and agreeing with what your customer is saying are two different positions. You need to first understand what your customer is saying before you can either agree or disagree with her. I'm assuming that you will understand and not necessarily agree with the objections that your customer raises. If you do agree with the objection, you either don't have a legitimate prospect or you need to go into customer service.

Consequently, when your prospect or customer tells you, "I just don't have the budget for this project this year," the first words uttered from your lips should be: "I understand what you are saying." You are not saying that you agree with them or that you even understand them. What you are relating to them is that you hear and understand what they are saying. Nothing more.

Step 3. *Isolate the objection from the rest of the sales process and uncover any other barriers to continuing on in your sales cycle.* I cannot stress enough that the approach to a customer's objection is where you will either shorten or lengthen your sales cycle. Immediately, after stating that you understand, follow up with this little discovery question: "Ms. Customer, bear with me for a moment. I realize that budget is a real issue to you. Hypothetically, if we could set aside the issue of your budget for a moment (actually create a visual by pretending with your hands that you are placing this issue to the side), what else do you see that might keep us from working together?"

Many experienced sales professionals have a difficult time getting this question out, but by asking this one question, you are asking the customer to tell you of any other hidden agendas she may have that would keep you apart. Understand this because if she says there is nothing else that she has concerns about, you have just closed the sale. All you need to do now is to resolve her budget problem in one of many creative ways you have at your disposal. Once you have satisfied this concern, the business is yours.

If, by chance, your customer replies to this question by stating that she also has worries about your ability to deliver on time, calmly state that you understand what she is saying, write it down on your notepad, and ask, "What else?" If there is nothing else, then proceed. If another objection appears, repeat this until the customer cannot come up with anything else. Then you ask for a commitment.

That's right. Ask for a commitment! Do not move on until you have clarified that if you address these objections to the customer's satisfaction, there is nothing else that would keep her from doing business with you. This is vital to shortening your sales cycle. You cannot skip this step. The best way to ask for this commitment is to say: "Ms. Customer, you have told me that budget and your unfamiliarity with our company are your two main concerns. Is that correct?" (Pause and wait for the answer. If you get a "yes," then proceed. If you get a "no," continue to question.) "So, if I understand properly, if I address those issues to your satisfaction, you don't see anything else that would preclude us from doing business?"

When she replies, "That's correct," what has just happened? She just committed to you to buy—if you satisfy her questions. The ball is in your court. Right where you want it. You are in charge of the sales cycle.

Step 4. *Explore the objection(s) one by one for underlying motives and let the customer tell you what to tell her.* Again, this is a classic point of compression. Use open-ended questions to let the customer tell you how to resolve her concern. I recommend that you begin this step by saying: "Ms. Customer, tell me about your budget process."

If you are dealing with a price concern, this is a perfect place to ask perception and comparison questions. A few good examples of these are

- Ms. Customer, what are you comparing my price against?
- Ms. Customer, why do you say our price is high?
- Ms. Customer, there are several components to this purchase besides price. Realistically, compared with the other components, where does price rank on a priority scale of 1 to 10, with 10 being the top priority?

Step 5. *Match your USP against your customer's concerns or objections.* This is easily accomplished because you have taken detailed notes and listened carefully for opportunities. The best way to start is to say, "Ms. Customer, now that I have a better feel for your concern about your budget let me address that in more detail. Our company has a unique and helpful program for customers just like you that also have budget problems. If we were able to delay billing for 60 days and then work a net 60 with you, how much of a favorable affect would that have on your budget?"

If the answer already lies in your proposal, but you are facing a misunderstanding, the best thing to say is, "Oh, Ms. Customer, I must have glossed right over that point. Let's take a moment and review the proposal again."

Step 6. *Confirm that you have properly addressed the objection and proceed.* This is the most important part to the Short Cycle sales professional. Always solicit the endorsement of your customer after you have answered her objection. The best way to solicit endorsement of your answer to the objection is to say, "Ms. Customer, does that answer your question to your satisfaction?"

In this particular instance, you want a "yes" or "no" answer. If the customer answers with a "no," then you need to simply say one of the following:

Tell me why.

From your perspective, tell me what part is missing.

Tell me what the ideal situation would look like to you.

Getting a "yes" achieves two very important steps in shortening your sales cycle:

1. The customer has told you that she is satisfied, and you should immediately move on to the next stage in your sales cycle.
2. You have just initiated emotional momentum within the customer that will help close the sale.

Short Cycle sales pros recognize these two opportunities and capitalize on them by gaining commitment for the next step in their sales cycle. Far too often I've seen professional salespeople fail to cash in on this critical moment. What happens most of the time when this occurs is that the customer will either stall or devise another objection. Result: The sale doesn't materialize.

SALES RACE RULE 17

Discover all customer concerns up front; formulate an implied understanding that if you successfully resolve these concerns in the mind of the customer, there is no reason not to proceed with the purchase; and then tackle each issue, one at a time, to your customer's satisfaction.

COMPRESSION CONCEPT: FOUR STEPS TO HELP YOU GET COMMITMENT FROM A STALLER

Earlier in this chapter, I defined a stall as a deliberate attempt to slow or stop your sales cycle. In all my years of training professional salespeople, I have observed that a stall is perhaps the most frustrating predicament that can occur. Regardless of the rationale of the staller, the exasperation of dealing with a stall sometimes creates distrust in the mind of the salesperson and unjustly ends the sales cycle process. Personally, I've been there many times and, as of the writing of this book, I find myself there now with two prospects. Since most of your stalls are going to revolve around a third-party or higher-authority referral, Exhibit 11-3 illustrates a proven Short Cycle Selling four-step process that will assure you of gaining something positive out of a stall.

Exhibit 11-3

STALL: *I can't go forward with this proposal until I have my boss's approval.*

Step 1: *Acknowledge the stall and ask to see her boss right now.* When you acknowledge a stall, be careful to not read in a negative connotation. Remember that many stalls are legitimate, and only patience will overcome them. Short Cycle sellers use this expression to acknowledge this stall: "Ms. Customer, I understand what you are saying. When could we speak with your boss?"

Even though you may not understand the true motive behind the stall, you *do* understand what the customer is saying. She is saying that she is stalling you for one reason or another. If the stall is blamed on a boss or another department, then the best way to end the stall and compress your sales cycle is to immediately ask or suggest that you meet the other party involved. Short Cycle sales professionals have found that if a customer makes a legitimate effort to put them in touch with her boss, their chances are very good. Generally this means that the customer has no problem with the salesperson helping the customer get what she wants. Once you have reached her boss, you will discover one of two things: either her boss is completely up to speed on your proposal or she will have no idea what you are talking about. In either case you are finally in front of the right person. As they say in the midwest, "Make hay while the sun shines."

Many times your customer, for whatever reason, will refuse to let you speak with anyone else. If you are denied this opportunity,

---

then proceed to step 2. You still can accomplish some form of sales cycle compression at this point.

Step 2. *Recheck key facts using open-ended questions.* It's been my experience that the facts that you need to recheck are buying time frame, likes and dislikes, and, most importantly, the decision-making process. Recheck the facts for two reasons:

1. Alleviate any misunderstanding on your behalf about the facts.
2. Hold the staller accountable for what she has told you. In this particular instance, you may have been purposely misled by the staller to believe that she can make the decision when indeed she can't without her boss's approval. You need to politely hold the staller accountable for misleading you. It just might shorten your sales cycle the next time you have to deal with her.

You accomplish this by saying one of the following:

Ms. Customer, perhaps I misunderstood you. According to my notes, I was under the assumption that you were the ultimate decision maker. (Then be quiet. Let the staller speak first.)

Ms. Customer, tell me again about the time frame for your purchase.

Ms. Customer, let's take a quick moment and review the things you like best about my proposal.

Step 3. *Review the benefits of the things she likes best about your proposal.* This is a vital step. The reason you review the benefits is because you are not going to be allowed to speak to the higher authority or third party and your customer must be your proxy salesperson. In other words, your customer must sell your proposition to her boss and she had better be well prepared. The key to step 3 is that you must get the customer to tell you about the benefits. In essence, you are getting her to rehearse for her presentation to her boss on your behalf. Don't tell her the benefits, but let her tell you. Of course, you may want to prompt her for any missing information.

Step 4. *Ask your customer for some form of commitment.* Here is the difference between Short Cycle sellers and the rest of the universe. In order to shorten your sales cycle and deal with the stall, you must ask for some form of commitment on behalf of your customer. I know exactly what you are thinking, "What kind of commitment can I get at this stage of the sales cycle? How can I get a commitment when the staller won't even let me speak to her boss?" I can tell you that there are several forms of commitment you can get your customer to make. My experience has shown me that professional salespeople who ask for a commitment here have shorter sales cycles and generally beat their competitors in the race for their customer's business.

Let's look at one way to ask for a commitment. "Ms. Customer, I am glad that you see so many benefits to you for doing business with us. It appears to me that you are sold on the idea." (Wait for a positive answer. If you don't get a "yes," then go directly back to step 2 and recheck your facts. The chances are you will get a positive answer.) "You will support it to your boss, won't you?" (Wait for the positive answer. She would look foolish to take you this far and not say "yes.") "That's great! When will you be presenting this to your boss?" (Quiet.) "That's great! When may I check with you on that day?" (Quiet.) "What can I provide to help you present this to your boss?" (Quiet.) "Since it is going to be about 10 days before you speak to her, let me suggest that the day before I will e-mail you this list of things you like about our proposal so that you will have it fresh in your memory. Okay?"

The Short Cycle salesperson gained two commitments from her customer that will help her deal with this stall. First, the customer did promise to support the proposition to her boss. Secondly, the customer agreed to prepare for her presentation to the boss by reviewing the e-mail being sent to her the day before she sees her boss.

THE BLADDER SCAN CASE

One of the most uncomfortable experiences that a hospitalized patient can endure is the insertion of a bladder catheter. In this respect, Tim Kartisek is a hospital patient's best friend. Tim sells a product to hospitals, clinics, and doctor's offices called the Bladder Scan. This outstanding product is an ultrasound-based machine that helps physicians and nurses determine if they truly need to insert a catheter into a patient. Besides the discomfort, this procedure runs the risk of creating an infection in the patient. The Bladder Scan accurately tells the appropriate medical technicians how much fluid is collected in a patient's bladder. A decision can then be made whether or not to insert a catheter. The Bladder Scan virtually eliminates the need for unnecessary catheterization procedures.

Tim Kartisek is a Short Cycle seller, and his territory is Maryland and Virginia. Recently, he encountered a stall on an important order for a Bladder Scan at a hospital in Baltimore, Maryland. The requisitioning department needed the equipment, but for some reason the procurement department was stalling. Tim was the recipient of the "It needs the hospital vice president's approval" stall. Like any good salesperson, Tim's main concern was for his customers who he saw as the doctors, nurses, and patients awaiting this equipment. Upon being presented with the stall by the hospital's materials manager, Tim immediately tried to gain some form of commitment, but was resisted. In fact, he couldn't even get the materials manager to call the hospital vice president to support the purchase. He knew that if he couldn't get some form of commitment, it could take weeks to get approval, if ever. After several days of no progress and discussions with his sales manager, Craig Middleton, Tim's tenacity resurfaced as he uncovered which hospital vice president was responsible for the endorsement. Getting nowhere with materials management, he ran the dangerous old "end around" play and it paid off. Seeking some form of commitment, Tim paid a visit to the hospital vice president. Based upon his explanation that doctors and patients were waiting for this machine, she immediately approved the expenditure and sent her consent to materials management. Along with the approved request, she sent a message that will probably prevent future stalls for Tim Kartisek and his Bladder Scan at that particular hospital.

The point of this case is that Mr. Kartisek kept seeking some form of commitment from the decision channel. He compressed his sales cycle significantly by finding a place to gain that commitment. Days after this stalling episode, it came to light that the materials manager deliberately stalled because he was concerned that Mr. Kartisek was pushing the order to meet a sales quota. Unbeknown to him, Tim Kartisek had exceeded his quota long before this took place. It doesn't matter what the staller's motives are, the result is the same: prolonged sales cycles.

SALES RACE WRAP-UP

Objectors and *stallers* have two distinctly different agendas. The objector should be viewed as a questioner, and the staller should be viewed as a stopper. The staller makes a deliberate attempt to slow or stop your sales cycle, while an objector's intent is to satisfy a legitimate concern or question that she has with your sale proposition. The staller may also have a legitimate concern, but the net effect on your sales cycle is to extend it. The staller and the objector are handled differently.

Short Cycle sellers retain control of the sales cycle and uncover all their customers' objections up front. Then they proceed to address each one individually. They move to the next stage in their sales cycle once they have gained the complete understanding and confidence of their customers.

As a Short Cycle seller, you should attain some form of commitment from a staller, even if it's an endorsement of your sales proposition to her boss. If that's the best you can do, then effective follow-up is your only recourse. There are many ways to control your follow-up using the latest in e-technology. This will be discussed further in Chapter 14.

MASTERING YOUR OWN SALES CYCLE

1. Here are the answers to Activity 11-1.

   S   My business partner is in Tanzania. I need her approval.

   O   There is no way I can pay that price.

   O   I've heard some bad things about your post-purchase service agreements.

   S   I have no idea where the purchase order is. I sent it upstairs for approval.

   O   If I can't get it by the 24th of this month, I don't want it.

2. Listed here are some of the most common objections that are confronted by Short Cycle sellers. On the lines provided, rewrite these objections in the form of the actual question your customer is asking.

Objection 1: Your price is 20 percent higher than your nearest competitor.

Your customer is really asking: _____

_____

Objection 2: We can't wait that long.

Your customer is really asking: _____

_____

Objection 3: I've heard some questionable comments being made about your customer service.

Your customer is really asking: _____

_____

Objection 4: But, I don't need all those features.

Your customer is really asking: _____

_____

Objection 5: It's our policy not to prepay anyone.

Your customer is really asking: _____

_____

3. For each of the five objections listed, complete three exploratory questions that are designed to uncover the actual concern of your customer.

Objection 1: Your price is 20 percent higher than your nearest competitor.

What _____

Why _____

Tell me about _____

Objection 2: We can't wait that long.

Tell me _____

What _____

How _____

Objection 3: I've heard some questionable comments being made about your customer service.

Who _____

Where _____

Tell me _____

Objection 4: But, I don't need all those features.

What _____

Why _____

How _____

Objection 5: We pay in 60 days, take it or leave it.

Who _____

How _____

When _____

CHAPTER TWELVE

S.A.F.E. CLOSING

It Means You Win

It's better to be S.A.F.E. than sorry (that you didn't get the business).

Joe Girard, one of the world's most successful automobile sales professionals, expressed that he always wondered why there is so much commotion about closing. In his book, *How to Close Every Sale*, Joe writes that from his perception, if you're in sales, closing "is your job!"

In order to facilitate Mr. Girard's concept and at the same time make your job easier, I have created a closing method that fits all selling styles. It is designed to help you, the professional salesperson, and your customer overcome the natural tension that occurs when you guide your customer to the transaction closure stage of your sales cycle. I refer to this method with the acronym *S.A.F.E.* or *S*alespeople *A*lleviating *F*earful *Ex*pectations. I will discuss this in greater detail later in this chapter.

Have you ever shopped for anything at a Nordstrom's store? If you have, you'll know exactly where I'm headed. If you haven't, let me tell you that its salespeople are more consultative than most so-called consultative business-to-business salespeople are. Personally, I've shopped in many Nordstrom stores in various cities. After carefully observing and analyzing their sales culture, it finally dawned on me that Nordstrom has a universal sales philosophy throughout its entire organiza-

174

tion. The prevailing attitude among its salespeople is that Nordstrom customers are expecting the sales professional to ask for the sale, so they shouldn't disappoint them. They ask for the business.

When is the last time you were the customer? Didn't you expect the salesperson to ask you for your business? Did he ask for your business or were you a victim of sales complacency? Along those same lines, when you are wearing your sales hat, closing the sale boils down to your perception of what your customers are expecting you to do. In other words, when you are conducting a sales presentation or presenting a proposal, how strongly do you feel that your customer is expecting you to ask him for a commitment?

From this perception, you will develop your closing philosophy. Some salespeople define their closing philosophy with expressions like "hard close" or soft sell. If your perception is that every customer is supposed to buy from you no matter what, but what they need is to be pushed, your closing philosophy will best be described as "hard closer." If your perception is that every customer is supposed to buy from you no matter what, but that your customer will tell you when he is ready to buy, then you probably would characterize your closing philosophy as soft sell.

Your closing philosophy then will govern your closing behavioral traits. If your closing philosophy is hard sell, then you probably will show a more assertive closing behavior than if your philosophy is soft sell.

In Activity 12-1, take exactly 1 minute and complete your thoughts about your closing philosophy and behavior. This is a timed activity for a reason, so be sure to be honest with yourself about the 1-minute time interval. Ready . . . begin!

Activity 12-1

My philosophy about closing is ———————————————————

———————————————————————————————

———————————————————————————————

———————————————————————————————

I outwardly exhibit this philosophy by the following closing behavior:

_____

_____

_____

Stop! Did you find this exercise difficult to complete within 1 minute? If you did, take comfort in the fact that in the 1000 plus times that I've conducted this drill, only a handful of people have stated that they've completed it without any problems. Your next thought probably is, "Why did I have a difficult time completing this activity?" The answer depends solely on how clear your perception is of what your customers expect you to do. This then defines your behavior.

One rule that I learned to be true some time ago has helped thousands of my clients and me to compress our sales cycles.

SALES RACE RULE 18

Your customers are expecting you to ask for their business. Don't disappoint them!

After you have sold an appointment, conducted a sales interview, prepared and presented your proposal, and negotiated a fair deal, you owe it to yourself to ask for the business. And, your customer knows it and expects that you will ask. It is not considered pushy or a hard sell to ask for what you have earned. Charlie Hasper, a former sales vice president of Clarke Floor Machine Company and one of the best salespeople I have ever met, told me, "Never be afraid to ask for what you think is yours." When you have done all that you can to earn it, the customer will give you the sign to ask.

SALES RACE RULE 19

Selling is a profession that can be likened to a romance; if you don't ask, there will never be a wedding.

COMPRESSION CONCEPT: CLOSING IS . . .

In your own sales career, you've more than likely seen many sales professionals who ask for the business so naturally that it just occurs without any thought. These pros unquestionably expect their customers to buy. It just happens. Have you ever noticed that they constantly lead their company in sales year after year? These sales professionals view the closing stage of their sales cycle as all true Short Cycle sellers:

1. *Closing culminates the current sales cycle and initiates a new sales cycle.* I've always had trouble with certain traditional sales jargon. As you know, I have an aversion to the word *objection*. I have the same feeling about the word *closing*. To me, a contemporary consultative and Short Cycle seller, the word closing implies the end, even though it often means you've *opened* a new account or relationship. I refer to the process traditionally called closing as transaction closure. Regardless of the business you're in, this transaction closure hopefully will be just the first of many with your new customer. Short Cycle sellers realize that when you close a transaction, you've just completed one business deal and prepared your customer for your next sales cycle. You have taken the first step in building a relationship. Also, at the point of transaction closure, your customer has expressed the utmost confidence and trust in you by awarding you with his money. This is a very positive time, and an ideal time to ask for a referral. If you ask at this time, your success rate will be phenomenal. That referral begins another sales cycle for you with another prospect.

2. *Selling is a helping profession. Therefore, closing is helping your customer satisfy a need and/or fulfill a want.* In order to shorten your sales cycle you *must* have this as an essential component of your closing philosophy. Your customer needs or wants what you are offering, and it's your job to carry out that obligation. Remember that no matter how powerful you perceive your sales skills to be, you absolutely cannot sell a business proposition to someone who does not need or want the item.

3. *In the transaction closure stage of your sales cycle, your role is to become a consultant to your customer.* Short Cycle sellers have discov-

ered that in order to compress the transaction closure stage of their sales cycle, they must adopt a consultative approach with their customers from the beginning. When you think of a consultant's job duties, two things come to mind: they get paid for what they know and they make suggestions or recommendations. The same is true for you, if you will become consultative at transaction closure. Outside of educators and ministers, the people who get paid for what they know generally make more money than the rest of the world. A few classic examples are physicians, consultants, lawyers, CEOs, talent agents, engineers, and certified public accountants (CPAs). If you are going to shorten your sales cycle, you need to position yourself in the same light as these other professionals. You need to become viewed as providing expert advice to your customer. Secondly, have you ever seen a consultant end a project without making some form of recommendation or suggestion to his client? Of course not, he would either be sued or run out of town. Well, the same is true for you. Don't finish your sales cycle without making that recommendation or suggestion. In your case, based upon your expertise, if the customer wants or needs it, recommend or suggest that he buy it.

4. *Closing is assisting your customer in his decision-making process.* The best Short Cycle sellers become part of their customer's decision-making process. It's just that simple. The means by which they become part of this decision formula is by gaining intimate knowledge of what transpires in their customer's decision-making process. When Short Cycle sellers diagram this process from data collected in a sales interview, they are able to identify points where they can assist their customers by providing consultative expertise.

5. *Sell to needs, close to wants.* As I discussed in Chapter 7, there are two dimensions to any customer purchase: needs and wants. These two classifications can be respectively assimilated with fact and feeling. Needs are fact, and wants are emotions or feelings. You must recognize that the prospecting, interview, proposal, presentation, substantiation, and referral stages of your sales cycle will deal predominantly with facts or needs. The negotiation and closing stages of your sales cycle revolve around the want or emotional aspect of your customer's decision-making process. To compress your sales cycle, you

must recognize that your customer experiences some tension or anxiety (emotion) when he first does business with you. This is the emotional side of buying. The anxiety is rooted in his insecurity about not knowing if you will deliver what you have promised. Typical questions that he is thinking, but probably leaving unexpressed, are

What will happen if this is a mistake?

How many people in my organization will be affected if this is a bad decision?

How will I look in the eyes of my peers if this doesn't work?

How will I look in the eyes of my boss if this doesn't work?

If this is a success, what can this do to better my career?

In order to be first in the sales race, your job is to ease these emotional concerns at the time of transaction closure.

6. *Ask, Ask, Ask, Ask, Ask.* To compress the transaction closure, you constantly must ask for the business. A startling fact was revealed to me recently in an audiocassette tape series entitled *The Aladdin Factor* by Mark Victor Hansen and Jack Canfield. They cite a study that shows that 46 percent of all sales professionals ask for the business once; 24 percent of the same salespeople ask the same customer for their business twice; 18 percent ask for the business three times; 12 percent ask the same customer for business four times. Only 4 percent will ask the fifth time. After 20 plus years in sales, I don't particularly find those facts startling, do you? However, what I did find surprising is that 60 percent of the business written is on the fifth time—60 percent! That statistic alone is enough to make you keep asking. Do you want to win the sales race by shortening your sales cycle? *Ask three times because the odds show that 82 percent of your competitors will not.* That's right! Eighty-two percent of your competitors have given up winning the sales race after they have been told "no" twice.

The final three words that best describe the Short Cycle sellers' closing philosophies are *frequently, enthusiastically,* and *sincerely.*

Ask for the business frequently! See the statistics just given.

Ask enthusiastically! The more energy you project, the shorter your sales cycle.

Ask with sincerity! You have to believe it's in your customer's best interest.

COMPRESSION CONCEPT: SALES RACE WINNERS KNOW WHEN TO ASK

If your customer is giving you buying signs, shut up and ask for the business! It doesn't matter that the sales cycle is not complete from your perspective. It only matters that the customer sees it as concluded.

SALES RACE RULE 20

What really counts is when the sales cycle is complete in the eyes of your customer.

This means that your sales cycle actually may be over prematurely. It may even end before you have even negotiated or closed the sale. I have personally witnessed this particular phenomenon many times. If you don't realize that the sales cycle is over, the result is usually very ugly. I have seen many 20-year sales veterans carry on and on and walk out of a sure thing with just another new friend, not another new customer. These seasoned sales professionals just extended their sales cycle, and they didn't even realize it.

The key question is, "How do you know when the sales cycle is done in the eyes of the customer?" The answer is fairly straightforward. Your customer will tell you with certain verbal and nonverbal signs. To shorten your sales cycle, ask for the business when you see or hear transaction closing clues.

Forget the sales cycle and ask for the sale when you hear your customer say any of the following:

I really like it.

How much is it?

What is your time frame?

What are your payment terms?

What other colors or sizes or package does that come in?

Who will do the installation?

Who will do the training?

Is that a firm price?

How long is that price good?

Let me give you an example of what should transpire. Your customer asks, "What is your time frame for installing this software?" Your response should be (use question-the-question from Chapter 7), "Mr. Customer, the more important question is, 'What is your time frame?'" Your customer responds, "I need it done within the next 60 days." Your transaction closure statement should sound like this, "If I can arrange that, can I count on your commitment?"

You will be able to shorten your sales cycle by asking for the business when you observe these nonverbal body expressions from your customer:

- *Your customer is reexamining the features of a product that you have just demonstrated to him.* This generally indicates to you that your customer is interested in this feature because he either did not understand the true value of that feature and now he does, or that specific feature is his main area of interest.

- *The customer enthusiastically explains the benefits of your service or product to someone else in his company (also known as selling for you).* Don't wait! Ask now! The customer has just taken over the selling job for you! Tell him what a great job he has done of explaining your business proposition and ask.

- *Constant positive head nods throughout your presentation.* How much more apparent does the customer need to be to tell you he is ready to buy? I have yet to conduct a sales presentation in which the customer deliberately tried to fool me into thinking that he was agreeing with me by nodding his head positively up and down. Most of those head movements are unconscious movements that truly reflect

181

what is going on in your customer's mind. If those nods are coupled with a smile and an attentive and upright body posture, ask!

- *Your buyer closely scrutinizes certain sections of your proposal for the second time.* This is akin to closely reexamining a specific feature of your demonstration. You might find the customer closely scrutinizing the terms, price, value-add, or features section of your proposal. Yes, you may find yourself facing an objection as a result of this close scrutiny, but once that happens the negotiation has begun and your odds of transaction closure are greatly in your favor. When you observe this occurring, ask, "Mr. Customer, you seem to be studying the terms section carefully. Tell me what specifically draws your attention to that area?"

- *Continued attentiveness and alertness.* It's the customer or prospect who is not attentive that portends indifference. If you have a prospect that has been continually attentive and alert, this signifies extreme interest, ask! When you feel that you've made your case, ask!

COMPRESSION CONCEPT: IT'S S.A.F.E. TO ASK

Short Cycle sellers know that there are as many anxieties and tensions inside their customers as there are inside themselves when it's about time to ask for the business. Your customer expects you to ask for the sale. He knows that you are a sales professional and that doing your job includes asking for the business. In fact, he is waiting for you to ask.

Many salespeople lengthen their sales cycles by putting off asking for transaction closure until *they* feel comfortable with it, rather than asking when the customer shows favorable signs. By waiting to ask, all you're really doing is building more tension on behalf of all parties involved. If you're a veteran salesperson, you are probably thinking right now that you can't understand how this would happen to someone with your experience, but it does. I've seen it happen right in front of me many times. In fact, it has happened to me. Veterans delay transaction close, just like rookies, because they expect the worst if they ask before *they* feel they are ready.

A few years ago, I developed a very elementary transaction closing method for sales professionals of all experience levels to help them avoid this sales cycle lengthening behavior. It is called S.A.F.E. transaction closing statements. S.A.F.E. is an acronym for *S*alespeople *A*lleviating *F*alse *E*xpectations. Its principal focus is to build a bridge over the salesperson's anxiety resulting from these false expectations. The primary false expectation most sales professionals face is that their customer will say "no" because

1. He is not ready to be asked.
2. He needs more time.
3. He needs more information.
4. I've never experienced a customer this ready to buy so early in the sales cycle.
5. He's never done business with me before.
6. He likes my competitor's offer better.
7. My price is too high.

Most salespeople encounter these paralyzing thoughts, even though their customer has given them all the right buying signs, and therefore they tend to deliberately prolong their sales cycle by not asking or overselling. Both of these behaviors, not asking and overselling, inevitably result in the customer stalling, objecting, or buying from a competitor. In any case, the salesperson runs a great risk of losing the sale.

S.A.F.E. transaction closing statements are designed to take both the seller and the buyer beyond the anxiety inherent in the transaction closure. Hundreds of my clients' salespeople have adopted them because of the comfort and confidence level these statements instill in them. Before you can start to successfully practice them, you must know that these S.A.F.E. transaction closing statements are built on four fundamental premises of all successful selling:

1. They are truly consultative in nature.
2. Selling is a helping and assisting profession.
3. Buying from you is a positive event.
4. The relationship between salesperson and customer is an alliance, not adversarial.

The actual words that I use in S.A.F.E. transaction closing statements can be classified within the four fundamental premises.

Consultative	Helping/Assisting	Positive	Alliance
Suggest	Try	When (not if)	We (not you)
Recommend	Guarantee	Feel good	Let's (let us)
	Your objectives	Results	Team
		Satisfy	Collaborative

When these words, or any form of them, are put into S.A.F.E. transaction closing statements, it looks like this:

Mr. Customer, let me recommend that we give this a try.

When we initiate this program, I guarantee we'll satisfy your objectives.

At this point, I normally suggest that we give it a try.

Let's team up and see what kind of results we get.

Mr. Customer, I feel good that we will get favorable results from this.

As a matter of course, let me recommend that you . . .

Let me suggest that we begin this collaboratively.

Again, the objective is to compress the sales cycle by overcoming the transaction closure anxiety, but at the same time, not relinquishing control of the sales cycle to your customer. These statements will provide you with confidence and put you at ease when your customer signals to you that the sales cycle is concluded.

Two additional thoughts that I will offer, in order to aid you in really making this transaction closure stage go smoother, are

1. You need to factor in the customer's behavioral style. For Bottom Liner people, don't forget to use terms like *the facts point to, it makes sense to me, the numbers add up,* or *your return on investment.* A good example of combining S.A.F.E. transaction closing with a behavioral approach would be: "Mr. Customer, the facts support my return on investment numbers. Let me suggest that we give it a try."

When asking Top Liner people, don't forget terms like *feels good, I feel I know your needs and wants, us, we, let's,* and *team.* Be sure to use the Top Liner person's first name when asking. It is less formal, conveys a stronger relationship, and Top Liners love hearing their names. A good example of factoring behavior into a S.A.F.E. transaction closing statement would sound like this, "Mary, we've been working together for some time now. I have a good feeling that you're going to be very happy with this. Let's give it a try."

2. The final point that I would ask you to consider in transacting a Short Cycle sale would be to practice silence. I have seen more sales blown by senior salespeople and rookies by overselling and overtalking. Once your customer gives you the sign that he is ready to buy, do two things: ask and be quiet.

If you don't remember anything else from this chapter, bear in mind that after you ask for the order, he who speaks first during silence, loses. It's a fact! If you speak first, right after you ask for the business, you run a very high risk of creating a distraction to your customer's thought process. Let them speak first. Keep silent no matter how long it takes. I've spoken first many times in my sales career, and I will personally attest to the fact that it creates a distraction and a much longer sales cycle. It is very hard to keep quiet when you realize that you have forgotten to say something, but after you ask for the business, it's too late to add on. You will lose (the order) if you speak first.

COMPRESSION CONCEPT: THE "NO" GAME PLAN RESTORES YOUR SALES CYCLE

It took me a long time to realize that as a professional salesperson, you do not necessarily have to take "no" as the final answer. It's totally up to you. It's your decision whether you have to accept "no" or try a "Plan B." I figure that after I have gone through the entire sales cycle and spent all that time preparing my client to do business with me, the sale is mine. Teaming that thought with Charlie Hasper's advice that you should never be afraid to ask for what's yours, I always enact the infamous Plan B if I'm told "no." I use it with discretion, but if I truly want the business, I institute Plan B.

Plan B has helped me close about 40 percent of the sales in which I have been told "no." Let me share with you what Plan B looks like. Try it the next time you are told "no."

The customer tells you, "Mr. Salesperson, I have decided to go with your competitor."

Step 1. Immediately respond with, "Please tell me why."

Step 2. Regardless of the answer, ask them, "Have you notified them (the competitor) or placed the order yet?" If they say "yes," then tell them you respect their decision and expect a chance the next time. If they reply, "No, we haven't had time to tell them. I wanted to tell you first." Then go to step 3.

Step 3. You need to realize that the deal is not dead yet and ignore the fact that your customer has already made a decision. You then quickly state one of the following:

So, you are saying that the only reason we are not going to do business is that . . .? How could we both get on the same page on this issue?

What would help get us over this concern?

I know you've made a decision, but hypothetically speaking, from your perspective, what would have to happen for me to earn that business?

Step 4. After you have asked these questions, be quiet! Let your customer speak. Then ask for the business by saying, "If I could do that for us, what would be the probability of us working together on this order?" Quiet!

Please don't misunderstand me. I'm not saying it works all the time, but I am saying that if your customer has based his decision on fair and unbiased facts and feelings, you've got a great shot at opening the deal up again. You still should remain in control of the sales cycle even if it appears over. However, if you feel that the decision was "wired" due to friendship or a bias, then don't waste your time. Ask for a referral and move on.

COMPRESSION CONCEPT: POSTCLOSING ANALYSIS COMPRESSES THE NEXT SALE

It is a fact that Short Cycle sellers do a postclosing analysis regardless of outcome. If they failed to get the business, Short Cycle sellers are adamant about not repeating the same mistake the next time. They are also resolute about modeling their positive behavior that contributed to a successful transaction closure. Both of these actions will have a shortening effect on your sales cycle. The time to do a postclosing analysis is right after the customer contact. Ask yourself these questions:

- Did my transaction closing behavior correctly reflect my closing philosophy?

- Did I observe silence? If no, why not?

- Did I try to initiate Plan B? If no, why not?

- Did I use the correct customer behavioral references?

- How could I have better rephrased my S.A.F.E. transaction closing statement?

- What signs did the customer give me to signal the sales cycle was over in his eyes?

- What buying signs did the customer give me that I ignored?

- How will I apply this to my transaction closure?

- What did I learn from this experience that will help me shorten my sales cycle?

By candidly answering these questions, you will become keenly aware of what steps you can take to shorten the transaction closing stage of your sales cycle. One final word of advice is to be very candid with yourself. Your degree of candor will affect your sales cycle and your income.

THE KRAFT FOODS CASE

Imagine how many packets of Kool-Aid you can stack in a semitrailer 40 feet long. That's a lot of Kool-Aid! Now imagine a 3½-mile-long line of 40-foot semitrailers parked back to back with each semitrailer full to the top containing packets of Kool-Aid. That is the way Pat Gaherty, strategic account retail sales manager for Kraft Foods, described the largest Kool-Aid sale ever made in history. Mr. Gaherty should know. He's the one who made that huge sale to one of the world's most prominent retailers.

Pat Gaherty has been in food sales with Kraft Foods for over 30 years. He now only handles the largest of the retail accounts and says that transaction closure in these sales is very difficult because of the sale size and profitability involved. Mr. Gaherty told me that his sales cycle to these larger retailers, especially on new items, is very long and complex, but he has found a way to exploit the process by using the concept presented in Sales Race Rule 18. Pat knows that these large retail customers are expecting him to ask for their business. In fact, he doesn't want them to forget that he's going to ask.

Mr. Gaherty said that he regularly practices a unique method to compress his sales cycle to the large retailers, especially in the closing stage. He calls it the "transaction closure setup." At every stage in Kraft's large retail beverage account sales cycle, Pat makes it a point to directly remind the buyer that at some time in that sales cycle he is going to ask that buyer for a commitment. He may tell a particular buyer several times that when the appropriate point in time arrives he is going to ask for the sale. Think about that for a minute. The buyer knows that Pat is not there for his health or therapy. He realized from the first appointment that Pat is going to ask for this huge commitment and still, Pat reassures him every step of the way that he will be asking. Using this routine of notification, Mr. Gaherty says that the buyers are much more prepared when the point of transaction closure arrives and there is actually much less tension. It's like Pat Gaherty says, "They know your purpose for being there is to sell them. They are expecting you to ask at some time in the sales cycle. Why not let them know in advance to be prepared because you are not going to disappoint them."

SALES RACE WRAP-UP

The entire concept behind Short Cycle transaction closure is that the customer is expecting you to ask for his business, so don't disappoint him. Closing a sale does not mean ending a relationship. Transaction closure means the start of a new sales cycle both with that particular customer and the referral that he has given you. It means that through a consultative role, you are helping your customer fulfill a want or satisfy a need. You are assisting your customer in the decision-making process.

Your customer will give you both verbal and nonverbal signs of his readiness to conclude the sales cycle. You need to be familiar enough with those so that you do not "kill the close." The four predominant transaction close-killers are

1. Not observing silence.
2. Overselling or overtalking when the customer is ready to buy.
3. Cliché closes, for example, sliding the pen across the desk and saying, "Press hard, there are 3 copies."
4. Poor communication or presentation skills (not benefit-oriented).

S.A.F.E. transaction closing statements are designed to take you and your customer beyond the anxiety involved in closing. They will alleviate any false expectations that you may conjure up in your mind. S.A.F.E. transaction closing statements are even more effective when you factor in the specific words and phrases that will attract the respective behaviors of the Bottom Liner and Top Liner customers. To even increase your chances of shortening your sales cycle using S.A.F.E. transaction closing statements, you must follow them with complete silence. Remember that he who speaks first loses.

This chapter's final two Compression Concepts that will help you shorten your sales cycle are

1. When a customer tells you "no," it's time to institute Plan B. Just because your customer has said "no" doesn't necessarily mean that the sales cycle is over.
2. Short Cycle sellers learn from their postclosing analysis. They neither repeat the same mistakes twice, nor do they fail to keep using statements that work.

MASTERING YOUR OWN SALES CYCLE

1. Based on the behavioral analysis you conducted on your customers in the Mastering Your Own Sales Cycle section of Chapter 8, pick three of those customers and write S.A.F.E. transaction closing statements factoring in the proper words for each behavioral style.

Customer name: _____

Behavioral style: _____

S.A.F.E. transaction closing statement: _____

_____

Customer Name: _____

Behavioral Style: _____

S.A.F.E. transaction closing statement: _____

_____

Customer name: _____

Behavioral style: _____

S.A.F.E. transaction closing statement: _____

_____

2. Who is the last customer that you sold? _____

What did you sell them? _____

Answer these questions about that transaction closing:

- Did my transaction closing behavior correctly reflect my closing philosophy? _____

- Did I observe silence? If no, why not? _____

_____

- Did I use the correct behavioral references? _____

- How could I have better rephrased my S.A.F.E. transaction closing statement? _____

_____

_____

- What signs did the customer give me to signal the sales cycle was over in his eyes? _____

_____

_____

- What buying signs did the customer give me that I ignored? _____

_____

_____

- What did I learn from this experience that will help me shorten my sales cycle? _____

_____

_____

CHAPTER THIRTEEN

FASTEST TIME WINS

Control Your Time and Shorten Your Sales Cycle

Resources that cannot be saved, conserved, or renewed are the ones we must utilize the most efficiently to take us to a higher standard of living.

Time is one of the most plentiful, yet precious resources that all of us have. Time governs so much in our lives. Our lifestyles are arranged around the proper allocation of this resource that we call time. Your birth certificate lists the exact time you were born. Your death certificate will list the exact time of death. The time in between the two is up to you!

Think about this one for a moment—just about every competitive sport has some element of time built into it. Downhill ski winners have the best times on the course. NASCAR, IRL, and CART drivers are judged on the time it takes to run a lap around their respective courses. There is only so much time allotted in a hockey, football, or basketball game. Major League Baseball is trying to reduce the time it takes to play a nine-inning game. The PGA players all have a tee time. One of the many things a sportscaster says about a tennis match is that it took four sets and 2 hours to play this match. Also, all televised sporting events take planned commercial time-outs.

Many of you may not remember, but in the 1950s and 1960s, a long time ago, television commercials used to be 60 seconds in length. Other than during the Super Bowl, when is the last time you saw a 60-second commercial? Pretty rare, aren't they? Why? Advertisers found that the attention span (the amount of time we can focus on the message of a commercial) has significantly decreased. Advertisers need to get their message across in less time. Most commercials now are 30 seconds in duration, at the longest. Networks have found that they can charge more money per second (time), by selling a 30-second spot versus a 60-second spot. They are able to fit more advertisers into the same commercial time frame.

Selling, like any athletics, is a time-based competitive profession. Selling, like advertising, is a matter of keeping customer focus for a specific time and message retention for a distinct time frame. What all three (selling, athletics, and advertising) have in common is that they are all about the measure and control of time.

SALES RACE RULE 21

Your sales cycle is a time-based event. Only your perception of time utilization is what keeps you from compressing it.

Try this little exercise to prove to yourself that time is a matter of your perception. Fill in the blanks with the first thought that comes to your mind. Use appropriate time measures, such as minutes, hours, days, months, weeks, and years, and be sure to quantify each answer (for example, 6 weeks or 60 minutes).

A long telephone call is _____

A short drive is _____

A quick sales cycle is _____

A drawn out problem is _____

"I'll be there in a little while," means _____

"I'll call you back in a bit," means _____

Now take these same six sentences and have two of your good customers complete them. Do not tell them your answers. Compare their
time perception to your perception. Where are the key differences? I
have a client who tells me that he'll get back to me in a bit. To me a
"bit" means at most 20 to 30 minutes. To her a bit means anywhere
from 3 or 4 hours to 4 or 5 days. A "long" telephone call to me is 2 to
3 hours. A long call to my wife, Ginny, is 20 to 30 minutes. A "quick"
drive to my colleague, Tom Rothrock, is 5 to 10 minutes. When I say
it's only a quick drive, I'm thinking about 20 minutes.

The point is that time is a matter of everyone's own perception. You,
as a reasoning and thinking human being, are able to create your own
thoughts. Those thoughts become your perceptions, and your perceptions do become your reality. That means that you have control over
your existence by making your perceptions anything you would like
them to be. If you are in doubt about this, start a discussion with one
of your customers of a different political affiliation or religious belief.
You'll quickly discover that her perception is her reality.

Since you are able to create your own reality through your perceptions, you are also able to control what your perception of time is and
how to best utilize that time. I can assure you that from my years of observing top sales achievers, they make the absolute best use of their
time compared to the marginal performers. Think about that last sen-
tence for a moment. Top sales achievers, "make the absolute best use"
of their time. When you *make* something, you are shaping it and therefore in control of it. For that very reason, I have titled this chapter
Fastest Time Wins: Control Your Time and Shorten Your Sales Cycle.
I don't purport that you can literally manufacture more time in a day
or month to sell your product or service. What I am suggesting is that
you can control your perception of how to best use your time. Making more time to sell implies a sense of control and discipline. I will
tell you that in the profession of sales, there is a direct correlation between your degree of self-discipline in the use of your selling time and
the amount of money you will earn.

COMPRESSION CONCEPT: OVERCOMING THE FOUR SKILL DEFICIENCIES THAT PROLONG YOUR SALES CYCLE

A sales professional's lack of self-discipline manifests itself in four self-defeating skill weaknesses that will seduce her away from accomplishing her predominant activities and Compression Objectives at each stage in her sales cycle. These four skill flaws are

1. Poor planning

2. Disorganization

3. Lack of delegation

4. Call reluctance

These four skill faults result in sales cycle limiting behaviors such as

Procrastination

Being "tied" to the telephone

Overcommitment—juggling too many activities

Scrambled priorities

Fire drills

Being "anchored" by corporate and administrative minutia

I can tell you without reservation that the primary reasons that any one salesperson has the above four skill weaknesses are that she does not realize the impact that these skills have on the length of her sales cycles. If she did, she'd master them very quickly. Secondly, since she does not have this awareness, she has never sought training or been trained to the necessary skill level. Ignorance is bliss, except in sales. Finally, no one, including her manager, has aptly addressed her skill development in these areas. In my experience, the third reason is generally because the manager also is weak in these areas, and I usually discover a case of the incompetent leading the incompetent. A sales manager who tells her salespeople to "do something, even if it's wrong" usually reveals her incapacity to perform these skills herself.

195

YOUR SALES CYCLE IS YOUR SALES PLAN

If I've read it once, I've read it at least 10 times over the years that "failing to plan means planning to fail." This has never been more true than when it is said about shortening your sales cycle. When you are not planning, you are reacting to events in the sales cycle, not controlling them. When you plan the events in your sales cycle, you are taking control by deciding what is going to happen, not reacting to what did happen. While you don't have to have the General Norman Schwartzkopf tactical planning mentality, you do have to plan three activities in order to control your sales cycle. They are Compression Objectives; desired time line; and monthly, weekly, and daily activities.

Compression Objectives

In Chapter 6 I discussed the concept of establishing Compression Objectives for each of your prospects and current customers. The only aspect that I would reiterate at this point is that by planning where you want the sales cycle to go next, you empower yourself with the control that you need to guide your customer there. That doesn't seem like too much to ask of you, does it?

Desired Time Line

Essential to any plan, sales or personal, is a time line. Plans are worthless without a specified time line. Can you imagine if during the War on Terrorism, Secretaries Powell and Rumsfeld decided to bomb Afghanistan on a "loose" time schedule? They would have just attacked al Qaeda when they felt like it or planned air raids at their convenience. The Allied efforts would have been a disaster because there would have been a total lack of control. The same holds true for your sales plan. Without assigning a definite time line to your planned accomplishments, you are not holding yourself accountable nor are you in control of your sales cycle.

Monthly, Weekly, and Daily Activities

Why do you think that day planners (especially electronic ones) have become so popular? They help salespeople in all worlds keep track (that is, control) of their monthly, weekly, and daily activities. The only thing they don't do for you is sit down and write a plan that consists of those activities. Once you realize that taking a few moments at the end of each month to plan the following month is actually saving you time, you'll make this a habit. Try this as a method to help you plan your monthly, weekly, and daily activities. It works great for me.

1. In the left-hand column of the table list the names of your prospects and current accounts.

Customer's or Prospect's Name	Current Stage of Sales Cycle	Compression Objective	Compression Objective Date	Transaction Closure Date
ABC Company				
Widgets Galore				
Minutia Mine				
XYZ Inc.				

2. In the column designated Current Stage of Sales Cycle, determine and write the stage in which your prospect or customer is currently positioned. This means the stage of your last or current contact with them.

Customer's or Prospect's Name	Current Stage of Sales Cycle	Compression Objective	Compression Objective Date	Transaction Closure Date
ABC Company	Demonstrate			
Widgets Galore	Prospect			
Minutia Mine	Substantiate			
XYZ Inc.	Interview			

3. In the middle column labeled Compression Objective, write the next stage in the sales cycle where you want to guide your customer or prospect.

Customer's or Prospect's Name	Current Stage of Sales Cycle	Compression Objective	Compression Objective Date	Transaction Closure Date
ABC Company	Demonstrate	Negotiate		
Widgets Galore	Prospect	Interview		
Minutia Mine	Substantiate	Negotiate		
XYZ Inc.	Interview	Presentation		

4. In the column labeled Compression Objective Date, write a realistic date that you wish to achieve the Compression Objective that you wrote in the previous column.

Customer's or Prospect's Name	Current Stage of Sales Cycle	Compression Objective	Compression Objective Date	Transaction Closure Date
ABC Company	Demonstrate	Negotiate	8/13	
Widgets Galore	Prospect	Interview	8/2	
Minutia Mine	Substantiate	Negotiate	8/26	
XYZ Inc.	Interview	Presentation	8/7	

5. Finally, to quote a famous golf expression, "Keep your eye on the ball." Keep your goal, the transaction closure date, always in front of you. By knowing when you want to close and what it is going to take to get there, you are in control of your sales cycle and not at your customer's whim. The final step to our elementary planning process is to enter the date you would like transaction closure in the right-hand column.

Customer's or Prospect's Name	Current Stage of Sales Cycle	Compression Objective	Compression Objective Date	Transaction Closure Date
ABC Company	Demonstrate	Negotiate	8/13	8/20
Widgets Galore	Prospect	Interview	8/2	9/7
Minutia Mine	Substantiate	Negotiate	8/26	8/31
XYZ Inc.	Interview	Presentation	8/7	9/2

6. Your plan is almost complete. All you need to do now is sort this table by the transaction closure date, putting the earliest date on top. This table clearly illustrates what your sales plan will be for August. You have spelled out the necessary activities that must take place by specific times in order for you to reach your sales goals. Now, book them in your daily planner and let that device worry about them.

Customer's or Prospect's Name	Current Stage of Sales Cycle	Compression Objective	Compression Objective Date	Transaction Closure Date
ABC Company	Demonstrate	Negotiate	8/13	8/20
Minutia Mine	Substantiate	Negotiate	8/26	8/31
XYZ Inc	Interview	Presentation	8/7	9/2
Widgets Galore	Prospect	Interview	8/2	9/7

Most of the sales cycle limiting behaviors that I identified in the first part of this chapter can be directly attributed to lack of planning. Procrastination is frequently the result of not knowing what to do next. Consequently, nothing gets done next, and the sales cycle goes on. Overcommitment and scrambled priorities can be just as devastating to your sales cycle time as procrastination. Overcommitment is caused by unrealistic sales activity expectations that you place on yourself. This simple planning guide will tell you when you can't do anymore. My personal experience with overcommitment has shown me that some of everything gets done, but none of it is completed successfully. Scrambled priorities are also a result of not knowing when things need to be done (lack of planning). Looking at the completed table, there is no doubt about what needs to be completed or when it needs to be completed. Your priorities are spelled out for you in a very objective manner.

GETTING ORGANIZED MEANS A SHORTER SALES CYCLE

Disorganization is a pitfall very common to those of us in the profession of sales. I wish I had a dollar for every salesperson that told me she had a true sales personality and part of that reputed behavior is disorganization and the related disdain for paperwork. I understand the dislike for paperwork, but I have no sympathy for those salespeople who are disorganized. One of the differences between a salesperson and a sales professional is their level of organization. Is it any wonder that the most successful salespeople in the world possess the ability to get and keep themselves organized no matter what they sell?

THE ORGANIZED SALES PRO CASE

One of the most successful salespeople I've ever had the privilege to work with is a gentleman by the name of Jim Webster. Jim is always on the list of top producers in total volume, gross margin, and new accounts. When I asked Jim what one key behavior that he attributed his constant sales success to, he said, "Being organized." Jim went on to tell me, "Organization is a daily effort. It's not just something that you ordinarily are. That daily effort puts me in control of my own sales destiny. I'm not reacting to events, I'm creating the events that occur." Jim then told me, "You just won't accomplish as much being disorganized. I've seen plenty of my competitors miss appointments, bid requests, and presentation opportunities because they are lost in a world of disorganization. They were in such disorder that they didn't even know what stage was next in their own sales cycle. I guess I had the shortest sales cycle in those cases. I got the business." Later in this chapter, I'll share some of Jim's secrets for staying organized.

I am both a reformed disorganized salesperson and a reformed cigarette smoker. Much like a reformed smoker points out to cigarette smokers the health hazards of tobacco, I point out the sales cycle hazards of disorganization to disorganized salespeople. My own personal experiences and observations through my sales training business have proven four points to me about disorganized salespeople:

1. Their numbers are plentiful. They might even be a significant majority.

2. No one has ever shown them how to be organized.

3. They have accepted disorganization as part of an inherent character flaw.

4. They have no idea that their lack of organization is robbing them of control of their sales cycle, thereby unnecessarily prolonging it.

Try this little exercise to determine your level of organization. Place a checkmark in the box next to the expressions below if you have said something like it in the last 30 days:

☐ I know it's somewhere here on my desk, I just saw it yesterday.

☐ Can you hang on a minute? I know it's on my desk somewhere?

☐ It may look messy to you, but the important thing is that I know exactly where everything is.

☐ Those are just papers from work. Throw them on the floor and hop in the backseat.

☐ I gave that book to someone, but I can't remember who?

☐ I put that message right here on my desk yesterday. Now I can't find it among all these papers.

☐ A clean desk is a sign of a sick mind.

☐ I just don't have enough time to make files for everything.

☐ I can't now, I'm too busy putting out fires.

☐ There is never enough time to get it all done.

If you checked two of the above, you need to get some help getting organized because your current behavior is costing you valuable time in your sales cycle.

There are two simple and very quick ways to remedy a bad case of disorganization.

1. *Make a list of daily activities and prioritize them.* Jim Webster credits much of his success as a Short Cycle seller to preparing a daily list of activities every afternoon for the next workday. Then he prioritizes each activity as a 1, 2, or 3. The "1" activities are his top priorities for the next day. They are the ones that *must* get accomplished; hence they are the first ones he works on. Jim makes prospecting and proposal devel-

opment "1" activities every day. The "2" activities are important and need to be completed that day, but they are not necessarily "must be accomplished first" activities. Good examples of "2" activities are sending out thank-you letters. Jim then lists his "3" activities as "accomplish today if possible." If they are not possible, then they go on tomorrow's list. Good examples of "3" activities are reading those articles in *Selling Power* or *Sales and Marketing Management*. You know you want to read them, but selling takes the "1" spot in your sales day.

Jim Webster gave me another pointer about his sales success. He says that keeping his professional sales skills honed is always a "1" priority in his life, but maybe not every day. When Jim buys a copy of *Selling Power* at his local bookstore, he scans the table of contents for articles of interest. He literally tears them out of the magazine and puts them in a to-read file in his desk. He then discards the balance of the periodical. When time permits, he pulls articles out of his to-read file and peruses them.

2. *Ask someone more organized than you to come into your office and show you her "organization system."* Why invent the wheel if someone already has? What higher compliment can you pay someone than asking to use her ideas? Realize that it is much better for your sales cycle to swallow your pride and ask for help than to continue on in a life of fire drills and overcommitment. I owe a great deal of my success in the last 10 years to my wife, Ginny. One day I became so frustrated at my lack of structure that she offered to go into my office on a Saturday and set it up like hers. One of the many things that I truly admire about her is her ability to make systems out of chaos. She spent a complete Saturday reorganizing, or should I say organizing, all of my files and so-called systems. On Monday morning she explained how I would be operating from that day forth. It worked, and almost instantly I noticed that I was in charge of my daily sales activities, not the other way around. Is her system the best? Who cares? For me it is the best because it is the only one that I know, and it saved me time from attending an "organize yourself" program or learning to do it myself by experimentation.

I've told many of my clients to identify someone in their lives that is more organized than they are and go ask for help. The ones who have taken this advice and asked for help are now reaping the benefits of shorter sales cycles because they are in control.

SHORT CYCLE SELLERS FIND WAYS TO DELEGATE

The second that I mention delegation as a way to compress sales cycles, every field sales representative in the world will look at me like I'm crazy.

I operate from an office in my home. Who will I delegate to? Abby, my 3-year-old yellow lab?

Jim, what planet have you been on? Haven't you been reading the newspaper? My company is downsizing and administrative people are the first to go. I don't have anyone to delegate to.

I'd love to delegate some of this paperwork, but my sales assistant at headquarters works with four other sales representatives. She doesn't have time.

I'm an independent sales representative. Who is going to pay for me to hire an administrative assistant?

I have a sales assistant, but I really can't trust her with handling the details. She's too new, and my customers don't know her.

My sales manager doesn't want us to bother the people in the office unless it's with order processing.

After I've made the sale, I'm afraid to let go in the post-sale stage because someone will mess it up.

I'm sure I haven't listed them all, but I will assure you that I've heard them all. I mean I've heard every, not just some but every, reason in the world why salespeople can't, won't, or refuse to delegate. To all of those thousands of salespeople who have told me this, I reply with the same line each time: "Your title is sales representative (account executive, account manager, regional sales manager, rainmaker), and you are paid to sell. That is the long and short of it. Contrary to popular belief, the more time that you make available to sell, the more you will sell. Control your selling time, and you'll control your sales cycle. It's just that simple."

"Okay, Jim, if it's just that simple, why don't you show us how?" I will, but not knowing each of your specific situations, I will present a solution that should address the most common circumstances. The first step in any event is to identify those tasks that need to be delegated. Many of you make the mistake of trying to identify whom to delegate to before you decide what needs to be delegated. If you are doing this, you are letting someone else's skill level dictate to you what tasks you need to perform and what tasks you can get rid of. Again, you are not in control of the activities that determine your sales cycle. So, make a list of tasks, activities, jobs, or events that you know would give you more time to sell. Let me give you one quick tip about this part of delegation. If you constantly delegate the worst, most miserable tasks that need to be performed, your luck at delegating will be limited. Other people dread doing those things as much as you do. Never delegate something that you would never do yourself.

Secondly, identify and select the proper person to delegate this deed to. Matching the job you are delegating with the available person, who has the best credentials in this area, is the way to accomplish this. The two most common mistakes that you may make are

1. Not looking outside your department.

2. Failure to look outside of your company.

When most salespeople talk about problems in delegating, they are referring to their own department. Take off the blinders, and look outside of your department. Personally, I would go to the customer service department first. They're trained to help, and just by the nature of the individual who applies for those jobs they are born helpers, and they probably know your customers. For technical matters, you should expect help from engineering, sales engineering, technical services, or information technology. It has been my experience that someone in one of those areas will assume responsibility for your delegated task.

What if you are an independent representative or a field representative without a staff to assist you? The same rule applies to you as it would to a factory salesperson at headquarters. Take off the blinders and look outside of your department or company. The best place to start is to look up and down your channel of distribution. Let's take a look at how

Michael Cucchiara, national sales manager for Hunter Industries, has coached his field salespeople to handle delegation using their channel of distribution.

THE HUNTER INDUSTRIES CASE

Hunter Industries is the world's leading manufacturer of irrigation equipment for commercial and golf applications. Their various channels of distribution are illustrated in Exhibit 13-1.

Hunter
↓
Wholesaler/dealer
↓
Irrigation/landscape contractor
↓
Property owner/golf course/municipality

Exhibit 13-1

As you can readily see, Hunter's domestic channel of distribution is not unlike most manufacturing concerns that distribute their goods via dealers. Hunter moves its goods to dealers, who in turn sell to landscape contractors, who install the Hunter products in the commercial buildings, golf courses, or municipalities. The only exception to that channel movement is if the property owners, golf courses, or municipalities have their own irrigation crews, and then Hunter dealers sell directly to those entities, bypassing the contractor.

There are times the Hunter salespeople are confronted with equipment problems on a new installation. Since they all operate from offices in their homes, they lack an administrative staff to delegate specific duties to or to help them put out "fires." Their biggest complaint was that right in the middle of a trade show or some important out-of-state dealer meeting, a contractor would improperly install a key component and the irrigation system would not work properly. Can you imagine a golf course in

Georgia or Nevada not getting water to the greens or fairways in the summer? Now, that's a "fire drill" if I've ever seen one. When this occurs, the contractor immediately calls his Hunter dealer for help. The dealer pushes the problem up-channel by calling the Hunter salesperson who is usually out of town. In the good old days, the Hunter salesperson would drop everything, change her plans, and rush to the "fire." Michael Cucchiara changed that routine very quickly. He trained his Hunter salespeople to delegate the problem back down the channel to the dealer. Between the dealer and the Hunter engineering group in San Diego, the problem was usually resolved. Michael found that the more times that he did this, the more proficient his dealers became at handling various problems and the fewer "fires" his salespeople faced. This meant they could spend more time selling and that meant that they were in control of their sales cycles. Michael proved what I have contended for years, that you can delegate outside your organization. All you need to do is look for the opportunity.

Finally, after you have identified whom you are going to delegate your task to, assign it using the proven delegation guidelines. Adhering to this method will ensure successful accomplishment of the delegated task.

1. Be specific on what you want accomplished and how you want the person to proceed.

2. Give the person a time frame within which you want the activity completed.

3. Give the person full authority and responsibility to do whatever it takes to complete the task successfully.

4. Be sure that upon completion, you pay kudos to the person you've delegated to and assure her that you will give full credit for successfully completing the task.

5. Conduct a debriefing with the person.

Once you have followed these guidelines and completed a successful delegation, less of your time will be required the next time you delegate to that person.

All the sales cycle limiting behaviors listed earlier in this chapter can be directly attributed to lack of delegation skills. It is difficult to let go the first time you delegate, but the rewards are much greater than the efforts. Remember that your objective is to make more time for you to sell, thereby giving you control of your sales cycle and income.

CALL RELUCTANCE DEFINITELY LENGTHENS YOUR SALES CYCLE

Charlie Johnson is from Red Oak, Iowa. Charlie is a Creighton University graduate, former college and high school athlete, and one of the most focused individuals I've ever met. I selected Charlie as one of my mentors in life. One part of Charlie's life that he doesn't talk much about is the years that he spent as a pilot and flight leader during World War II. Charlie is one of those heroes who led missions over enemy territory, literally looked the enemy in the eye, and faced life-or-death situations at times. The lives of his crew members rested squarely on his shoulders every day. Charlie has told me some of the events he faced during the war, and I can say that Charlie is a very brave man. Charlie is also a top-producing salesperson. He began his sales career at Burroughs and retired from Industrial Chemical Laboratories. He was always one of the top two salespeople in the company.

From what I've just told you about Charlie Johnson, it shouldn't be too difficult for you to imagine that he isn't the kind of salesperson who would let anything or anyone intimidate him. And, you're right. Charlie doesn't let anything come between him and success. Charlie and I still meet for lunch or breakfast occasionally, and recently we discussed the topic of call reluctance. Can you imagine that a man who had repeatedly led others into battle would have thoughts that might keep him from making a harmless sales call? He admitted that he did, but he also told me that it is a completely natural thing for salespeople to have these self-doubting notions. The reason that Charlie was always a top producer is that he overcame these potentially paralyzing thoughts by remaining focused on his mission. Charlie told me that he never once allowed his negative thought process control his actions. He learned early on that he controlled his thought process, not the other way around. When is the last time that you led a group into a battle for their lives? The point is that if it's natural for a man as courageous as Charlie Johnson to have negative thoughts about making sales calls, why wouldn't it be natural for all the rest of us?

The answer is that *it is natural* for the rest of us to have self-doubts about making sales calls. I've been selling for a long time, and it still happens to me. The difference between Charlie and some of the rest of the world is that Charlie never let call reluctance control him. He controlled it.

Call reluctance reveals itself in many different sales cycle elongating behaviors. Some of the most common are

1. *Procrastination.* You put off making prospect calls or introducing new services or products to current customers.

2. *Being "tied" to the telephone.* This does not refer to when you are making sales appointments, but to when you are handling service issues or making dinner plans, taking football pool reservations, or talking with the same customers that you did last week.

3. *Being "tied" to your computer.* This refers to time you spend sending and receiving unproductive e-mails, performing Web searches, or engaging in busy work.

4. *"Anchored" by corporate and administrative minutia.* You put a priority on internal matters over external matters and on inward focus versus outward focus.

Can you see now the devastating effect that these behaviors can have on your sales cycle?

We're all guilty of them, but that's okay as long as you recognize them and take control. In order to take control, you must identify whether it is fear of rejection or fear of failure that causes your behavior. The difference between fear of rejection and fear of failure is that in fearing rejection we have a tendency to put the blame on someone else, like a customer or prospect. Fear of failure focuses on whether you have the competency to be successful.

Here are some ideas that have helped me control my anxieties resulting from fear of rejection and failure:

1. Write a calling plan for every day of your sales week. Include a specific number of calls on prospects and list their names, addresses,

telephone numbers, and your Compression Objective. Do this task before you do anything else in your day. When you have successfully completed the calls, reward yourself with a treat.

2. Use your microcassette recorder to make a self-help positive affirmation tape. Use phrases like

I am a good prospector.

I am experiencing more success than before.

XYZ Company is going to buy from me.

The authors of *Chicken Soup for the Soul* have recorded an outstanding audiotape series entitled, *The Aladdin Factor*. It is a marvelous tape program, and it specifically addresses salespeople and their fear of rejection when asking for an appointment or business. My favorite two expressions in this whole tape program are

Ask, ask, ask, ask, ask, ask.

Some will, some won't, so what, someone else is waiting (to be asked).

Make these two expressions part of your minicassette tape self-affirmations. For 30 days, listen to your tape first thing upon rising in the morning and last thing before you go to bed at night.

3. Plan massive action and begin tomorrow by calling more prospects than you've ever called before in a single day. Stay focused on this task, and call hundreds of prospects until you reach your comfort level again.

4. Quickly visualize every call before you pick up the telephone. Anticipate rejection statements and develop a scripted positive response. Write that response down on a piece of paper in front of you.

I practice these four techniques when I feel call reluctance coming on, and they do put me back in control of my sales cycle.

SALES RACE WRAP-UP

The biggest obstacle to shortening your sales cycle is you. Your thoughts, perceptions, and actions as they relate to your concept of time are determining factors in your ability to compress your sales cycle.

The lack of self-discipline is exhibited by four skill weaknesses that prolong your sales cycle. They are

Poor planning   Lack of delegation

Disorganization   Call reluctance

Your sales plan directly correlates to your sales cycle. In order to be successful with a sales plan, you must be specific and objective and the plan must be written. Disorganization is another time waster and will rapidly lengthen your sales cycle. The best ways to conquer disorganization are to make a daily to-do list and prioritize it and ask someone more organized than you to show you her organization system.

By controlling your selling time, you will control your sales cycle. One way to make more time to sell is to delegate nonessential duties and tasks. Candidates for you to delegate to must be trustworthy, conscientious, and desirable of the responsibility. They may be found up- or down-channel. They don't necessarily have to be within your organization. Once you have identified the tasks to be delegated and the person to whom you are going to delegate, follow the five simple guidelines I've presented in this chapter.

Finally, call reluctance is a behavior that, if left unchecked, will result in long sales cycles and eventually lead you into a career in customer service or marketing. Call reluctance generally originates from fear of rejection and fear of failure. These fears manifest themselves in paralyzing behavioral patterns such as habitual procrastination. The four best ways to take control of these fears are

1. Write a daily calling and prospecting plan.

2. Make self-affirmation tapes and play them twice a day.

3. Plan and execute an action plan.

4. Utilize visualization techniques.

MASTERING YOUR OWN SALES CYCLE

Use the given tables for your worksheet, and write your sales plan using the six-step procedure.

Step 1. List the names of your prospects or customers.

Customer's or Prospect's Name	Current Stage of Sales Cycle	Compression Objective	Compression Objective Date	Transaction Closure Date

Step 2. Identify and record their current stage positions in your sales cycle.

Customer's or Prospect's Name	Current Stage of Sales Cycle	Compression Objective	Compression Objective Date	Transaction Closure Date

Step 3. Enter their respective Compression Objectives.

Customer's or Prospect's Name	Current Stage of Sales Cycle	Compression Objective	Compression Objective Date	Transaction Closure Date

Step 4. Enter the dates you will accomplish each Compression Objective.

Customer's or Prospect's Name	Current Stage of Sales Cycle	Compression Objective	Compression Objective Date	Transaction Closure Date

Step 5. Enter a transaction closure date.

Customer's or Prospect's Name	Current Stage of Sales Cycle	Compression Objective	Compression Objective Date	Transaction Closure Date

Step 6. Re-sort the table by earliest transaction closure date.

Customer's or Prospect's Name	Current Stage of Sales Cycle	Compression Objective	Compression Objective Date	Transaction Closure Date

On the lines provided, list two names and telephone numbers of people more organized than you. What date will they be able to help you get organized?

_____   _____

_____   _____

Identify and write on the lines provided five tasks or duties that you can delegate. Next list to whom you will delegate them. If applicable, list someone up- or down-channel from you.

Task	Delegate

SALES TECHNOLOGY AND AUTOMATION = SHORTENED SALES CYCLES

Technology is only as good as the user will allow it to be.

Let me begin this chapter by telling you that there are many technologies available today that will shorten your sales cycle. You can use e-mail, Web conferences, Web sites, streaming videos, sales force automation, and customer relationship management. In this chapter, I won't address the use of videoconferencing.

Many clients have asked me which software technology, sales force automation (SFA) or customer relationship management (CRM), is better. Let's begin this discussion by clarifying the original differences between sales force automation and customer relationship management. Today, those terms are bandied around as synonyms, but in all actuality, their origins were quite different. Sales force automation software was designed primarily to aid a salesperson in automating his sales cycle. Customer relationship management software evolved directly from the customer service aspect. Customer service software enabled organizations to manage and track their service functions better.

Sales force automation and customer service software companies were pumping out products that utilized the same data, but were kept in different, nonintegrated systems. In other words, it was very likely that the sales department and customer service department of your company each had separate customer data files that contained virtually the same information. Neither department really shared this data, but they both claimed that they needed a proprietary database. This dilemma probably came to light when sales would talk to a customer and that customer would mention that he had just spoken to a customer service representative who promised him the exact opposite of what sales had just promised him. Or, it might have been just the opposite situation, where customer service said it couldn't perform a task for the customer and the customer called back, asked for sales, and sure enough got what he wanted. Ever happen to you?

To make a long story short, the sultans of SFA and customer service software soon decided to produce multitask systems in which all users could share a common customer database and conduct their own work through this database. They referred to this as "enterprise-wide" and declared enterprise-wide as "good." Soon the companies producing SFA software repositioned their offerings to include customer service and renamed them CRM systems. The reposition was readily accepted in the marketplace because, after all, combining communal databases into a multifunctional system that could be used company-wide (enterprise-wide) made good business sense. In summary, CRM was created when SFA and customer service finally joined forces.

CRM Magazine reported that over 70 percent of all sales forces are not using their already installed sales force automation and customer relationship management software systems.

Think about the staggering implication of this when you measure it in wasted dollars and cents. Literally, there must be hundreds of millions of dollars of SFA and CRM software just sitting on servers and hard drives not being utilized to shorten sales cycles. The interesting fact is that this vast waste goes well beyond the information systems realm. If hundreds of millions of dollars of software are lying idle, what about the millions upon millions of dollars that are being wasted by salespeople in unproductive time and lost sales? Those lost sales and unproductive hours are referred to as *opportunity costs,* and there are plenty of opportunity costs to you that are associated with finishing second in any particular sales race.

After many years of selling and installing various SFA and CRM systems, and training clients on them, I have come to the conclusion that there are seven primary reasons that salespeople dread these systems. Which of the reasons listed below fits your rationalization for not using your system?

1. *Poor training.* It always amazes me when a client invests tens of thousands or hundreds of thousands of dollars on CRM software but skimps on the training aspect. It's like giving a hungry person a fishing pole with no bait. Epicor Software, a $220 million company in Irvine, California, produces a CRM system. Epicor's director of marketing, Greg Horton, says that his experience substantiates my rationale that lack of training is a primary reason for CRM failure or misuse. Mr. Horton says that most good CRM training not only shows the salespeople how to use the CRM system, but why they should use it. It's been my experience that the "why to use it" is the motivation for the "how to use it." Salespeople must understand that these systems are tremendous aids in shortening their sales cycles. Mr. Horton goes on to say that lack of training also greatly affects the performance of the information technology (IT) department at companies that install CRM systems. If your IT department doesn't understand your CRM system or lacks training support resources, you can usually go to the software manufacturer's Web site to obtain a telephone number or URL address for help. You may have to pay for the telephone charges, but if you don't, one of your competitors will, and finishing second place in the sales race stinks!

2. *Mistrust of management's intent.* Greg Horton relayed to me that many salespeople refuse to utilize CRM because they are suspicious of management's intent. They feel that it is another tool by which management can watch over or micromanage them. These same salespeople are filling out manual call reports and sending them to

their managers. What's the difference? The difference is the speed between mailing or faxing a call report in and the speed of entering the data on a computer and having it available to management immediately. That's the only difference, but it's an important one. It pertains directly to the speed at which your manager can respond to you with assistance or guidance in closing a sale while your competitor's manager awaits U.S. Mail delivery or an administrative assistant to take him your fax.

3. *Lack of top management support or insistence on use.* Another major reason that CRM systems fail is lack of top management support. If management does not mandate it, the system fails. It's just that simple. In fact, many times top sales management is caught in a technology gap; hence, they fail to understand that CRM is a primary tool in shortening sales cycles. These senior executives may not possess any technology literacy, so they ignore it. I know several CEOs and senior sales executives who don't even have a computer in their own offices. What do you suppose their sales technology is like? In fact, I was asked by a top executive of one of the world's leading providers of financial data for stockbrokers what would happen if their salespeople wouldn't use a CRM system after they installed it? His major concern was how he would look to other top executives in his organization if he was part of a decision to buy CRM and the sales representatives didn't use it. This reminded me of the tail wagging the dog. Obviously, he would have never mandated usage of his CRM. I wanted to scream at the top of my lungs, "Look, buddy, you're in charge here, not your sales representatives." Needless to say, I abruptly packed up my briefcase and ran as fast as the wind. This deal was bound for disaster, and I didn't want to be part of it.

4. *Animosity toward the information technology department.* Jeff Lewis, a CRM expert in San Jose, California, cited that he feels that sometimes there exists a definite animosity between field salespeople and their respective IT departments. Jeff said that his experience shows that some field salespeople view CRM as a burden and something imposed upon them by the IT department. Greg Horton from Epicor told me that this animosity usually stems from the fact that IT departments don't want to add an additional burden to their staffs for a CRM

system that the IT department had very little input in choosing. IT departments have a rule of thumb that they usually need to have one support person for every 30 to 40 CRM users. This can be a huge load for an IT department especially when salespeople, by nature, will call first with questions instead of trying to figure it out on their own.

5. *End user indifference.* A Short Cycle salesperson knows that a customer who is indifferent to his sales proposition is more difficult to sell than one who is totally opposed to his sales proposition. Jeff Lewis tells me that this is very much the case with getting a commitment from field salespeople to use a CRM system. Jeff says that a salesperson's indifference is the absolute worst mental state he could encounter when he works with his clients. They just don't care one way or the other, and generally speaking, no one can make them care.

6. *Cumbersome and difficult to use.* Just the nature of adding another administrative task to a salesperson's day is enough to make him revolt. That's exactly what many sales managers have done by installing certain CRM systems. I am intimately familiar with a multibillion dollar company that had a group of software people in their IT department design a CRM system. Not only had none of the IT people ever sold a single item before, but also they never even asked the sales, marketing, and customer service functions about the design, operation, or databases of their new system. It was developed in-house, and they spent months upon months and millions upon millions of dollars to deliver this fiasco to their sales team with no formal training. The results were massive insurrection and system failure. It was a terrible burden to enter or retrieve data. No one used it until the CEO, who never had a need to use it, mandated use and based compensation on up-to-date entries. The result was more spending to train salespeople and then change the system and train them again. If your CRM is burdensome, dump it. What's the lesson here? If your IT department is developing a proprietary CRM, run to your CEO and enlighten him. There are systems out there that are designed to shorten your sales cycle, not prolong it with hours upon hours of screen changes, error messages, and "data hide and seek."

7. *Lack of organization skills.* Salespeople carry a stigma about being disorganized and hating paperwork. It is supposed to be the "nature of the beast." Many have convinced themselves that it is true and use this as an excuse not to utilize a CRM system. Well, the good news is here! Software companies have made their systems so flexible and scalable that even the most disorganized person will find it easy and simple to retrieve data that they typically would have lost. That alone is a sales cycle shortening event for disorganized salespeople and should be a powerful motivator for embracing the use of a CRM system.

SALES RACE RULE 22

Employing CRM sales technology will give you an edge in the race to your customer because, on average, 70 percent of your competitors that have it aren't using it.

COMPRESSION CONCEPT: WHAT A GOOD CRM SYSTEM CAN DO TO SHORTEN YOUR SALES CYCLE

From both my personal and my clients' experiences, I will tell you that using a CRM system will definitely shorten your sales cycle, but don't take my word for it. In this section, I'll prove it to you.

Many CRM systems track and report what they call a *sales pipeline.* The sales pipeline is an imaginary pipeline, not unlike a gasoline or oil pipeline, through which prospects and customers flow. Your prospects enter the pipeline with the first appointment and progress through the pipeline with each customer event that transpires. Then, hopefully, they exit the pipeline as a customer as illustrated in Exhibit 14-1. Many systems will automatically track this progression for you based on your entries and predetermined pipeline events.

CRM Pipeline

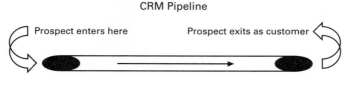

Exhibit 14-1

Does anything sound familiar to you? You are correct if you have associated the CRM pipeline with your sales cycle. CRM systems automatically track your customers, each and every one of them, through your sales cycle, that is, the CRM system pipeline. They can be prospects, or they can be current customers who are in a new sales cycle. In either case, CRM systems will automatically compare your customers' movements through your sales cycle based upon your entries and the stages of your sales cycle. What that means to you (sound familiar?) is that anytime that you wish, you are able to see what stage is next for each of your customers. It gives you a great overview of your sales cycle and reminds you of the next stage or what your compression objective should be. If you handle multiple accounts and are continuously prospecting for new ones, and most of you are, this provides you with a true leg up on your competitors. It will enable you to get to the finish line first.

Let's take a look inside the CRM pipeline based on the stages of the generic sales cycle that we presented in Chapter 1. I will show you *compression activities* that most CRM systems offer to help you shorten your sales cycle. Exhibit 14-2 represents this generic sales cycle as presented by a CRM pipeline.

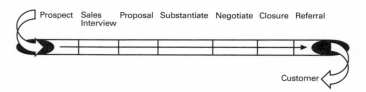

Exhibit 14 - 2

Prospect

In the prospect stage of your sales cycle, CRM systems can do everything from control how many prospects that you are working on at one time to automatically mailing or e-mailing multiple introductory letters to those prospects. These clever systems even tell you when it's time to call on those prospects and can conduct an automated marketing plan based on your prospect's profile and market segment. In other words, while you are out calling on new and current customers, your CRM system is automatically conducting a marketing campaign to those prospects and customers who you have already entered into the pipeline. In fact, one CRM system will forecast your chances of closing a pipeline prospect based on the prospect's responses to your marketing events. Who wants to spend time with a customer or prospect that is not moving down the pipeline? This particular CRM system allows you to concentrate on the "A" prospects immediately, while the system automatically markets to the "B" and "C" prospects. Talk about shortening your sales cycle!

I was speaking to a client who is a senior vice president of a large regional bank. She is responsible for business development (sales). The discussion topic was account planning and shortening her bankers' sales cycles. I explained to her that the sales cycle is different for each product that her division offers. Loans, trusts, and investments all have different sales cycles. This senior vice president preferred that her bankers sell loans as an initial entree to their customers. The next thing she wants them to sell is trust services. After they have sold their customers both loans and trust services, she wants them to sell investment services. I asked her two questions:

1. How do your bankers tell where they are in the sales cycle with any given customer?

2. How do your bankers know what to sell their customers after a loan was closed?

She was stumped. I recommended that she begin a search for a CRM program that could be tailored to help her bankers' track their multiple customer dealings. She should look for a system that has the potential to automatically enter customers into the next product offering's sales cycle or pipeline once they have been sold a service. I showed her that just by perusing their CRM customer profiles and purchase history, her bankers could tell what services to sell next. The same goes for you.

Sales Interview

Some CRM software companies have systems that contain prospect and customer profile databases. Most of these databases easily can be tailored to your specific customer market segments. This data is collected during your target market research and your sales interview. I've heard many sales representatives say that it takes too much of their time to enter this data. They use the excuse, and it's nothing more than an excuse, that they should be out in front of customers belly to belly and face to face, not hooked to some keyboard entering data. Generally these comments come from salespeople who are disorganized and don't keep complete written records anyway. The next thing they know, a competitor has penetrated one of their customer's vale of loyalty and is selling them something he should be. Why? There may be many reasons, but more than likely he didn't have the information that pointed to that particular want or need. Why? Again, he didn't keep good records.

Some CRM systems' ability to allow you to identify and reach "A" prospects first is a real sales cycle compressor when it comes to the sales interview. The advantage is that you will be calling on the prospects that *want* to grant you a first appointment.

CRM system customer profiles can be easily designed to provide you with the correct open-ended questions to ask your customers. These questions are usually based on the input of many other successful salespeople in your industry. They are questions that are designed to solicit the customer information you need to record to make yourself as successful as these top guns. Talk about shortening both your learning curve and sales cycle!

Proposals and Demonstrations

Most good CRM systems have proposal generators in them that automatically spit out a formal proposal once you have fed in the required data. This wasn't always the case, but the more contemporary systems now contain this feature. If you are a field sales representative, you no longer have to rely on an administrative assistant or corporate department to crank out proposals for you. It is entirely possible for you to be at a customer's facility, collect the data you need to generate a proposal or conduct a demonstration, enter the data into your CRM system on your laptop, and print a formal first-class proposal right on the spot. A few CRM systems contain a customized format for proposal generation. Others tout that their system contains a quotation generation component. In fact, one system contains a quotation generator that is designed to automatically become the order entry document once the sale reaches transaction closure. Again, both of these are tremendous sales cycle compressors since you are able to deliver an instant proposal, engage the customer in negotiations, and close the transaction before a competitor enters the picture.

Substantiate

This is one stage of your sales cycle in which CRM may not play a very large compression role. If you have a substantiation stage in your sales cycle, about the best way to utilize CRM to compress it is to substantiate your competencies in your two-letter introductory series in the prospecting stage. One other quick way to substantiate your competencies is to have the ability to develop, print, and deliver an immediate proposal from your CRM. Many of your customers will find that very impressive. That act alone may be enough to substantiate your professional competencies without your prospect having to experience a longer chain of events to prove it. A little later in this chapter I will show you how to use other sales technology to shorten the substantiation stage of your sales cycle.

Negotiation

As you may recall from Chapter 10, preparation is a key to successfully negotiating a sale. You may also remember from Chapter 10 that the party with the most information usually negotiates from a stronger position. Also, I've told you that 85 percent of the time you engage a customer in negotiations and keep them there, you will walk away with the business. CRM is a tremendous tool to shorten the negotiating stage of your sales cycle. By utilizing the customer profile, customer activity records, and enterprise-wide call reports, you will be armed with significant data to bolster your position in the negotiation. Be sure to read the call report section and check for all entries from all departments that may have talked with your customer. You just might find that one piece of information crucial to putting the deal together. As I mentioned earlier in the Proposals and Demonstrations section of this chapter, a good

CRM system will contain a proposal or quote generator. That alone will allow you to hasten your move into the negotiation stage because you can readily print the proposal and start the negotiations. Remember that once you've reached the negotiation, you stand an excellent chance of closing the transaction.

Transaction Closure

All the CRM systems in the world are designed with the *intent* to help you get to the transaction closure stage as fast as possible. Their purpose is to provide you with the information and marketing automation to assist you through your sales cycle. Some are much better than others at achieving this objective, but this is not a case of implementing just any system because having one is better than having none at all. There are specific systems that will get you to the end of the sales cycle quicker, but at that point, you are on your own. CRM systems will not ask for the order. It's up to you. Remember that your customers are expecting you to ask, so don't disappointment them.

Referral

As in transaction closure, the CRM system can only take you to a certain point in your sales cycle. There is not a CRM system in existence that will automatically assure referrals for you. However, the stronger CRM systems can be customized to automatically send out a form letter or e-mail to your customers after transaction closure to solicit referrals for you. It is always best to include this referral request in the thank-you correspondence that is automatically generated for you after the sale. You can arrange for these CRM systems to ask for the referrals, but you must follow up the letter personally to guarantee those referrals. Once you have received them, they should be input into your system as leads or suspects.

It is up to you to utilize these tools. Keep in mind that of the salespeople that have CRM at their disposal, 70 percent are not using them. This gives you a tremendous advantage right now, but it won't last forever. As CRM systems evolve and become more utilitarian, that 70 percent will drop rapidly. It's time to step ahead of your competitors.

COMPRESSION CONCEPT: OTHER SALES TECHNOLOGIES THAT WILL HELP YOU SHORTEN YOUR SALES CYCLE

Besides CRM systems, there are many tools available to assist you in shortening your sales cycle. My favorites are Web conferencing, streaming video, e-mail, palm devices, and the use of a well-designed Web site. I'm very sure that I don't need to explain e-mail, Web site, or even streaming video, so let's begin by examining Web conferencing.

The Virtual Meeting

Web conferencing is commonly referred to as the *virtual meeting*. It's primarily used to shorten your sales cycle in the demonstration/proposal/presentation stage. Also, it can be very effective in substantiating your professional competencies. You as the sales professional can conduct a sales presentation without ever leaving your office. Your customers can have people from multiple geographic locations attend without the added travel expense and time away from their offices. This is an excellent tool for international customers or prospects. These virtual meetings work great! Once your prospect or customer agrees on the time, you control it from there. I've found that many times, it is much easier to set up a short Web conference with multiple attendees than it is to schedule a face-to-face meeting. Don't get me wrong. I'd much rather have a face-to-face meeting, but if it's going to require waiting a long time to get a face-to-face meeting, I'm going to resort to a virtual meeting. It is a tool designed to shorten your sales cycle.

The mechanics of a virtual meeting are quite simple. You conduct the meeting through an electronic presentation uploaded to a Web conference provider's site, and you communicate through a conference call service. You don't leave your desk, and the prospects don't leave theirs. The prospects call up the provider's URL address and get the electronic presentation on their computer screen. They dial your conference call provider, enter a preassigned code, and they are in the meeting. You control the presentation using the same principles I discussed in Chapter 9. If you've never experienced it, you must give it a try. Remember that because you do not have face-to-face contact with your prospect or customer, you cannot read their nonverbal body signs or facial expressions. This means that you must design feedback questions for your audience that will give you some feel for what they are thinking.

I've found the following to be very effective in achieving instant feedback:

Who feels differently about that?

Who wants me to slow down?

Who wants me to speed up?

What are your thoughts, Mr. Prospect?

In your opinion, Mr. Prospect, what do you feel are the strong points so far?

In your opinion, Mr. Prospect, what do you have concerns about so far?

These should be familiar questions to you. They are some of the same questions that you should be using in a face-to-face sales presentation to elicit interactivity. The only difference is that on a Web conference, you will need to constantly employ them.

Streaming Video

The use of streaming video has become much more prevalent since the costs of broadband connections have become affordable. Many of your business-to-business customers will already be hooked up to a broadband line or some form of digital subscriber line (DSL). Mr. Earl Pettet, director of sales administration for Streaming Media Corporation of Englewood Cliffs, New Jersey, says that streaming video can quickly give your customers or prospects an idea of whether you will fit into their defined set of alternative suppliers. Mr. Pettet goes on to say that streaming video gives you a huge advantage over your competitors because your customers and prospects can actually meet you through your message on the video and observe your product or service at work. The best way that I've seen streaming video used is by noting the Internet address for the video in your two-letter introductory series. Many prospects will find it nonthreatening to view you in the comfort of their own office on their own time schedule. After they view your video, it will be much easier to sell that initial appointment. Also, they will be able to have all the decision influencers, regardless of their location, view the streaming video. Talk about shortening your sales cycle and giving you a head start in the race to your customers!

E-Mail

You may take your e-mail service for granted, but never underestimate its prominence in helping you become a Short Cycle seller. As I discussed in previous chapters, e-mail will aid you in shortening your prospecting and presentation stages. You can request your prospect's involvement before and after your presentation via e-mail. It is a tremendous tool. If you don't think it plays that important of a role in your sales life, answer this question for me, "What is the first thing you generally do when you enter your office in the morning?" Check your e-mail? I told you so!

Palm Devices

I'm all for anything that facilitates compression selling techniques, including the use of palm devices. I can make two appointment entries in my manual day planner in the time it takes a palm device owner to enter one. And, yes I can retrieve appointment information in my manual day planner faster than palm device owners can retrieve their data. What I cannot do is enter addresses, telephone numbers, e-mail addresses, and appointments in my manual day planner and upload them to my desktop. I cannot access my e-mail from my manual day planner like many palm device owners can from their apparatus. Are those important activities to me? You bet they are. Are they activities that will shorten my sales cycle? Absolutely!

Web Sites

Finally, if you are not on your employer's Web site or you do not currently have a Web site, I urge you to take advantage of the many free offers that exist and develop one of your own. Will it bring a multitude of prospects to you? Yes, but only if you drive them there to see what you are offering. The best way to drive prospects to your Web site is to put your Web site address on your business cards, stationery, e-mail signature, and your voice mail. If properly designed, your Web site will shorten the prospecting and substantiation stages of your sales cycle because you will be able to query prospects, and that data can be downloaded to your CRM. With the continuously lowering costs of streaming video, your Web site would be a great place to introduce yourself and your USP. I have found that one of the best-kept secrets with America's salespeople is what they do for a living. Yet, their success is dependent upon people knowing who they are and what they do.

SALES RACE WRAP-UP

A very succinct recap of this chapter is provided in table form. The "X" in a particular column shows you the sales technology currently available and the areas where it can best be utilized to shorten the generic sales cycle used throughout this book.

	CRM	Web Conferencing	Streaming Video	E-Mail	Palm Device	Web Site
Prospect	X		X	X	X	X
Sales interview	X				X	
Demo/proposal	X	X	X	X		
Substantiate		X	X	X		X
Negotiate	X			X		
Transaction closure		X		X		
Referral	X			X	X	X

Based on the table, I would have to say that the three tools that are most used in helping you shorten your sales cycle are CRM systems, e-mail, and streaming video. However, if you currently have an underutilized CRM system then you can see why your competitors may be winning your sales race.

MASTERING YOUR OWN SALES CYCLE

1. Because most sales cycles are different, put the stages of *your* sales cycle in the left column of the table, starting in the second row. Then read across the top line of the table and put an "X" in the cell corresponding with the stage of your sales cycle that that particular technology can help you shorten. If you do not use a certain technology listed on the top line, assume that you will and complete the exercise.

	CRM	Web Conferencing	Streaming Video	E-Mail	Palm Device	Web Site

2. Now, referring back to the table, list each stage of *your* sales cycle in the left column of blanks that follow. On the corresponding lines on the right, list what technology you can use in each stage and the specific predominant activities that this technology can help you compress. See the example.

Sales Cycle Stage	Technology and how it can help shorten this stage
Prospecting	Streaming video—drive prospects there to view services
	CRM—use two-letter introductory series to targets

229

Sales Cycle Stage	Technology and how it can help shorten this stage

CHAPTER FIFTEEN

MARKETING WILL HELP YOU FINISH FIRST

Like selling, other marketing activities are tools that can shorten your sales cycle.

Many marketing departments in the corporate world would be hard pressed to explain their own sales cycles and how their jobs impact the various stages of those sales cycles. In fact, many times the marketing plan is developed separately from the sales plan and the result is total lack of synchronization and purpose. While marketers do understand that their job is to position their product and services with customers and prospects, I have yet to see a formal marketing plan, that lists shortening the sales cycle as one of its objectives. The intent may be there, but as in so many marketing plans that I read, it is never spelled out in writing. Failure to write this out as an objective, means failure to address it specifically in the marketing plan.

If you work for an organization that has a formalized marketing function, what do you suppose the reaction of the marketing manager would be when you asked her about her perception of your sales cycle? Unless she came up through the sales ranks or right out of business school, my bet is that she'd either ask you to elaborate or explain to her exactly what you meant by sales cycle. She might even defer that question to your sales manager. If she does understand your sales cycle, then how would she respond when you ask her what marketing activities she's planning in order to compress each stage in your sales cycle?

In my career, I've witnessed and participated in the development and writing of many marketing plans. The sales plan, generally included in the marketing plan under the promotion and personal selling section, rarely, if ever, includes input from salespeople on how their sales cycle can be shortened. As a sales representative, you are asked to provide information concerning your sales forecast each year for the marketing plan. However, I've never seen or heard of a marketing manager ask, "Hey, Ms. Sales Rep, what kind of things can we include in the marketing plan for next year that will specifically shorten your sales cycle?"

There are many answers to this question. In fact, if you do not have a marketing department, you still can do some of these marketing activities yourself and reap the benefits of shortening your sales cycle. One of the major ways that a marketing plan can shorten your sales cycle is by helping you favorably affect your customers' perceptions.

SALES RACE RULE 23

Your customers' perceptions are their own respective realities. Change their perceptions and you change their realities. Make your sales race a battle of perception, not product!

COMPRESSION CONCEPT: AFFECT YOUR CUSTOMERS' PERCEPTIONS BY POSITIONING, NOT BY PRODUCT FEATURES

As we discussed earlier in Chapter 8, selling is a profession of changing customers' perceptions of your product or service, your company, and you. My experience shows that the most successful Short Cycle sellers practice *perception adjustment* religiously. They are constantly working toward instilling a favorable and consistent awareness in their customers' eyes. Marketing executives refer to this as *positioning*. In political circles, it is often referred to as "putting a spin on." Regardless of what you call it, basically it all boils down to trying to affect your customers' perceptions so that they see you as you want to be seen. You are trying to make your reality their reality.

THE POSITIONING BY CHANGING PERCEPTION CASE

Baking soda has been a staple (necessity) on grocery shoppers' lists for many years. Homemakers all over the world require baking soda to bake cookies and other wonderful delights. In fact, baking at home was in high fashion right up until the latter middle part of the twentieth century. What happened then would have a profound and everlasting influence on companies like Arm & Hammer, the largest retail seller of baking soda.

In the latter part of the 1900s, it became an economic necessity for many homemakers to seek employment outside of the home. The era of the mother working outside the home and the dual-income family was born. Paychecks became more important than cookies to many families. What effect do you suppose this trend had on home baking? You're correct! Baking soon became a thing of the past in many households because working mothers didn't have time to spend baking.

What did Arm & Hammer do to counter this trend in the household-baking segment? They used a marketing strategy referred to as *product line extension*. In other words they tried to find alternative uses for baking soda to extend that product's life cycle. In my opinion, what they did was just short of genius. Arm & Hammer *positioned* baking soda as a cleaner and deodorizer. New uses for an old product were introduced to the homemaker and household buyer. Baking soda became a refrigerator and carpet deodorizer, kitchen sink cleaner, vegetable and fruit cleaner, toothpaste additive, and antiacid. In fact, Arm & Hammer took their positioning of baking soda one step beyond just another cleaner and deodorizer. They positioned it as a *natural* cleaner and deodorizer that will not scratch or harm porcelain and is *safe* for use on foods. By positioning Arm & Hammer baking soda as a natural cleaner, the company created a perception of household and environmental safety. What do you suppose this did to the sales cycle of the sales representatives selling baking soda?

If you doubt the success of Arm & Hammer's positioning efforts, next time you speak to someone in their forties or fifties, ask them two questions:

1. What product does Arm & Hammer make?
2. What is the product's primary use?

A majority of these people will tell you that Arm & Hammer is the "baking soda company" and the primary use of the product is baking. Now ask the same question of people in their twenties and early thirties. A majority of them will tell you Arm & Hammer makes baking soda that is used primarily in toothpaste and cleaning products.

If you'll notice in their advertisements, Arm & Hammer doesn't go into the specifics of how baking soda cleans. In fact, I'd be willing to bet you that most of its users couldn't tell you what chemical properties make it clean. Also, I'd be willing to wager that most of the loyal baking soda customers who tear off a top of a box and place the box in the refrigerator could not tell you how it deodorizes. Why do they buy it if they don't know how it works? They buy it because Arm & Hammer has told them it works and has positioned itself as a very credible source for consumer products. Arm & Hammer doesn't sell those household products based on the chemical workings of baking soda. They are not selling cleaners, deodorizers, or product properties that make baking soda clean so well. They don't tell you that it has a certain pH level or a specific gravity that is conducive to cleaning products. In other words, Arm & Hammer doesn't try to affect your perception with product features. They sell you on safety, clean sinks, clean vegetables (free of *E. coli*), and fresh-smelling refrigerators and carpets. That is known as *positioning* the product for different uses.

Is it a different product than your mother or grandmother used in her cookie recipe? No. Is it packaged differently? In some cases, yes. In some cases, no. Was the consumers' perception of baking soda altered? Yes! Did Arm & Hammer's household sales of baking soda increase? It had to! Did they extend the product life cycle of baking soda? Yes! Does this mean that they were successful in their positioning efforts? Absolutely! Did positioning have a favorable and profound effect on the sales cycle of baking soda? Without a doubt!

By sending a consistent positioning message via advertising, sales literature, samples, pricing points, sales aids, and distribution plans, marketing departments can have a profound effect on your sales cycle. But, they must be aware that shortening the sales cycle is one of their goals. I guarantee that if you have a discussion with your marketing department manager about shortening your sales cycle, she will look at these activities in an entirely different light.

How should marketing determine what that consistent positioning message should be? Marketing needs to ask your customers what their current perception is and why they feel that way. Among other things, marketing needs to ask customers about:

You	Your product or service
Decision process	Billing procedures
Shipping	Product or service use
Product demonstration	Best communications methods
Pricing	Promotional events
Customer service—complaint resolution	

Marketing should then compare the answers to these questions to how it wants the organization to be perceived. In the areas where there is a discrepancy between the desired perception and the customer's reality, marketing has to ask the customer hypothetically what it would take to change her perception from point A to point B. Once they have this data, marketing needs to ask the sales force what impact these misperceived notions have on their sales cycles and what sales feels will take the customers' perceptions from point A to point B. Then, and only then, marketing can develop a *positioning strategy* that will shorten your sales cycle. In a way, hasn't marketing just asked the customer to tell it what needs to be turned around and repeated it back to the customer in the form of a *positioning statement*? Absolutely!

COMPRESSION CONCEPT: OTHER MARKETING ACTIVITIES SHOULD BE AIMED AT HELPING YOU SHORTEN YOUR SALES CYCLE

Many marketing departments ask themselves, "What kind of materials and activities make it easier for our sales staff to inform customers about our product?" They seem to focus on the *ease of telling* product features and benefits, not giving direct thought to helping you shorten your sales cycle. Ease of telling and Short Cycle Selling are not synonymous by any means. Ease of telling is product-feature focused and Short Cycle Selling is outcome based.

Since there are many activities that fall under the umbrella of marketing, there are some more questions that you need to ask yourself about marketing's role in Short Cycle Selling. Let's examine a list of questions you need to ask yourself, in order for you to understand how to help your marketers develop activities that bring about maximum sales cycle compression.

1. Looking at my company from a potential customer's standpoint, what promotion activities would raise my awareness level?

2. If I were about to have my first appointment with a prospect, what role would marketing play in helping me prepare my prospect for that appointment?

3. What marketing activities would have the biggest impact in helping me communicate my USP and provide meaningful differentiations between my competitors and me?

4. If I were a customer, what supplier marketing action would help me to substantiate the professional competencies of that supplier?

5. If I were a customer, what marketing communications would be most effective at drawing my attention?

6. If I were my customer, what type of proposal would stimulate me to act?

7. What types of market data would help a customer, involved in negotiations with me, see things from a perspective more favorable to me?

8. If I were one of my customers, what kind of product demonstration would convince me to buy? (Most marketing departments develop demonstrations that exhibit product features. They get caught up in the product-versus-product battle and forget to factor in what interests the customer. They totally neglect to ask themselves, "What will favorably affect the customer's perception in a way that the sales cycle will be shortened?")

9. How can marketing help me get my customer involved before a presentation or demonstration and keep them involved afterward?

10. From my customer's perspective, what kind of inducement or reward could a marketing department offer to encourage referrals?

Notice that many of these questions are written to stimulate thought about the customer's perception. In fact, with a slight change in wording, these are questions that you or your marketing department might want to ask your customers.

Let's take a look at what I've seen some of my clients' marketing departments do to help their sales professionals shorten their sales cycles. For consistency purposes, I will use the generic sales cycle presented in Chapter 1. Please note that lacking a formal marketing department does not preclude you from trying some of these ideas.

Prospecting Stage

- *Timely qualified leads.* The most common complaint that I hear from salespeople is that the leads generated by marketing are either too old or not qualified. To solve this problem, one of my client's marketing managers took leads from the floor of an international trade show every 4 hours and e-mailed them to the corporate marketing department for qualification and assignment to sales. That way, their booth visitors were contacted the first day that they returned from the show. Talk about shortening the sales cycle! Another client had a marketing policy that any requests from a Web site "hit" were distributed to sales within 2 hours.

- *Share national account data via CRM.* One client of mine sold to a national account with multiple geographic locations. Despite the fact that one manager was assigned to coordinate all the sales efforts of the many sales representatives for that account, marketing management decided to share all the sales data enterprise-wide on their CRM system from each customer location. When they began that procedure, their sales representative in Portland, Oregon, realized that his counterparts on the east coast were selling a wider array of products than he had been selling to the customer's division in his territory. The Portland representative printed this report and took it to the regional buyer of his national account and immediately he added two more products in his region. By providing enterprise-wide access to the purchase activity, marketing facilitated Short Cycle Selling.

Sales Interview

- *Put multiple USPs on server.* A large banking client of ours has several divisions, such as business, personal, trust, strategic account, and corporate. Each division has its own multiple Unique Selling Propositions. Marketing put all of these on the main server so that all bankers had access to all USPs before they went on a sales interview. It was a tremendous idea and paid huge dividends to their bankers.

- *Put a list of open-ended questions on the server.* I recommended to another client, who had more than his share of rookie sales professionals, to put a list of open-ended questions on the company's server. That way all his salespeople had access to questions that were key in the sales interview. The marketing department stepped in to complete the job, and the results were outstanding! Not only did it cut the learning curve of his new representatives, it simultaneously reduced their sales cycle time.

Demonstration/Proposal/Presentation

- *Web seminar selling.* Seminar selling is where marketing rents a meeting room, offers a continental breakfast, provides an "expert" from your company to make a presentation or demonstration on an issue of current concern within your industry, gives away a radio, and you sell like hell at the coffee breaks. Most last only 2 to 3 hours, but you'll lose at least one-half of a day by the time it's all over. You probably have read that seminar selling is one of the effective ways to find prospects, and in many industries it is. Try this one for a different twist on seminar selling. Have your marketing department invite your prospects and customers to a seminar in the privacy of their own offices—a Web seminar. Once they have registered, confirm both by e-mail and mail. Send them a crisp 1-dollar bill to buy coffee and a coupon for a doughnut at their local doughnut shop. Have your expert speak for 30 minutes, and follow it up with a brief question-and-answer session. After the seminar, immediately call all the participants you've invited and arrange an appointment. With Web seminars, your attendance will more than likely be higher and you can invite prospects from literally all over the world. Most Web conference services will give you a free trial. See The Resource Center at the back of this book.

Substantiate

- *Highlight successful customer outcomes on your Web site.* Again, this creates an air of success, competency, and accomplishment. You do not need to reveal the details, just provide enough information to substantiate that it actually occurred. Because this is a Web site, you will want to have marketing constantly update these customer outcomes to exhibit your competencies with other clients.

Negotiate

- *Provide a resource for data.* Marketing by its own definition embodies market research and data collection. As I mentioned in Chapter 10, one of the two best tools to shorten the negotiation stage of your sales cycle is to have abundant information. I have suggested to many marketing executives that they accumulate an up-to-date database on all competitors. That way they can arm you with the facts when you enter a customer negotiation session. This task is predicated upon the information that you, the salesperson, feed back to marketing. The facts that you should collect revolve around

Pricing	Promotional activity
Key personnel	Acquisition rumors

Customer list (you know who they are)	Rumors about new products or services
Payment terms	New distribution points
Product line	Value-added activities

You can probably add to this list by asking yourself, "What type of information do I wish I had at my disposal during the last difficult negotiation?"

Transaction Closure

- *Value-added activities to offer as trade-offs.* When is the last time you were about to close a transaction and you had nothing more to give, but wished you were in a position to say, "Ms. Customer, if I give you this, can we begin?" I have one medical equipment client whose marketing group put all their salespeople in a position of never being without having that one final "thing" to give in order to get the business. This client sold to physicians, and its marketing department developed a series of short training workshops that addressed such issues as time management, stress management, customer service, and conflict resolution for nurses and medical office personnel. If the negotiations evolved down to only one issue or became stalled, then our client's sales representatives would offer these training workshops at no charge in order to close the transaction. Your value-added ideas don't need to be as sophisticated as these, but if you will take time to ask your customers what activities, unrelated to your business, would help their business, you will discover a bountiful agenda of value-added opportunities.

Referral

- *You'll get more of the type of behavior you reward.* This simple behavioral principle is put to good use by one of my clients to stimulate his customers to give referrals. His marketing person developed a simple, but effective gift plan in which the value of the gifts escalated with each referral given. All of his tokens of appreciation are business-type novelty items that carry his logo. This year, he starts with a nice pen for the first referral and the top item is an attaché case given for 10 referrals. The referrals must end in a sale. At the beginning of each year his marketing person announces a new referral reward plan via e-mail to all his current customers and, yes, his prospects. The results have enabled him to operate purely on a referral basis. This is another prime example of marketing helping salespeople shorten their sales cycles.

COMPRESSION CONCEPT: USING MARKETING TO ATTACK THE MARKET FROM ALL ANGLES

THE PUSH AND PULL MARKETING CASE

Jeff Carowitz is the vice president of marketing for Hunter Industries. He is one of the few marketing managers that I have met who is focused on shortening the sales cycle for his company's sales representatives. Hunter, first mentioned in Chapter 13, is the world's leading manufacturer of commercial irrigation equipment. Exhibit 15-1 illustrates Hunter Industries' traditional channel of distribution. In an effort to shorten his sales representatives' sales cycles, Jeff Carowitz employs both *push* and *pull* marketing concepts. Push marketing consists of providing the Hunter sales professionals with the marketing tools, such as special terms, pricing, and incentives, to motivate Hunter wholesalers to sell more Hunter products. These marketing activities literally compel the wholesalers to push the Hunter line to the end user, the irrigation contractor. By concentrating the push effort on distributor incentives, they stimulate the distributor to sell Hunter, in lieu of a competitor's brand.

To compress the sales cycle even further, Mr. Carowitz employs pull marketing tactics aimed at the end user of Hunter's products, the irrigation contractor. These include purchasing incentives, field trips to the Hunter San Diego manufacturing campus, and value-added activities such as seminars on managing collections and receivables. The objective of these marketing events is to stimulate contractor brand awareness and demand so that contractors begin to request Hunter products from the wholesale level. These requests for Hunter products require the wholesalers to stock more Hunter inventory, thereby pulling the product through the channel of distribution. It works beautifully. Hunter gets requests every day from distributors that want to sell the Hunter line because their contractor customers are inquiring about it.

Exhibit 15-1 Push versus Pull Marketing

Hunter's Golf Division national sales manager, Mike Lamson, readily validates the Jeff Carowitz push and pull strategy of marketing. He is the first to say that his salespeople's cycles would be much longer without such marketing assistance.

SALES RACE WRAP-UP

Your customers' perceptions are their realities. Therefore, if they perceive your organization as being difficult to do business with, it becomes factual that you are difficult to do business with. Whether you work for a company that has a large marketing department or you are a self-employed independent sales representative, your marketing efforts should be aimed at two outcomes:

1. Favorably affecting your customers' perceptions.

2. Shortening each stage of your sales cycle.

You can favorably affect your customers' perceptions through determining what their current opinions are and comparing them to how you want to be viewed. Then assist your marketing department by helping them draft a consistent positioning strategy that will change your customers' viewpoints.

Shortening the sales cycle is usually not listed as an objective of a marketing plan. Many marketing managers will not ask you what marketing tools you need to compress each stage of your sales cycle. It is up to you to ask yourself what marketing events will help you shorten your sales cycle. In this chapter, I listed several marketing activities that my clients use to condense their sales cycles. You do not need a huge marketing department to implement these ideas with your organization.

MASTERING YOUR OWN SALES CYCLE

1. If you have a marketing department or person responsible, take your Mastering Your Own Sales Cycle section from Chapter 1 of this book and review your sales cycle with him or her.

2. Once you have completed step 1, brainstorm what marketing activities you can use to shorten your sales cycle. Be specific and make a list for each stage.

3. List three of your top customers and three of your top prospects on the lines provided.

Customers	Prospects
_____	_____
_____	_____
_____	_____

4. How do you want them to perceive you? List five words.

_____

_____

_____

_____

_____

5. Call the decision maker or several key influencers for each customer and prospect listed and ask each of them the questions listed below:

- What marketing activities would raise your awareness level of our company?

- How could we have helped (can we help) you be more prepared for our first appointment?

- Tell me what you think is the best way for me to distinguish myself from my competitors.

- How can we best demonstrate our professional competencies to you?

- What marketing communication method is most effective at drawing your attention?

- Tell me the best way to format my proposals. What data should be included?

- Hypothetically speaking, of course, if you were going to demonstrate my product, what would you do to make the demonstration more powerful?

- How do you feel about giving me referrals? What would be a good way for our company to show its appreciation for this?

6. Compare the answers to the way you want to be perceived. Using this comparison, what kind of positioning strategy do you think you will need to affect their perception of you?

CHAPTER SIXTEEN

HONE YOUR MENTAL GAME

Put Your Racing Face On

Hold a visual image of the sales success that you want, and that image will become reality!

The profession of selling is like no other profession in the world. What is it about selling that makes it so unique? Is it the competitiveness or the freedom to plan your own day? Could it be that the compensation is usually the highest when compared to others in the organization? Is it the fine restaurants, hotels, and golf courses? Maybe it's the company car, traveling, and an expense account that drive people to sell.

When I ask professional salespeople what they like most about their jobs, a majority of the successful ones tell me it's three things:

1. *The thrill of making the sale.* For a successful veteran sales representative, the personal delight from making the next sale is as strong as the excitement of making the very first sale.

2. *Recognition for being the best or selling the most.* For years I've attended sales award ceremonies at which plaques, checks, trophies, trips, and gifts are awarded to the top performers. Two thoughts always cross my mind when I attend these programs: it always seems to

be the same people getting these awards year after year, and I can closely predict which rookies will be up receiving recognition next year.

3. *Compensation is tied to effort.* Besides being a professional athlete or a top executive, salespeople are in about the only profession where a majority of their compensation should be tied to performance. The successful and confident salespeople tell me that they wouldn't want it any other way.

Is the selling profession for everyone? Absolutely not! My wife, Ginny, is a speech therapist and audiologist by education. She is 50 percent owner in our business and handles the financial and information aspects. She tells me that she feels queasy when she even thinks about the remote possibility of having to pick up a telephone and call someone for a sales appointment. Ginny is thankful for the fact that selling is not a part of her job. Many nonselling friends have told me that the actual thought of making a sales presentation in front of a group makes them weak-kneed. I've met many customer service managers who have told me that they love working with customers, but they couldn't imagine asking someone for an order. They perceive the closing stage to be pushy. In the course of a year, I interview many different professionals such as engineers, bankers, chemists, and accountants. They tell me that if they had to get up every morning and meet with people whom they don't know and try to sell them something they don't want, life would not be worth living. Others have asked me how I survive without a salary. Still others have told me that they could not take "no" for an answer. The rejection would put them in a tailspin that would culminate in deep depression.

For those reasons alone, my sales friends, we deserve to be compensated better than most other professions. If the truth were known, it would reveal some pretty interesting secrets about those of us who love to sell. The world would know that it is a difficult job, but we love doing it. They would discover that "the thrill of the kill" (transaction closure) is worth more than the compensation. There would be a stark realization that many nights we sleep in a motel and eat fast foods. Two secrets revealed would be that many of us don't play golf every week or go to the afternoon matinees at the local theater. And, perhaps the world would be most surprised to find out that we do take rejection personally. We just know how to handle it.

SALES RACE RULE 24
You're the only one who can do it for you!

COMPRESSION CONCEPT: KNOW YOUR SELLING SELF

Randy Austad is the former executive vice president of operations for one of the world's largest catalog golf sales companies, Austad's Golf in South Dakota. If you travel by air, you probably have seen Austad's advertisements in the various airline magazines. When the Austad family sold the business, Randy pursued his true professional love, assessing behavior in the workplace. Ever since high school and college days, Randy was intrigued by what made people tick. Behavioral differences between successful salespeople and those less successful especially fascinated him. After years of study, Randy Austad concluded that sales success could be predicted by a simple formula. Austad's model for sales success formula is expressed as

$$S + (B \times A) = \text{Results}$$

The formula reads *skills* plus *behavior* times *attitude* equals some form of *sales results*. The S in the formula represents skill level, which can be acquired or taught, the B represents the behavioral aspect of each salesperson, and the A is the influence that attitude has on the salesperson's behavior. In Randy's formula, all the components are variable. Change the level of intensity of any of the three ingredients either up or down, and the impact on the results will be profound. Notice that attitude has a multiplying effect on behavior. This is very much the case in practicing Short Cycle Selling. I have presented you with 16 chapters of skill areas in which any one of them can result in Compression Selling. How positive an attitude you possess will directly affect the behavioral change that will encourage you to shorten your sales cycle. Randy Austad knows that success in selling is behaviorally driven.

Today, Randy Austad is regional vice president of Profiles International in Waco, Texas. Profiles International is owned and run by Jim Sirbasku, CEO, and Bud Haney, president. Their business is recognized as America's fastest growing company in the workplace behavioral assessment industry. They are known for their cutting-edge behavioral assessment products and innovation. Randy's business card displays his job title, not as regional vice president, but as "Assessment Guru." Randy Austad and Profiles International help sales professionals get better at selling. How? They afford sales professionals like you and me an opportunity to learn about our own strengths and weaknesses and compare those against other successful salespeople. This is called a *normative* comparison or assessment, which is much more insightful than its counterpart, the *ipsative* assessment. Jim, Bud, Randy, and their team of Ph.D.s and sales experts have developed The Profiles Sales Indicator, used to develop sales professionals at all levels.

It is a behavioral assessment, which measures five critical sales behaviors that are necessary for sales success. The Profiles Sales Indicator measures your

Competitiveness: desire to win versus being cooperative.

Self-reliance: need for autonomy versus collaborative.

Persistence: ability to overcome tension to finish versus succumbing to doubt.

Energy: preference for risk, adventure, and challenge versus being harmonious.

Sales drive: what matters most, results or process?

Randy Austad highlights three crucial areas where this assessment will assist in shortening your sales cycle. They are:

1. You will understand yourself much better because your sales strengths and weaknesses are highlighted on the ensuing reports. Mr. Austad is adamant about focusing personal development plans on your strengths

rather than weaknesses. His research shows that you will gain more and quicker professional growth by developing your strengths rather than focusing development efforts on your weaknesses.

2. From gaining a better insight into yourself, you will also be able to understand and relate better to your customers. Also, the information presented in Chapter 8 about identifying Bottom Liner and Top Liner behaviors will become much more meaningful to you.

3. You will be able to establish much stronger relationships with your manager and your peers. You will understand why you react to them the way you do. Your management can either play a significant role in helping you shorten your sales cycle or, for some unknown personal or political reasons, make you jump through hoops.

Pure and simple, the results will give you an edge in the sales race to your customer.

COMPRESSION CONCEPT: FOCUS ON SHORT CYCLE SELLING SUCCESS

Throughout this book I have drawn analogies between the professions of athletics and sales. As you can see from the list of the five sales success qualities that Profiles International measures, all are apropos to athletics. In fact, when many professional athletes retire from their sport, they join the ranks of sales professionals. Why is that? They love to compete, and that's what we're all about—competing for customers, recognition, dollars, and being number one in our company or industry.

Besides having his own thriving psychology practice in the northern suburbs of Chicago, Dr. Jeffrey Fishbein is team psychologist for a noted Major League Baseball team. He works with professional baseball players at all playing levels within the organizations. Dr. Fishbein specializes in performance enhancement through a training program that he developed specifically for professional athletes. My son, Todd, was a professional baseball player and went through Dr. Fishbein's training, with the rest of the Montreal Expos' players, during his first spring training after being traded to the Expos. Knowing sales as well as Todd does, he felt Dr. Fishbein's program was very applicable to sales development. After spending considerable time with Dr. Fishbein and reviewing his program, I was so impressed that I wanted to share it with you in this book.

Dr. Fishbein's F.O.C.U.S. program has five key concepts which are

1. *Fortitude*

2. *Optimism*

3. *Confidence*

4. *Understanding*

5. *Strength*

Fortitude

Dr. Fishbein points out to us that some of the most important aspects of fortitude are

1. *Focusing on that which you can control.* Focus on controlling your sales cycle by practicing the principles that I've set forth in this book. Take control of all stages in your sales cycle by segmenting, using open-ended questions, preparing for negotiations, using S.A.F.E. transaction closing statements, and getting referrals.

2. *You have a choice on how you respond to adversity.* As sales professionals, we face adversity more often than most professional athletes do. Daily, we encounter rejection, rudeness, loss of self-esteem, and events that go awry creating many forms of stress and pressure. Dr. Fishbein is correct about us having a choice of how we react to these forms of adversity. We can react terribly and let these sales cycle events control us. Or, we can counter with a terrific response and take control of our sales cycle regardless of the adversity in it. I keep a small sign taped on my computer where I can see it every morning that I'm in my office. It reads: *You have a choice today. Terrible or terrific.*

3. *When things are not going well, think of playing (selling) well.* The next time you are struggling with a slow month or perceive that you are in a sales slump, step back, take a deep breath, and think back to how you felt during a good month. Once you have that feeling, focus on it and use it to drive your negative thoughts away.

Optimism

Dr. Fishbein tells us that in order to be an optimist, you must

1. *Explain situations to your benefit.* Identify how you will make sense out of losing a sale or closing a huge sale. In other words, how do you choose to explain good or bad events in your sales cycle? Do you wish to attribute a poor sales performance to someone else or will you accept responsibility for it?

2. *Use your power to choose your response.* You have many choices, but perhaps the most important is how you view the situation you have created for yourself. Optimists choose to see the positive, remember the positive, and act positive.

3. *Use your abilities to challenge yourself.* Use your skills to challenge false beliefs and better your current situations. Your sales performance will improve when you learn to rely on your thought process to provide the change you need.

Confidence

In this part of Dr. Fishbein's F.O.C.U.S. program, he stresses the importance of two key concepts: value yourself as an individual more than as an athlete or salesperson; and, lacking self-confidence leads to self-doubt and decreased performance. From speaking with Dr. Fishbein, I can tell you that sales slumps and hitting slumps in baseball seem to have a correlation to self-doubt.

The F.O.C.U.S. program provides some resolutions for those of us who occasionally come upon a bout of self-doubt.

1. *Use positive self-talk.* Once again we find that your thoughts will control your behavior. I will tell you that the best way I've found to utilize self-talk is to record my positive thoughts on a minicassette recorder and play them to myself on my drive to work every morning. Also, I never leave town without my minicassette recorder. I have recorded many tapes, and I change the messages regularly to fit the situations that I encounter. Positive affirmations work!

2. *Act "as if" or "fake it until you make it."* Both Drs. Jeffrey Fishbein and Wayne Dyer are huge on acting as if you have already accom-

plished your success. Take a moment and do this little exercise with me. Visualize yourself as being a successful salesperson. Imagine what it feels like to be the salesperson that always gets to the customer first. That's it. Now, how would that person act? What would that salesperson say and do? How would he feel always getting the business? What kind of reward would that person give himself? Once you have that feeling, start to act that way. Emulate how you feel the successful seller would behave.

3. *Remind yourself of your strengths and develop those further.* In order to build your confidence, dwell on your strengths. Selling is a profession of confidence. Your customers can read your level of confidence in your nonverbal expressions. Displaying confidence is a key behavioral trait in shortening your sales cycle. People buy from people who they like and trust. Confidence begets your customer's trust in you. As Randy Austad, from Profiles International told you, maximum growth comes from working on your strengths. By working on your strengths, you will be constantly reminding yourself of them, thereby building maximum self-confidence.

4. *Deal with your fears.* It's difficult for many of us to think of any professional athlete as fearing anything. However, I will tell you that anytime you are in a profession where self-performance is crucial to survival, fear is a key factor. Professional athletes and salespeople predominantly fear failure. Dr. Fishbein gives you several ways to control this fear:

   a. *Accept the fact that failure is part of sales.* Failure is part of hitting a baseball, acting, and all human endeavors. If you can accept this as reality, it will be easier to react to such events and fear them less.

   b. *View the situation rationally.* In other words, if you don't land this key prospect, will it ruin your sales year? Probably not.

   c. *Release your fear of the outcome.* Focus on each stage of your sales cycle and your Compression Objectives. Don't worry about the outcome because it will have a paralyzing affect on you.

   d. *Take risks.* Dr. Fishbein is not advocating reckless abandon, but he is saying that athletes and salespeople need to take some risk in order to advance. For salespeople it means having a cake, with your business card prominently displayed on it, delivered to a top prospect who will not return your calls. It means asking your customers what you can do outside of your business to help them improve their bottom line. It means self-deprecating humor. It's a fact that salespeople who take calculated risks will shorten their sales cycles.

e. *Be decisive.* Salespeople who are indecisive never become number one in their company or industry. They are the ones who lengthen their sales cycles. Do you want to exude confidence? Be decisive.

Understanding

In the F.O.C.U.S. program, understanding relates to how you feel and think, as well as to how the mind and body work together to achieve successful performances. It deals with understanding how to control your mental state through various techniques. Relaxation and concentration are key factors in athletic performance enhancement just as they are in sales accomplishment. The keys most pertinent to sales in this facet of F.O.C.U.S. are

1. *Remain present, positive, and process-oriented.* This is very applicable to Short Cycle Selling success. Your present goal is to guide your prospect to the next stage in your sales cycle. Be positive that your customer will follow you to the next stage. Stay within the Short Cycle Selling process.

2. *Focus on what you can control.* You can control your sales cycle, and that's what Short Cycle Selling is all about. I have given a process in which you can take and maintain control of your sales cycle.

3. *Practice.* How do you suppose that Tony Gwynn, one of the greatest contact hitters in baseball history, became such a great hitter? Practice, practice, and more practice. Tony was usually the first one at the ballpark each day. It has been said by many Major League Baseball announcers that before each game, Gwynn would take batting practice off a hitting tee and off a pitching machine, before he even went on the field for the pregame live batting practice. He had each

of his games at bat videotaped, and after every game he would watch these tapes in slow motion to analyze his swing. Tony carried out this practice ritual for his entire career. My questions to you are "What form of practice are you conducting to become a champion Short Cycle seller? Do you listen to tapes in your car every day? What kinds of role-playing are you doing with your sales manager? When is the last time you read a self-improvement book? How often do you mentally rehearse a closing statement?"

Strength

You would expect a section on strength improvement in any performance development program for professional athletes, wouldn't you? Dr. Fishbein's strength component of his F.O.C.U.S. program for athletes deals with mental, not physical, strength. Because of the competitive and self-reliant behavioral traits required to be successful in both professional athletics and sales, this section will stimulate an abundance of thought on your behalf.

Dr. Fishbein attributes mental success in athletics to perseverance, responsibility, and desire. Can't the exact same thing be said of becoming a successful salesperson? Absolutely!

Perseverance means keeping your momentum moving at all times toward your goals. In Short Cycle sales this means staying with your CRM system until it does become a tool to compress your sales cycle. It means performing the precall preparation and segmentation efforts. Perseverance in Short Cycle Selling is indicated by information and data collection prior to a customer negotiation. It means asking for the appointment or order more than one time.

Who is responsible for your current sales success level? You! I cannot tell you how many times I've heard sales professionals try to blame their managers, customers, business conditions, or even their families for their limited sales success. By reading this book, you have indicated to me that you know you are responsible for your own success. You are preparing yourself for better times ahead.

In selling, the best predictor of success is past performance. I say this because the best sales professionals are not born that way. Sales excellence is a learned behavior that comes from practice, thought, dedication, and desire. One of my favorite expressions is "once a sales winner, always a sales winner." How can I be so sure of that? It's simple. You don't get anywhere in life without dedication and desire. I've witnessed it with all my successful clients and independent business owners such as my friend, Jack Loughrey, who has a thriving janitorial supply business in Minneapolis; Dr. Jeffrey Fishbein, who has a flourishing psychology practice; Laurie Harper, my literary agent, who has an outstanding agency practice; Bob Brown, who has a strong Colorado ReMax 3000 Inc. real estate business; Ron Robinson, who owns a well-established maintenance contracting company; and many, many more. Two common denominators exist in each of these instances: dedication and desire. Once you have learned this lesson, you will always desire to be a winner. That's how I am so sure that the best predictor of sales success is past sales success.

To conclude this section on Dr. Fishbein's F.O.C.U.S. model for performance development, top athletes and top sales people make many sacrifices to get where they are. You will have to also. Remember the next time you pass up a chance for free tickets to a ball game or symphony, that no one but you is responsible for this action. It is your choice whether you are terrible or terrific, a success or a failure, stronger or weaker, happy or discontented.

SALES RACE RULE 25

You become what you think about.

Several months ago I ordered a cassette tape series from Nightingale-Conant. The speaker was Mr. Ed Foreman, and the tape series was entitled *Fully Alive, Fully Human.* In these tapes Ed Foreman tells you how to make every day a great day. He tells you to listen to his entire tape series 20 times and you will reap some great rewards. Mr. Foreman, I spend many hours in an automobile every year, and I have listened to your tapes at least 10 times. You are correct, sir. The rewards are bountiful.

Let me tell you what I do on a daily basis as a result of Mr. Foreman's advice.

1. The first thing I do each morning is eat breakfast while I read a motivational and inspirational book. I have given up the newspaper at breakfast, and that alone helps me start the day on a positive note. I have made this a habit.

2. As soon as I pull out of my driveway at 6:00 a.m. every morning, I begin to listen to my microcassette recorder. I play one of the many positive affirmation tapes that I have made for myself. My daily agenda determines which tape I play. All of the tapes are motivational and keep me thinking about sales success. You do become what you think about. These self-made tapes are only 6 or 7 minutes in length.

3. If I still have time on my drive to the office or the airport or a client's office, I listen to a cassette from one of the various nationally known speakers and motivators. My favorites are Dr. Wayne Dyer's tapes and *Selling Power Live* by *Selling Power* magazine. Every time I climb into my car, I plug in a tape. This is a habit.

4. Usually, my first stop is at the 7-Eleven near my office for a small cup of coffee. I'm sure there are better places to buy coffee than 7-Eleven, but I really like the people who work there. Every morning without fail, Muhammad, the manager, will invariably ask me how I am. I've learned to say "terrific" or "fantastic." I no longer respond with "It's too cold or too hot or business is slow." I have learned that I have a choice—to be terrible or terrific—and if I have a choice, and I do, I prefer terrific. How about you? This has become a habit for me.

5. I have made walking 3 miles each night a habit of mine. Not only do I sleep better, but also it relieves the tension from the day's rushing and running around.

6. Finally, every evening, the last thing I do before I shut off the lights in our bedroom is read from that inspirational or motivational book again. Maybe I'll read just a few paragraphs or maybe I'll get hooked and read several pages or chapters. As a result of making this a habit, I have read seven great books in the last 6 months besides continuing to build our business and write eight more chapters in this book.

Now, I leave you with one last power thought about Short Cycle Selling:

Success consists of getting up one more time than you fall.

Todd Kasper, Yale '99

SALES RACE WRAP-UP

Winning and recognition motivate sales professionals. Skills, behavior, and attitude are three factors that determine a salesperson's career path. Profiles International measures a salesperson's success on five personal behavioral traits:

Competitiveness

Self-reliance

Persistence

Energy

Sales drive

Profiles International has found in its studies that by measuring differing levels of each of these behaviors and comparing them against other successful salespeople, it can reasonably and accurately predict sales success.

We can apply Dr. Jeffrey Fishbein's model for performance development for professional athletes to professional salespeople. Both occupations require people who are very self-reliant and competitive. Dr. Fishbein's F.O.C.U.S. model is made up of five key concepts:

*F*ortitude

*O*ptimism

*C*onfidence

*U*nderstanding

*S*trength

Finally, you become what you think about. You will be a Short Cycle seller if you work on developing your sales strengths following the process that I have presented. Like building muscle, building your Short Cycle Selling skills will require repetition and practice. It's your choice—terrible or terrific!

Good luck and good Short Cycle Selling!

MASTERING YOUR SALES CYCLE

Write a personal development plan using the format provided here.

1. dentify the top three priorities in your own personal performance development.

      1. _____

      2. _____

      3. _____

2. Take each priority that you've identified and assign a start date for improvement and a date you will complete your development program.

_____   _____   _____

_____   _____   _____

_____   _____   _____

3. List those people whose help you will enlist to assist you in bringing these priorities to fruition.

_____   _____

_____   _____

4. How will you reward yourself when you accomplish each priority?

_____

_____

5. What sacrifices do you anticipate making in order to successfully achieve these priorities?

_____

_____

THE 25 SALES RACE RULES
THAT ENSURE YOUR SHORT CYCLE
SELLING SUCCESS

1. Short Cycle sellers know that there is no substitute for a good account management plan.

2. The absolute number one quickest way to beat your competitors through the sales cycle is to ask your current accounts for help.

3. Keep it brief. The more you talk, the more chance you have of prompting an objection.

4. More than likely your prospect or customer will not give you the appointment unless you give her a benefit for seeing you.

5. You, as the professional salesperson, set the Compression Objective for each customer or prospect.

6. It is not necessary to follow all the stages in a sales cycle if your customer or prospect is ready to buy. Go to the close, but don't forget that after the close is the referral stage of your sales cycle.

7. By establishing Compression Objectives for each stage of your sales cycle, you, not the customer, control the sales cycle.

8. Let the customers tell you what to tell them in your proposal or presentation.

9. Seventy percent of the sales appointment should be spent listening, 20 percent should be spent questioning, and 10 percent should be spent addressing only the specific things customers tell you that they need to know.

10. After you have recommended, suggested, or asked for any form of customer commitment, never be the first one to talk. Always let the customer or prospect answer, even if it takes several seconds.

11. As a professional salesperson, it is your job to favorably affect your customer's perception of you, your company, and your products or services.

12. Make your customer play an active role in your presentation, demonstration, or proposal before, during, and after the event.

13. To best way to engage your customer is to conduct a presentation that is 50 percent customer interactive and 50 percent relaying your business proposition (telling).

14. Regardless of your particular sales cycle, once you have engaged a customer or prospect in negotiations, you have a better than 85 percent chance of closing the sale. If you don't "put the deal together," you must assume full responsibility.

15. Never grant a concession, no matter how insignificant, without getting something in return, no matter how insignificant.

16. If you are granted a concession, capitulate immediately by giving a concession, regardless of size.

17. Discover all customer concerns up front; formulate an implied understanding that if you successfully resolve these concerns in the mind of the customer, there is no reason not to proceed with the purchase; and then tackle each issue, one at a time, to your customer's satisfaction.

18. Your customers are expecting you to ask for their business. Don't disappoint them!

19. Selling is a profession that can be likened to a romance; if you don't ask, there will never be a wedding.

20. What really counts is when the sales cycle is complete in the eyes of your customer.

21. Your sales cycle is a time-based event. Only your perception of time utilization is what keeps you from compressing it.

22. Employing CRM sales technology will give you an edge in the race to your customer because, on average, 70 percent of your competitors that have it aren't using it.

23. Your customers' perceptions are their own respective realities. Change their perceptions and you change their realities. Make your sales race a battle of perception, not product!

24. You're the only one who can do it for you!

25. You become what you think about.

THE RESOURCE CENTER

I diligently keep myself focused on sales success, and I want you to do the same. Here are some great sources of inspiration and motivation that I want you to explore:

SALES SKILLS, CAREER, AND PERSONAL DEVELOPMENT

Mr. Jim Kasper, Author
2280 S. Xanadu Way, Suite 320
Aurora, Colorado 80014
www.salestrainers.com
www.shortcycleselling.com

Mr. Randy Austad, Assessment Guru: Mr. Austad's expertise is helping you determine your sales behavioral strengths and capitalizing on them.
4949 South Syracuse, Suite 300
Denver, Colorado 80237
profiles@qwest.com

Dr. Jeffrey Fishbein, Ph.D.: Dr. Fishbein's model for performance enhancement is proven in both sales and professional athletics.
1500 Shermer Road, 320 E
Northbrook, Illinois 60062
focusdoctor@attbi.com

Dr. Wayne Dyer, Ph.D.: Dr. Dyer's work is great reading for your morning and evening "positive inspirational" moments.
C/O Hay House, Inc.
P.O. Box 5100
Carlsbad, California 92018-5100
www.successlists.com/wayne-dyer/

Mr. Ed Foreman: Mr. Foreman is an excellent source for life strategy and common sense advice. He provides tremendous motivation.
Executive Development Systems, Inc.
3818 Vinecrest Drive
Dallas, Texas 75229
Toll Free: (800) 955-7353
Local: (214) 351-0055
Fax: (214) 351-5024
edf@edforeman.com
www.edforeman.com

Nightingale-Conant: This is the best source for motivational and sales tapes. This company has an excellent inventory and usually ships immediately.
6245 W. Howard
Niles, Illinois 60714
(800) 525-9000
www.nightingale-conant.com.

PROFESSIONAL SALES JOURNALS AND PERIODICALS

Both of the following professional periodicals are must reads on a regular basis. Monthly, both periodicals offer great ideas for shortening your sales cycle and improving your sales skills. Personally, I subscribe to both and encourage you to do the same.

Selling Power Magazine
P.O. Box 5467
Fredericksburg, Virginia 22403-0467
(800) 752-7355
www.sellingpower.com

Sales and Marketing Management Magazine
770 Broadway
New York, New York 10003
(800) 821-6897
www.smm.com

RECOMMENDED READING

Brown, Les, *Live Your Dreams,* New York: Avon Books, 1992.

Chopra, Deepak, *The Seven Spiritual Laws of Success,* San Rafael, CA: Amber Allen Publishing, 1993.

Dyer, Dr. Wayne, *You'll See It When You Believe It,* New York: Avon Books, 1989.

Gschwandtner, Gerhard, *Timeless Super Achievers,* Fredericksburg, VA: Personal Selling Power, 1998.

Gschwandtner, Gerhard, *123 Super Sales Tips,* Fredericksburg, VA: Personal Selling Power, 1997.

Kennedy, Daniel S., *The Ultimate Success Secret,* Phoenix, AZ: Kennedy Inner Circle, Inc., 1999.

Robbins, Anthony, *Awaken the Giant Within,* Fireside, 1991.

Robbins, Anthony, *Unlimited Power,* Ballantine Books, 1986.

CRM AND SFA PROVIDERS

Clientele by Epicor: Clientele is a complete CRM solution.
195 Technology
Irvine, California 92618-2402
www.clientele.epicor.com

Deuxo.com: This is a unique software that guides you in successfully turning a suspect into a prospect based upon specific marketing activities.
1745 Shea Center Drive, Suite 350
Highlands Ranch, Colorado 80129
(303) 382-1245
www.deuxo.com

Salesforce.com: This is a complete CRM solution.
The Landmark@One Market
Suite 300
San Francisco, California 94105
(415) 901-7000, Fax: (415) 901-7040
www.salesforce.com

WEB CONFERENCING PROVIDERS

SalesTool.com: This is a basic Web conferencing service for very reasonable price. They are very reliable.
9769 West 119th Drive, Suite 2
Broomfield, Colorado 80021-2560

PlaceWare: This is an excellent provider with all the bells and whistles. They are very reliable.
295 N. Bernardo Ave.
Mountain View, California 94043
www.PlaceWare.com

Streaming Media

Streaming Media Corporation: This is a very talented group of people who provide streaming media services. They are extremely reliable and respond quickly.
6446 South Kenton Street, Suite 130
Englewood, Colorado 80111
www.smc.net

Short Cycle Selling Web Site

Author's quarterly Web conferences are scheduled to discuss your particular Short Cycle Selling situations. Check the Web site for details.
www.shortcycleselling.com

INDEX

A.R.E.B.A., 55–64
  activity, 64
  approach, 57
  ask, 59–60
  benefit, 58–59
  case study, 61–62
  explain, 58
  goals, 55–56
  reason, 57–58
  Web site, 62–63
  when used, 62
Account management plan, 45
Achiever bottom liner, 105, 107,
  110–112, 113–114
Action-based activities, 70–72
Aggressiveness, 16–17
Aladdin Factor, The, 179, 209
Anderson, Russell, 46
Appointments, 85
  (*See also* A.R.E.B.A.)
Arm & Hammer, 233–234
Austad, Randy, 247–248, 252, 261

Behavioral assessment, 248–249
Behavioral styles
  (*see* Bottom liner; Top liner)
Black, Tom, 115–116
Board of directors, 44
Books, 263
Bottom liner, 103–114
  how to identify, 110–113
  overview, 104
  questions to ask, 111–113
  S.A.F.E. statements, 184
  sales cycle stages, 113–114
  sales negotiation, 150
  substyles, 105
Brand identification, 5
Brown, Bob, 255
Brown, Scott, 151, 152
Business banker sales cycle, 8

Buying behaviors, 28

Call reluctance, 17, 207–209
Canfield, Jack, 179
Carowitz, Jeff, 241–242
Case studies:
  Arm & Hammer, 233–234
  Bladder Scan case, 170–171
  Farmer's Insurance Group,
    115–116
  Hunter Industries, 205–206,
    241–242
  Industrial Chemical of Arizona,
    30
  Kraft Foods, 188
  organization, 200
  participant engagement, 130–131
  pharmacological drug company,
    72–74
  Sage Products, 150–152
  Spectranetics, 61–62
  USA.NET, 85
  Vectra/Zions Bancorp, 45–47
Cathcart, Jim, 103
Chisholm, Jeana, 45, 46
Close-killers, 189
Closing the appointment, 59–60
Closing the sale, 174–191
  activities, 175–176, 190–191
  ask for the sale, 176, 179–180
  behavioral style, 184–185
  body expressions, 181–182
  case study, 188
  close-killers, 189
  hard close/soft sell, 175
  nature of, 177–180
  plan B, 185–186
  postclosing analysis, 187
  S.A.F.E., 182–185
  silence, 185
  when to ask, 180–182

Cold call, 56–60
Commitment-based activities, 70–72
Competition, 15–26
  activity, 25–26
  competitive analysis, 19–24
  external, 18–19
  internal, 16–18
Competitive analysis, 19–24
Competitive analysis matrix, 21–24
Competitive factors, 20–21
Competitive forces, 20
Competitiveness, 248
Compression concepts:
  ask for compression objective,
    94–95
  behavioral styles, 103–115
  closing, 177–182
  competitive analysis, 19–24
  compression objective, 67–70
  compression questions, 88–92
  concessions, 147–149
  CRM, 219–224
  customer internal opportunity
    analysis, 43–44
  customer's action-based activities,
    70–72
  customer's perception, 102–103
  differing sales cycles, 8–9
  marketing, 236–241
  objectors, 157–169
  plan B, 185–186
  positioning, 232–235
  psychological program, 249–255
  question-the-question technique,
    92–94
  race winning discovery strategy,
    80–84
  referrals from customers, 47–49
  S.A.F.E. closing statements,
    182–185
  sales negotiations, 138–150
  sales presentation (customer
    involvement), 121–133
  segmentation and target process,
    30–33
  self-assessment, 247–249
  skill deficiencies, 195–199
  stages of sales cycle, 2–7
  stallers, 160–162, 166–169
  training customers, 50–51

Compression objectives, 2, 65–77
  activity, 77
  case study, 72–74
  customer's action-based activities,
    70–72
  moving through stages of sales
    cycle, 67–70
  profiling, 67
  Web conferencing, 75–76
Compression questions, 88–92
Concentration, 253
Concessions, 147–149
Confidence, 16, 17, 251–253
Consultative approach, 72, 95
Consultative close, 59–60
Consultative selling, 4
Contact information (see Resource
  Center)
Control of sales cycle, 11
  conceding control, 67
  sales negotiations, 149–150
Cooperator top liner, 104, 108,
  109–113, 114–115
Counselor approach, 72
Credibility, 5–6, 11
CRM (see Customer relationship
  management)
CRM pipeline, 219–220
Cucchiara, Michael, 205
Current accounts:
  new business, 40–44
  referrals, 47–49
  training the customer, 50–51
Customer-centered, 67
Customer-focused, 67
Customer internal opportunity
  analysis, 43–44
Customer relationship management
  (CRM), 214–224
  negotiation stage, 223–224
  proposals and demonstrations,
    222–223
  prospect stage, 220–221
  providers, 263
  referral, 224
  sales interview, 221–222
  sales pipeline, 219–220
  substantiate stage, 223
  transaction closure, 224
Customer service software, 214–215

Customer specific competitive analysis, 19–24
Customer wants/needs, 78–98
 activities, 97–98
 ask for compression objective, 94–95
 case study, 85
 compression questions, 88–92
 information gathering, 81–83
 question-the-question technique, 92–94
 reality check technique, 91
 sales interview, 87–88
 scenario planning, 83–84
 strategy, 80
 talking too much, 86–87
Customer's perception, 101–103, 232–235

Daily activities, 255–256
Daily list of activities, 201–202
Decision makers, 3
Dedication, 255
Delegation, 203–207
Demonstration/proposal/presentation stage, 4–5
 (See also Sales presentations)
Demonstrations (see Sales presentations)
Desire, 255
Differing sales cycles, 8–9
Direct benefit statement, 59
Discovery process (see Customer wants/needs)
Disorganization, 199–203
Ditka, Mike, 80
Dragnet, 106
Dyer, Wayne, 251, 256, 261

E-mail, 227
E-selling (see Technology)
Ease of telling, 236
Energy, 248
Enthusiasm, 121–123
Epicor Software, 216
Extended post-presentation connection, 133
External competition, 18–19

F.O.C.U.S., 249–255

Facilitator, 127
Farmer's Insurance Group, 115–116
Fear of rejection/failure, 208–209
Fears, 252–253
First appointment (see A.R.E.B.A.)
First-time sale, 10
Fishbein, Jeffrey, 249–255, 261
Foreman, Ed, 255, 262
Fortitude, 250
Frequency of purchase, 11
Fully Alive, Fully Human, 255

Gaherty, Pat, 188
Girard, Joe, 174
Goodwill call, 70–71
Gwynn, Tony, 253–254

Haig, Alexander, 107
Haney, Bud, 248
Hansen, Mark Victor, 179
Hard close, 175
Harper, Laurie, 255
Hasper, Charlie, 176
Hook on the back statement, 148, 149
Hopkins, Tom, 4
Horton, Greg, 216–217
How to Close Every Sale (Girard), 174
Hunter Industries, 205–206, 241–242

Idea person top liner, 104, 108–115
Immediate post-presentation connection, 131–133
Implied benefit statement, 59
Industrial Chemical of Arizona (ICA), 30
Industry life cycle, 6
Information gathering, 81–83
Information sources (see Resource Center)
Initial prospect contact (see A.R.E.B.A.)
Intelligence data, 33
Internal competition, 16–18
Internet (see Technology)
Interview stage, 4
 (See also Customer wants/needs)
Introspection (see Mental game)

Johnson, Charlie, 207–208
Journals/periodicals, 262

Kartisek, Tim, 170–171
Kasper, Todd, 249, 257
Kraft Foods, 188

Lamson, Mike, 242
Lewis, Jeff, 217–218
Limiting behaviors, 195
Logical bottom liner, 104–107,
    110–114
Loughrey, Jack, 255
Lycos.com, 33

Market characteristics, 28
Market presence, 5
Market segmentation, 27–39
    activity, 38–39
    advantages, 29–30
    buying behavior, 28
    case study, 30
    market characteristics, 28
    research, 33–34
    steps in process, 30–33
    unique selling proposition, 34–36
Marketing, 231–244
    activity, 243–244
    case study, 241–242
    customer's perception, 235
    demonstration/proposal/
        presentation, 238
    goals, 242–243
    negotiate, 239–240
    positioning, 232–235
    prospecting stage, 237–238
    push/pull, 241–242
    questions to ask yourself, 236–237
    referral, 240–241
    sales interview, 238
    substantiate, 239
    transaction closure, 240
    Web seminar selling, 238–239
Matrix development, 21–24
McCandless, Alan, 151–152
Medical equipment manufacturer
    sales cycle, 9
Meet me in the middle statement, 148,
    149
Mental game, 245–258
    activity, 258
    confidence, 251–253
    fortitude, 250

optimism, 251
self-assessment, 247–249
strength, 254–255
understanding, 253–254
Middleton, Craig, 170
Mistakes, 66
Moroni, Bob, 85

Narrowing the universe, 33
Needs, 87–88
Negotiation (*see* Sales negotiations)
Networking chance meeting, 56
New business, 40–54
    account management plan, 45
    activity, 53–54
    case study, 45–47
    current accounts, 40–44
    customer internal opportunity
        analysis, 43–44
    defined, 40
    referrals, 47–49
    training the customer, 50
New Strategic Selling, The
    (Heiman/Sanchez), 33
Nightingale-Conant, 255, 262
Nordstrom, 174–175

Objectors, 157–166
    (*See also* Stallers/objectors)
Obstacles (*see* Stallers/objectors)
Open-ended question, 87–88
Open-ended question close, 59–60
Opportunities, 24, 41–42, 43–44
Optimism, 251
Organization, 199–203
Overcommitment, 199

Palm devices, 227
Participative management, 3
Participative sales presentation,
    123–133
    favorable buying decision, 124
    post-presentation connection,
        131–133
    pre-presentation involvement,
        125–127
    presentation engagement, 127–131
Past performance, 254–255
Perception, 101–103, 232–235
Perception adjustment, 232

Periodicals/journals, 262
Perseverance, 254
Persistence, 248
Personal development plan, 258
Personality traits, 16–17
Pettet, Earl, 226
Plan B, 185–186
Planning:
    activities, 196–199
    compression objectives, 196
    desired time line, 196
    sales negotiations, 141–142
Positioning, 232–235
Positive self-talk, 251
Post-presentation connection,
        131–133
Postclosing analysis, 187
Practice, 253–254
Predictor of success, 254
Predominant activity, 2
Presentations (*see* Sales presentations)
Priorities, 201–202
Private banking, 45–47
Procrastination, 199
Product line extension, 233
Product sellers, 157–158
Profiles International, 248
Profiles sales indicator, 248
Profiling, 67
Projection technique, 99–101
Proposals (*see* Sales presentations)
Prospect profile, 7
Prospect stage, 3–4
Prospects, 3–4, 7, 50–51
    (*See also* A.R.E.B.A.)
Psychology (*see* Mental game)
Pull marketing, 241–242
Purchase influencers, 3
Push marketing, 241–242
Pushy salespeople, 16–17
Putting a spin on, 232

Question-the-question technique,
        92–94

Race winning discovery strategy, 80
Rapport-building questions, 88
Reagan, Ronald, 107
Reality check technique, 91
Realm, 48–49

Reference books, 263
Referral stage, 7
Referrals, 47–49, 240–241
Rejection, 15
Relationship Selling (Cathcart), 103
Relaxation, 253
Repeat sale, 10
Reputation, 11
Research, 33–34, 81–83
Resource Center, 261–264
Robinson, Ron, 255
Rothrock, Tom, 194
Rules (*see* Sales rules)

S.A.F.E. transaction closing
        statements, 182–185
Sage Products, 150–152
Sales cycle, 1–14
    activity, 12–14
    conditions affecting the stages,
        10–11
    demonstration/proposal/presenta-
        tion stage, 4–5
    (*See also* Sales presentations)
    differing cycles, 8–9
    interview stage, 4
    (*See also* Customer
        wants/needs)
    moving through the stages, 67–70
    negotiation stage, 6
    (*See also* Sales negotiations)
    prospect stage, 3–4
    referral stage, 7
    substantiate stage, 5–6
    transaction closure stage, 7
    (*See also* Closing the sale)
Sales drive, 248
Sales force automation (SFA) (*see* Cus-
        tomer relationship management)
Sales interview (*see* Customer
        wants/needs)
Sales negotiations, 137–155
    activity, 153–155
    advantage of getting this far, 138
    arguing, 144
    ask customer to negotiate, 138–140
    case study, 150–152
    concessions, 147–149
    customer involvement, 140–145
    customer's behavioral style, 150

Sales negotiations (*continued*)
  frequent contact, 143
  information, 145
  issues to discuss, 143–144, 149–150
  planning, 141–142
  time deadline, 145–147
Sales objectives, 66
Sales opportunities, 24, 41, 43–44
Sales pipeline, 219–220
Sales presentations, 120–136
  activity, 136
  enthusiasm, 121–123
  participation, 123–133
    (*See also* Participative sales presentation)
  predominant activities, 134–135
  virtual presentation, 133–134
Sales race winning discovery strategy, 80
Sales rules, 259–260
Sales success formula, 247
Sales technology (*see* Technology)
Salespeople, things they like about their jobs, 245–246
Scenario planning, 83–85, 141
Scrambled priorities, 199
Segmentation (*see* Market segmentation)
Self-assessment, 247–249
  (*See also* Mental game)
Self-assuredness, 17
Self-confidence, 16, 17
Self-defeating skill weaknesses, 195
Self-discipline, 194
Self-pride, 16, 17
Self-reliance, 248
Self-satisfaction, 17
Self-starters, 16
Self-talk, 251
Selling for you, 181
Selling Power Live, 256
Seminar selling, 238–239
SFA (*see* Customer relationship management)
Shepard, Mike, 151–152
Short cycle selling Web site, 264
Shortening the sales cycle, 192–213
  activities, 193–194, 201, 211–213
  call reluctance, 207–209

case studies, 200, 205–206
  delegation, 203–207
  fear of rejection/failure, 208–209
  organization, 199–203
  overcommitment, 199
  planning, 196–199
  procrastination, 199
  scrambled priorities, 199
  skill deficiencies, 195
Silence, 95, 185
Sirbasku, Jim, 248
Skill weaknesses, 195
Soft sell, 175
Spectranetics Corporation, 61–62
Stallers/objectors, 156–173
  activities, 162, 172–173
  case study, 170–171
  distinguishing objections/stalls, 161–162
  handling objections, 162–166
  handling stallers, 166–169
  objectors, 157–160
  stallers, 160–161
Strategic account-planning meeting, 45
Straw issues, 142
Streaming video, 226–227, 264
Strengths, 252
Substantiation stage, 5–6
Suspects, 4

Target selling, 37
  (*See also* Market segmentation)
Technology, 214–230
  activity, 229–230
  CRM, 214–224
    (*See also* Customer relationship management)
  e-mail, 227
  palm devices, 227
  research, 33–34, 81–83
  streaming video, 226–227
  summary, 228
  virtual meeting, 225–226
  Web conferencing, 75–76, 225–226
  Web seminar selling, 238–239
  Web site, 62–63, 227–228
Tenacity, 16, 17
Third-party referral, 161

Time, 192
   (*See also* Shortening the sales
      cycle)
Time deadline, 145–147
To-do list, 201–202
Top liner, 103–115
   how to identify, 110–113
   overview, 104
   questions to ask, 111–113
   S.A.F.E. statements, 185
   sales cycle stages, 114–115
   sales negotiation, 150
   substyles, 109
Trade-off statement, 142, 148, 149
Transaction closure (*see* Closing the
     sale)
Transaction closure setup, 188
Two-letter introductory series, 56

Unassertive sales race losers, 17
Understanding, 253–254

Unique selling proposition (USP),
   34–36
USA.NET, 85
USP, 34–36

Value-added activities, 240
Vectra Bank, 45–47
Virtual meeting, 225–226
Virtual sales presentation, 133–134
Visualization technique, 209, 252

Wants, 87–88
Web conferencing, 75–76, 225–226
Web conferencing providers, 264
Web seminar selling, 238–239
Web site, 62–63, 227–228
Webster, Jim, 200, 201–202
Wine, Don, 30

Zero response, 50–51
Zions Bancorporation, 45–47

About the Author

Jim Kasper is president and founder of Interactive Resource Group. Mr. Kasper has 25 years of practical experience in direct sales, sales management, sales training, and marketing. He holds a Bachelor of Science in Economics and a Bachelor of Science in Political Science from Carroll College in Waukesha, Wisconsin. Jim also holds a Master of Business Administration degree from Northern Illinois University. For over 10 years, he has been an assistant professor of marketing at Regis University and is the recipient of the Faculty Excellence Award, an honor bestowed by Regis students. He teaches marketing, advertising and promotion, channel management, and consumer behavior.

Mr. Kasper has conducted customized sales skills training for such companies as Amoco, Chase Manhattan, Honeywell, Corning, Gannett, AT&T, and Adaptec.

Jim and his wife of 30 years, Ginny, have resided in the Denver area for over 25 years. They have one son, Todd, a graduate of Yale University, a former professional baseball player, and a financial specialist for the Royal Bank of Canada.